Kari Palonen
At the Origins of Parliamentary Europe

Kari Palonen

At the Origins of Parliamentary Europe

Supranational parliamentary government in debates of the Ad Hoc Assembly for the European Political Community in 1952–1953

Verlag Barbara Budrich
Opladen • Berlin • Toronto 2024

All rights reserved. No part of this publication may be reproduced, stored in or introduced into a retrieval system, or transmitted, in any form, or by any means (electronic, mechanical, photocopying, recording or otherwise) without the prior written permission of Verlag Barbara Budrich. Any person who does any unauthorized act in relation to this publication may be liable to criminal prosecution and civil claims for damages.

You must not circulate this book in any other binding or cover and you must impose this same condition on any acquirer.

A CIP catalogue record for this book is available from
Die Deutsche Nationalbibliothek (The German National Library)

© 2024 by Verlag Barbara Budrich GmbH, Opladen, Berlin & Toronto
www.budrich.eu

ISBN   978-3-8474-3066-7 (Paperback)
eISBN 978-3-8474-3201-2 (PDF)
eISBN 978-3-8474-3232-6 (EPUB)
DOI   10.3224/84743066

Verlag Barbara Budrich GmbH
Stauffenbergstr. 7. D-51379 Leverkusen Opladen, Germany
86 Delma Drive. Toronto, ON M8W 4P6 Canada

Cover design by Bettina Lehfeldt, Kleinmachnow, Germany
Cover picture credits. NB/MP / Alamy Stock Photo

Table of Contents

1	**A momentum of double politicisation**	9
1.1	A parliamentary alternative for European integration	9
1.2	The Ad Hoc Assembly	10
1.3	Politicisation as a perspective on Europeanisation	12
1.4	Supranational politicisation	14
1.5	Parliamentary politicisation	16
1.6	Research agenda and practices of analysis	20
1.7	Plan of the book and acknowledgements	23
2	**Parliament in post-war European projects**	25
2.1	Post-war pro-European projects	25
2.2	The Hague Congress	27
2.2.1	The 'Political Report' and the 'Political Resolution'	27
2.2.2	'European Deliberative Assembly'	32
2.3	'European Parliamentary Union'	34
2.4	A professorial draft for the European Constitution	35
3	**The Council of Europe**	38
3.1	The Concept of Europe in the Treaty of London	39
3.2	The Consultative Assembly	40
3.3	A federalist critique: André Philip	44
3.4	Committee plans for supranationalism	46
4	**European Coal and Steel Community (ECSC)**	48
4.1	From the Schuman Declaration to the ECSC	48
4.2	The Paris Treaty	51
4.2.1	The High Authority	52
4.2.2	The Common Assembly	54
4.2.3	The Council of Ministers	57
4.3	The Common Assembly plenum in September 1952	59
4.3.1	Opening declarations	60
4.3.2	The Rules of procedure	63

4.3.3	Parliamentary powers of the Common Assembly	66
5	**Setting up the Ad Hoc Assembly**	**68**
5.1	The political impulse	68
5.2	Remarks on studies on the Ad Hoc Assembly	71
5.3	The Ad Hoc Assembly debate in the Common Assembly	74
5.4	Constitution-writing by parliamentarians	77
5.5	The members of the Ad Hoc Assembly	79
5.6	The organisation of the Ad Hoc Assembly	84
5.7	The Ad Hoc Assembly as a parliamentary institution	89
6	**The Politics of Naming**	**90**
6.1	Naming rhetoric	90
6.2	Naming disputes	91
6.2.1	European Political Community	91
6.2.2	Self-naming of the Ad Hoc Assembly	95
6.2.3	European Parliament	97
6.3	Naming the polity	102
7	**A supranational polity**	**105**
7.1	A colourful conceptual history	105
7.2	Supranationalism in early European integration	107
7.3	Supranationalism in the Ad Hoc Assembly	108
7.3.1	Against nationalism	108
7.3.2	Supranationalism vs. intergovernmentalism	110
7.3.3	The delegation paradigm	114
7.3.4	The parliamentary condition	117
7.3.5	Europeanisation as freedom from dependence	119
7.4	Supranational policies	121
7.4.1	Economic policies	121
7.4.2	Foreign policy	124
7.4.3	Full and associated members	126
7.5	Supranational politicisation	127

8	**The European Parliament**	131
8.1	Histories of parliamentarisation	131
8.2	The Parliament of the Community	132
8.2.1	The organisation of Parliament	133
8.2.2	The bicameral system	140
8.2.3	Legislation and initiative	142
8.3	The Peoples' Chamber	145
8.3.1	Direct elections	145
8.3.2	Proportional or majority representation	151
8.3.3	The distribution of seats	155
8.4	The Senate	158
8.4.1	A parliamentary chamber	158
8.4.2	Parity or balancing of seats	162
8.4.3	Membership and term length	164
8.5	Towards a supranational parliament	168
9	**The European government**	170
9.1	Council of National Ministers	170
9.2	The European Executive Council	176
9.2.1	Composition, powers, activity	176
9.2.2	Election and parliamentary responsibility	178
9.3	A draft for a European parliamentary government	185
10	**Towards a supranational and parliamentary Europe**	190
10.1	Parliamentary virtues of the Ad Hoc Assembly	190
10.2	Proposals for empowering the Parliament	192
10.2.1	The Vedel Report	192
10.2.2	The Spinelli Project	200
10.3	The legacy of the Ad Hoc Assembly	205

References 210

Index of actors 219

Index of concepts 221

1 A momentum of double politicisation

This book analyses a historical momentum that combines two projects for politicising the European order – supranationalism and parliamentarism – which were joined in the debates of the so-called Ad Hoc Assembly from September 1952 to March 1953. The Ad Hoc Assembly, formally the 'Ad Hoc Assembly Instructed to Work Out a Draft Treaty Setting up a European Political Community' drafted a Constitution for the European Political Community (EPC) and, in doing so, combined the two politicisation projects in a unique way to propose a supranational parliamentary government for six European countries. My aim is to write the history of this double politicisation project for European integration and to discuss the political theories included in it.

1.1 A parliamentary alternative for European integration

The European Parliament (EP) is today regarded as the most important supranational parliamentary institution in the world. For parliamentary scholars, the EP is still lacking many criteria of a parliamentary government, although it has gained new powers in the European Union (EU). My point is to recover a parliamentary alternative from the past for West European integration, one originally proposed by parliamentarians from the 'Europe of the Six' (member states of the European Coal and Steel Community) when debating a constitutional draft for the EPC in the Ad Hoc Assembly's plenum and committees.

Applying parliamentary principles to a supranational polity was an unprecedented objective. Acting as a parliamentary-style institution, the Ad Hoc Assembly members sketched out different ideas as well as specific proposals on how to realise a supranational parliamentarism for the EPC. Many of the proposals were not included in the Assembly's Draft Treaty of 10 March 1953, although some of them were realised later, and others remain on the agenda for parliamentarising the present EU. The parliamentary character of the debates is shown in the willingness of the Ad Hoc Assembly members to listen to the arguments and occasionally to change their stands, largely independently of the party affiliation or nationality of the members.

In his *Liberty before Liberalism* Quentin Skinner reminds us of the value of 'bringing buried intellectual treasure back to the surface' (1998, 112). The Ad Hoc Assembly's debates on the constitutional draft offer me an excellent case of lost treasures in parliamentary and supranational politics. Max Weber emphasises that, among the unrealised possibilities, there are what he calls 'objective possibilities' which could have been realised (esp. Weber 1906, 269–

275), and historians should always include them in their judgements about the past. For politicians, the situation is always open for *Chancen,* that is, for possibilities, opportunities, occasions or options (see Weber 1904, 145–146; Palonen 2010 and Tribe 2023), and these existed also for the parliamentarians debating in the Ad Hoc Assembly. This study of unrealised 'objective possibilities' analyses not merely abstract constructions, but a thoroughly debated project for choosing a parliamentary alternative for a supranational Europe.

The debates of the Ad Hoc Assembly contain a range of ideas and proposals worth considering for the parliamentarisation of the EU today. The *Wertbeziehung* (in the sense of Weber 1917a) of this study consists of the superiority of the parliamentary style of politics over others, such as presidential regime, government by experts, intergovernmental negotiation assembly or plebiscitarian populist movements. Besides a system of government, the parliamentary way of doing politics (see Palonen 2018) includes procedural, rhetorical and temporal aspects of debating politics based on members who are free from dependence (in the sense of Skinner 1998). These wider aspects of parliamentary politics were rather implied, if not made explicit, by the Ad Hoc Assembly.

1.2 The Ad Hoc Assembly

The first supranational institution in Europe after the Second World War was the European Coal and Steel Community (ECSC), based on the Treaty of Paris from 1951. Its parliamentary angle was the Common Assembly, which could, by a qualified majority, dismiss the executive High Authority by a vote of no confidence when debating the annual report. As marginal as this possibility appeared, it nonetheless opened a perspective on extending parliamentary government to a supranational level. When the Common Assembly met in September 1952, it immediately attempted to act like a real parliament, seeking to increase its own powers within the ECSC.

The Ad Hoc Assembly was a proto-parliamentary institution, set up by the Council of Foreign Ministers of the six ECSC member states (France, West Germany, Italy, Belgium, Luxembourg and the Netherlands). It was composed of members of the Common Assembly, complemented with a few additional parliamentarians from France, West Germany and Italy as well as observers from Council of Europe member countries outside the ECSC.

The ECSC ministers gave to the Ad Hoc Assembly the task of drafting a Constitution for the European Political Community (EPC). This new political community would serve as a political backup for the ECSC and the European Defence Community (EDC), which the six governments had agreed to launch.

The point was to avoid the weaknesses of the still-intergovernmental Council of Europe with its merely advisory Consultative Assembly, and of the ECSC, in which the supranational executive, High Authority, was not a government of politicians and was exposed only to weak parliamentary control. After thorough debates, the Ad Hoc Assembly's majority agreed that the Constitution of the European Political Community should be based on a supranational parliamentary system, on a European Government responsible to a European Parliament.

For instituting a supranational parliamentary government, no direct historical or theoretical models were available. For writing the Draft Treaty for the European Political Community, the Ad Hoc Assembly was obliged to be politically innovative. A solution as to how to apply the principles, institutions and practices of parliamentary government at the supranational level had to be invented and deliberated. The Ad Hoc Assembly members created an agenda for debating the setup of such a system of government, and the debate itself saw moves put forward for different alternatives regarding the parliament, the electoral system and the election and dismissal of the European government; ultimately, institutions and procedures were chosen for establishing a parliamentary government for Europe.

The Ad Hoc Assembly, with its debates and the Draft Treaty of 10 March 1953, marks a unique event in the history of the European integration. The details of its work never attracted much interest among European integration or parliamentary scholars. Nonetheless, the debates and documents of the Ad Hoc Assembly have been collected and are available in a digitised form at the website of the European University Institute in Florence. The EUI archive is, of course, a sign that a scholarly interest in the politics of the Ad Hoc Assembly could be expected (see section 5.2).

With this background knowledge, I decided to write a book on the politicisation of the concept of Europe – restricted to the six ECSC member states – based on debates and documents of the Ad Hoc Assembly. As a Weberian style of political theorist willing to speculate with my own political imagination, I want to study the Ad Hoc Assembly's work as an exemplar of parliamentary debate and to interpret its debates and documents as an extraordinary application of the idea of parliamentary government to a supranational polity. With this study, I hope to contribute to the conceptual history and political theory of supranational and parliamentary politics, analysing the debates and documents of the Ad Hoc Assembly as the still most comprehensive full-scale project for a European parliamentary government.

1.3 Politicisation as a perspective on Europeanisation

The guiding conceptual principle of this book lies in the claim that Europeanisation is to be understood as a politicisation of an existing order, of a regime based on nation-states and intergovernmental relations between them. The alternative proposed by the Ad Hoc Assembly was for the creation of a supranational parliamentary polity. I consider this double, parliamentary-cum-supranational momentum to be an exemplar of politicisation of the European integration.

Since the 1980s, I have written extensively on the conceptual history of politics as an activity-concept (versus politics as a sphere-concept, see esp. Palonen 2006, 2021) and on ideal-typical reflections on the aspects of this concept (esp. Palonen 2003). From this perspective, politicisation does not signify extending 'the boundaries of the political', as Charles S. Maier (1987) put it, in relation to other sphere-concepts, such as law, economy or religion. When politics is considered as an activity, as in 'dealing with the contingent event', to quote John Pocock (1975, 156), then politics can also be found elsewhere than in what is traditionally considered politics, or 'polity' in the sense of Karl Rohe (1978/1994). The conceptual history of politics in connection with the democratisation and parliamentarisation of polities (see Steinmetz 2018), especially since the second half of the nineteenth century in Europe, can be written in terms of rhetorical *topoi* concerning politics as an activity (see Palonen 2006, 2012, 2021).

Rohe interpreted the German concept of *Politik* with three English nouns, to all of which the adjective 'political' was related, namely 'politics', 'policy' and 'polity' (1978/1994, 61–81). I revised his triad by interpreting the activity of politics in terms of a concept of contingency corresponding to Max Weber's concept of *Chance*, related to opportunities, occasions or options as well as realisable 'objective possibilities' (see Palonen 1998, 2010). My interpretation includes the aspect of *politicking*, as a rhetorically neutralised expression à la W.B. Gallie (1973). With these moves, I understand the activity of politics as an umbrella concept for a typology consisting of four aspects: politicisation, polity, politicking and policy (Palonen 2003; on applying this scheme to Weber's *Politik als Beruf,* see Palonen 2019a).

In this scheme, I understand *politicisation* as initial move that qualifies an action as political. From the activity perspective, politics is not 'already there' as a part of the 'nature' of an object or as a distinct parcel in the garden of concepts. On the contrary, what is called politics will be seen as the result of politicisations, that is, of a variety of contingency-opening moves of the actors as well as of contingency-identifying and -legitimising interpretations of existing states of affairs or trends.

In my 'Four Times' article (2003), I also discussed the relationship of the other aspects of politics to politicisation. To put it shortly, *polity* is a result of combining past moves and experiences of politicisation into what appears as a legitimate range of contingency; this can, however, be challenged by new politicising projects, which can gain legitimacy and thereby alter the polity. Each politicising move opens specific *Chancen* for *politicking*, or playing with these *Chancen* in actual use of the occasions and opportunities for action. *Policy* refers to a distinct normative-finalistic form of politicking, aiming at a coherent line, plan or programme, which is not always better than an opportunistic use of situations.

An exemplary and explicit form of moves for politicisation lies in setting a question onto a parliamentary agenda as a contingent and controversial item to be debated *pro et contra;* the debate follows specific procedures, for example, going through different debating rounds in plena and committees, concluding in a vote on a resolution, which can be regarded as the final step in the debate. Agenda-setting might require specific procedures, time schedules and ways of formulating the question. The politicising potential of moving an item depends on its novelty and scope or reach as well as the ambition level of the item. Parliamentary agenda-setting provides the model for the less-regulated politicisation of new topics onto the agenda of debate in different contexts.

Politicisation can also occur less intentionally, as a politicising interpretation of some realised or ongoing changes of phenomena, including changes in the modes of thinking. Such an identification and judgement of an existing situation or historical trend opens new ways of politicking for the participating actors. A politicising interpretation of changes can dispute what is legitimate or practicable in the polity in question. In this sense, we can also speak of the politicisation of the experience or imagination of persons.

With this conceptual perspective, it is easy to understand how both the introduction of a supranational level and the parliamentarisation of supranational forms of politics are politicising moves. Supranationalism brought the political acting and thinking of European institutions to a new level, delimiting the powers and competence of the nation-states and creating new complex relationships between them and the European level. 'Level' can be understood both in the sense of a spatial metaphor of a broader or higher range for doing politics, and as a temporal concept of a demand to give to the European way of acting politically a different quality than the established practices of the member states. The question is not merely of a greater complexity, but of replacing the identity rhetoric of a nation-state by opening debates on what a politicised concept of Europe would be like and how it could be realised in different types of debates on institutions, procedures and practices.

The history of the parliamentarisation of government in Europe (see, for example, Turkka 2007; Selinger 2019; Ihalainen, Ilie and Palonen eds 2016; Benôit and Rozenberg eds 2020) itself marks a history of politicisation of the ways of dealing with issues in an openly contingent and controversial manner. The setting up of a representative assembly is already a major step towards parliamentarisation of the polity and empowering it to elect and dismiss government is decisive for being able to speak of a parliamentary form of government (see Bagehot 1867/72, Weber 1918). The democratised form of parliamentarism presupposes the election of parliament by universal suffrage of all citizens. The parliamentary character of an assembly also depends on criteria such as fair procedures for thorough debates, the existence of a rhetorical culture capable of weighing the strengths and weaknesses of items for debate, the freedom of members from dependence (free mandate, free speech, freedom from arrest, free and fair elections) as well as enough of fair distribution of parliamentary time (see Palonen 2018).

This analytical and conceptual historical perspective on European politicisation has hardly anything to do with current studies of specialists on the EU's 'politicisation' since the 1990s, which have been marked by the rise of right-wing populist parties turning against the pro-European 'permissive consensus' (see, for example, De Wilde and Zürn 2012; Zürn 2016). Cécile Robert also contests the view by emphasising the expert powers of the European Commission as a form of de-politicisation, regarding their 'expertise as a way of doing politics [while] pretending not to' (2021, esp. 205–206). In more general terms, some of my close colleagues have also highlighted how European integration has, from its origins, been a political project (see Kauppi, Palonen and Wiesner 2016; Wiesner ed. 2019 and 2021; Haapala and Oleart eds 2022). This perspective on politicisation unifies the topics of supranationality and parliamentarism in a way that has very seldom been discussed in the scholarly literature (see, however, Guerriri 2014 on the ECSC's Common Assembly).

1.4 Supranational politicisation

The project for the European Political Community marked a politicisation through the challenge it posed to the nation-state paradigm by aiming at institutionalising a supranational European polity (for the six ECSC member states). It is an excellent example of a radical agenda-setting project that was shifting the unit of the polity itself. The idea of a supranational European polity with its own governmental and parliamentary institutions was new, and for the founders, it was unclear to what extent the citizens were ready to such politicising shifts in their thoughts and opinions in order to convincingly legitimise the new polity-level.

A supranational polity requires of institutions and procedures independent of those of the nation-state. Even if the ministers and officials of a supranational parliament are also citizens of the member states, they must not be bound by an imperative mandate or by a veto power on the part of the member states, for only then may they enjoy a freedom from dependence corresponding to Skinner's concept of neo-Roman liberty (1998). Only such freedom enables the members of supranational institutions to think in 'European' terms.

In an ambitious sense, supranationalism aims at a de-nationalisation of politics and at de-legitimisation of the nation-state as the primary and quasi-natural polity. Supranational Europeanisation has required a constant struggle not only with nationalist thinking, but also with the inertia of vested interests, routines and conventions in existing polities, which must be overcome or neutralised. The point lies in the moment of break with the past, with the 'mythology of parochialism', to quote Quentin Skinner (1969) again, with a willingness to face an unknown future when institutionalising a supranational polity-level.

This politicising perspective on Europeanisation is not teleological: it dispenses with the projection of a future European unity. Europeanisation neither requires a consensus between political actors but presupposes procedures and rhetorical practices for dealing with the disputes regarding the dimensions of politicisation. The different styles or degrees of de-nationalisation can in principle be dealt by the parliamentary style of raising objections and making revisions.

My approach comes close to the view of Ulrich Beck and Edgar Grange on opening a new level of power struggle, implying the loss of many of those valid at the national level:

Mit der Europäisierung ist ein neues Machtspiel eröffnet worden, mit dem die alten, nationalen Machtspiele ihre Regeln und Grundbegriffe, ihre Substanz verloren haben, auch wenn einige politische Akteure sie immer noch weiterspielen. Kurz gesagt: Die Dauerkonflikte, die mit der Europäisierung zugleich geschürt wurden und gezähmt werden sollen, beziehen ihre politische Brisanz gerade darauf, dass die politischen Akteure gezwungen sind, ein neues Spiel zu spielen. (Beck and Grange 2004, 208–209)

The Ad Hoc Assembly hardly ever spoke about politics in the language of playing games. However, when facing the task of constructing supranational parliamentarism, playing with the political imagination was required from them, even if this was presented as a concern for stability and security.

When understood as politicisation, Europeanisation was moved from ideas and identities to procedures, practices and institutions. The forms of European de-nationalisation have not been settled into classical models such as federalism. A European 'we-consciousness' should not be understood as a common ground for action, but as a regulative idea, for which different options and institutional settings could be possible and worth debating. The political idea of Europe presupposes multiple and contested visions and interpretations.

The supranational organising principle is opposed to the intergovernmentalism characteristic of the 'Westphalian' order of great powers. The intergovernmental principle still shaped the League of Nations, the United Nations and their suborganisations, the OEEC, the NATO and, as mentioned, the Council of Europe. The European Political Community was intended to be supranational also in the legal sense of a unit that can sign international treaties and agreements.

Supranational Europeanisation still left important powers to the member states. The most common justification for the supranational polity in this context was member states' agreeing to transfer a part of their sovereignty to the supranational polity. This required a demarcation of powers and competence as well as a procedure for dealing with disputes concerning them between the member state and European polity levels. The 'question of Europe' was expected to be a part of the domestic controversies of the member states.

1.5 Parliamentary politicisation

Historically, the parliamentary element played at most a secondary role in the post-war European movement. The supranational element in the European Coal and Steel Community was the High Authority, initially without a controlling parliamentary institution: the Common Assembly was only introduced after negotiations with the member states. In the later stage of European integration, the increased powers of the European Commission, a successor of the High Authority, have also been repeatedly defended against the Parliamentary Assembly, later renamed the European Parliament (see Schorkopf 2022; Robert 2021). For this reason, the work of the Ad Hoc Assembly, combining the parliamentary momentum with the supranational one, was exceptional.

To speak of the parliamentarisation of a new type of polity is to refer to a different politicisation than that of changing the political system of a country from a constitutional monarchy, a presidential system or a rule of officialdom (*Beamtenherrschaft*) to a parliamentary system (Weber 1918, 235–258). The immediate objective of European parliamentarisation was to overcome the intergovernmental model of most international institutions as well as the model of a non-partisan expert government.

A difficulty with the Europeanisation of the parliamentary style of politics was the historical link between parliament and national representation both in Westminster and in the continental European polities. Parliament in such a view refers not to a political practice of debating *pro et contra* but to a unified 'people' behind it. Edmund Burke's strong defence of parliamentary autonomy in his speech to the electorate in Bristol rendered the deliberative assembly in a 'national' context: 'Parliament is a deliberative Assembly of one Nation, with one Interest, that of the whole' (Burke 1774, §105). In France, the representing *la nation une et indivisible* was even stronger, which has made deliberation *pro et contra* à la Westminster difficult to accept (see Gunn 2009), even the parliament's name was Assemblée Nationale, and the Frankfurt Parlament of 1848 was officially called Nationalversammlung.

The assumption of the parliament as only a national institution was also a major obstacle for Britain to join supranational institutions, including the ECSC. In the British concept of representation, there have been strong 'mimetic' features (see Conti 2019). An alternative vision, as it is formulated by Frank Ankersmit, understands that representation itself is a political act that creates the represented and the representatives (see esp. Ankersmit 2002, 115), which can be regarded as a condition for an independent debating parliament. In this sense, 'parliament' refers to a way of doing politics in a 'parliamentary' manner, independently of whether on national, subnational or supranational level.

A supranational parliamentary government could not simply imitate the forms, practices and historical experiences of parliamentarisation. The route to parliamentary government has varied radically from country to country, and there exists no single set of criteria for judging whether a government fulfils to a sufficient degree the requirements for parliamentary government. It would be necessary to consider the given criteria in order to distinguish the parliamentary way of doing politics from other ways (see Palonen 2018).

There are some political criteria to distinguish an estate diet from a parliament. Historically, they refer to how the British Parliament lost its estate character in the late Middle Ages and how the revolutionary French parliament broke with the preceding assemblies. They are marked by the freedom of members from dependence, or Skinner's neo-Roman concept of liberty (1998, 2002). The free, as opposed to imperative, mandate was a major dimension in these breaks (see Müller 1966, for France Tanchoux 2004), as well as freedom of speech in parliament (see Colclough 2005), freedom from arrest (parliamentary immunity) and free and fair elections (see Hexter 1992). Since the First World War free and fair parliamentary elections included universal male and female suffrage.

The parliamentary way of doing politics is characterised by its rules of procedure. These have been developed in Westminster since the seventeenth century and codified since the eighteenth century in the works of John Hatsell, Jeremy Bentham and Thomas Erskine May (see Redlich 1905 and Palonen 2014a). The Westminster style of parliamentarism has a multi-stage debate in plenum and in committees as the core of parliamentary process of politics, with the last step in debate being the final vote itself (see Griffith and Ryle 2003, 86).

The Francophone procedure, despite many similarities (see Pierre 1887), has always regarded debate merely as a preparation to the final decision by vote (see the discussion in Palonen 2019b). Complementary to this procedural aspect lies parliamentary rhetoric, in which aesthetic eloquence is subordinated to political judgement, and the unit of rhetoric is not a speech, but a debate (see Palonen 2016).

Furthermore, parliamentary politics is also that of playing with time as a key element of political action. Time is built into the key parliamentary moves, from agenda-setting via presenting a motion to debate in multiple regulated stages, through interrupting the smooth advance of a motion by amendments, adjournments, raising questions of order, later the *clôture* for terminating the debate, and so on. From early on, Westminster has recognised the limits to parliamentary time, and it has proposed different regulations to deal with it. With parliamentary powers over everyday questions and with the democratisation of suffrage and membership, the scarcity of parliamentary time tended to paralyse parliaments, and new rules for distributing parliamentary time more fairly were required (See Redlich 1905; Vieira 2015; Palonen 2014a and 2018). The length of parliamentary sessions and the restrictions on speech and debate times radicalised the government vs. opposition divide in parliament, more recently with provisions in Westminster to strengthen the cross-party initiatives of backbenchers (see Wright 2012, Evans ed. 2017). An important consequence of the longer and more intensive parliamentary time after the Second World War was the professionalisation of the practices of parliamentary politics (See Borchert 2003, Palonen 2023).

Parliamentary-style politics contains other questions of how parliamentary government should be applied to a supranational polity. One of the lessons of the revolutionary parliament in the English Civil War was that a parliament itself cannot govern – such attempts have later in French been called pejoratively *régime d'assemblée* – but instead, parliament must appoint from among its members an executive committee, a government or a cabinet, as the political core of government is called in Britain (see Bagehot 1867/1872).

British history in the decades after the Glorious Revolution of 1688/89 contains a number of political innovations which together provided necessary conditions for the parliamentary government of Westminster. The monarch and the court retained a 'dignified' part in government, whereas the cabinet formed the 'efficient' part of it (Bagehot 1867/72, 9–10). The cabinet included the appointment of a Prime Minister and cabinet ministers from among the members of the Houses or Parliament (Selinger 2019), the formation of parties and, through them, the government versus opposition divide in parliament (Kluxen 1956; 1983, Skinner 1974). For the latter, a decisive feature were the first attempts to dismiss government by purely political grounds, as manifested in Sandys' Motion in 1741 (Turkka 2007); however, the principle that a cabinet that has lost the confidence of the parliamentary majority must resign or dissolve the parliament was finally affirmed only after the First Reform Act in 1835 (Andrén 1947). Only after that did the term 'parliamentary government' became a regular one (see Grey 1855), while in the twentieth century scholarship the possibility of a parliamentary majority dismissing a government became a standard criterion for parliamentary government.

Westminster concepts have played a remarkable role also in continental European parliamentarism, although its fates and experiences have differed widely. A major divide has been between the British style of gradual and partly unintended forms of politicisation through parliamentarisation versus the conscious creation of parliamentary constitutions, which took place especially in the new states created after World War I, frequently without permanent success.

In the context of analysing issues constitutive for parliamentary government, such as bicameralism, the electoral system, simple vs. qualified majority and so on, I shall invoke the French and German historical experiences, political constellations and distinct institutional devices either as parallels or as contrasts to the motions taken up in the Ad Hoc Assembly. Support for specific 'national' arrangements might then appear as tacit moves to oppose or to restrict supra-nationalism.

Europeanisation also set new requirements for politicking: in domestic assessments of the European dimension; in negotiations between the European and member-state level; and within the European institutions themselves. A supranational parliament cannot be realised as a project of officials and experts without first hearing the political voice of the citizens, that is, without democratisation. European-level parliamentary debate and representation based on free and fair elections with universal suffrage are the key institutions for democratisation, in addition to the role played by human rights, citizenship, citizen initiatives and experiments with advisory assemblies elected by sortition.

The Ad Hoc Assembly's constitutional draft also gave impetus for revising judgements on the political significance of parliaments in post-war Europe. There had been claims that parliaments would be outdated or replaced by planning, a claim made by ideologues among the Social Democrats and, in a more technocratic version, by Gaullists in France (see Roussellier 2015). For a neo-Marxist, the parliament had suffered an 'involution' and become only a façade in the capitalist states (Agnoli 1967). In the student movement, the longing for direct, participatory democracy, frequently in combination with old *Räte* or workers' council models, was offered as an alternative to parliamentarism (see e.g. Gottschalch 1968). Moderate forms of devaluing parliamentary politics were included in the *Parteienstaat* thesis of Gerhard Leibholz (1951) as well as with Jürgen Habermas' hopes for pre-parliamentary public activities of the *Öffentlichkeit* (1962).

I have contributed to arguments against the alleged decline of parliamentarism (see Palonen 2021b; Palonen, Rosales and Turkka eds 2014; Palonen and Rosales ed. 2015; Turkka and Soininen eds 2012). The debates of the Ad

Hoc Assembly show that conservative, liberal and social democratic parliamentarians from West European countries offered, with the rise of supranationalism, a new defence of parliamentary government, and that these bear a closer examination. Their parliamentary experiences and identities tended to view officials and experts with suspicion, while placing trust in parliamentary institutions' procedures and practices to hold governments, officials and experts in check.

1.6 Research agenda and practices of analysis

In this volume, I analyse the politicisation of European integration through the debates and documents of the Ad Hoc Assembly in three different contexts of scholarship. The first concerns the parliamentary dimension in post-war projects of European integration. This deals with the key projects of that time, such as the Hague Congress for Europe in 1948, the Treaty of London, which established the Council of Europe, and the early Common Assembly of the ECSC, including its first attempts at parliamentarisation.

The second context lies in the political theory and conceptual history of parliamentarism. The EU studies have so far seldom gained the interest of parliamentary scholars and vice versa. My interest in the topic extends the focus on parliamentary studies during the last 15–20 years. In *Parliamentary Thinking* (2018), I discussed other criteria for evaluating parliamentary and political qualities besides the formal presence of a parliamentary government alone, but taking also into account such aspects as procedures, rhetoric, freedom from dependence, and playing with time: these aspects are built into the parliamentary style of doing politics. Although the questions of formal parliamentary government were a clear priority in the Ad Hoc Assembly, parliamentary time and excluding imperative mandates were also an inherent part of the debates, and by implication, also the politics of procedure and the rhetorical practices.

A consequence of supranational Europeanisation, as planned for the European Political Community was dissolving the classical divide between domestic politics and foreign policy, characteristic of the Westphalian order (on the initial discrepancy see, for example, Koselleck 1959). The supranational Europeanisation applies disputes at the level of the European polity, whereas parliamentarisation contests governments' monopoly in the inter-polity relations by applying the distinct parliamentary form of deliberating between alternative courses of action over diplomatic negotiations concerning the borders and the distribution of resources. This also brings up the question of the problem of counting vs. weighing votes, and of the majority principle as opposed to plural votes, and veto powers for some participants (see Weber 1917b, 167–172).

I have left out of the study traditional historians' questions, such as: following the fate of the constitutional Draft beyond its passing in the Ad Hoc Assembly in March 1953; and how and why the European Political Community was rejected by the French Assemblée Nationale, which for years was a major blow to European integration. Such topics have been discussed in several studies (such as Kapteyn 1962, Forsyth 1964, Griffiths 2000, Rittberger 2005, Krumrey 2018). Consequently, I shall concentrate exclusively on the debates and documents of the Ad Hoc Assembly as marking an important, early strand of thinking about Europe in supranational and parliamentary terms.

Nonetheless, and this marks third perspective on the Ad Hoc Assembly, I do notice comment on several later decisions of EU institutions, if they are clearly related to the Draft Treaty and items debated by the Ad Hoc Assembly. In the final chapter I speculate, against the background of later parliamentarisation projects, on the prospects for parliamentarisation of the EU today in relation to the debates in the Ad Hoc Assembly.

There are different 'methodological' alternatives for studying the Ad Hoc Assembly's debates and documents from a politicisation perspective. One is to take the text of the treaties and related documents as the point of departure for comparing the Draft Treaty with other post-war European treaties or programmatic proposals. More interesting would be to compare the draft versions of the treaties and proposals, analyse the alterations made in the drafts and speculate on the grounds for making the alterations. This would be the perspective of a constitutional theorist (see Schorkopf 2023).

As the debates of the Ad Hoc Assembly in plenum and in committees are available, however, it is possible to look at the topic from the angle of key treaty-related topics in the archived debates. My preferred strategy as a conceptually and rhetorically oriented parliamentary scholar lies in focusing on the debates themselves. Instead of concentrating on the final documents, a study of the parliamentary style of doing politics requires analysing the debates, regarding documents as the contingent results of debate, and including moves in debate which never gained a majority in the vote. In this sense, the debate analysis deepens the 'history of losers' perspective characteristic of this study and renders intelligible the shifts in the formulations of the draft versions. Studying debates could thus contribute to identifying politics-in-action by rendering the moves, arguments and debate constellations more intelligible. An additional advantage of the debate-focused approach is that it raises interest in the details, including those politically relevant concepts and topics which arose as by-products of thematic debates on the items, but which relate to wider political controversies.

The topical foci of the debates must be compiled selectively in order to avoid the morass of empiricism. I have used the *topoi* of supranationalism, parliamentarism and the themes and concepts linking them together as the selection principle, in part, following their presentation in the constitutional draft. This perspective allowed me to thematise the *topoi* and their mutual links in the debates – including differences between the specific sites of the debate within the Ad Hoc Assembly – and then follow how they were included, modified or excluded.

For accentuating the politicisation perspective, I begin the analysis of documents and debates with an additional level of thematic abstraction, namely the rhetoric used in the politics of naming. For an unprecedented supranational European polity, the actors – already at the time of the early Council of Europe and of the ECSC – were obliged to name the institutions and the principles by which they would follow or break with tradition. It is, for example, informative to examine the expression 'European Parliament' – when, where, how and by whom it has been used, and how its political significance was altered in debates up to and including the Ad Hoc Assembly.

The key concepts around parliamentarism and supranationalism can be taken as indications of how far the actors go with the politicising of Europeanisation. At the same time, any use – or absence of use – of the parliamentary and supranational vocabulary may be considered as politicking when referring to the specific contexts and audiences of the debate. The tactics employed oblige me to consider the parliamentarians as 'innovating ideologists' in the sense used by Quentin Skinner (1974).

In my procedures and practices of textual interpretation (see Wiesner, Haapala and Palonen 2017), the study of the politics of naming introduces an abstract, but illustrative focus for interpreting the parliamentarism and supranationalism in the Ad Hoc Assembly's project for a Constitution for the European Political Community. The focus will then be sharpened or narrowed to analyse the debates around the Constitutional Draft and their changes during the half-year period in 1952/53.

My twenty-year study of parliamentary politics has equipped me with a political imagination concerning the parliamentary way of doing politics, and I am applying this imagination to the present volume as well. This includes the Weberian way of discussing items in the context of the various *Chancen* it contained and, when the item is in the past, its 'objective possibilities', that is, what was a realisable possibility, although not realised in the actual case (see esp. Weber 1906). This is a further reason why I have chosen for this study the specific combination of supranationalism and parliamentarism as discussed in the Ad Hoc Assembly. The wider questions on later history and the prospects for parliamentary supranationalism, as proposed by the Draft Treaty, will be discussed in the final chapter.

1.7 Plan of the book and acknowledgements

First, I want to specify what I am not doing. This book is neither a history of the Ad Hoc Assembly nor a constitutional commentary on the Draft Treaty and its origins. My focus on the political momentum connecting supranationalism and parliamentarism has made my reading of the sources and my discussion of the topics selective. I have practically left out the legal status of the Political Community entirely as well as that of the advisory Economic and Social Council, as they were not immediately relevant to the problems at hand. I have only touched upon the relationship to the inclusion of the European Coal and Steel Community and the European Defence Community, although this was extensively debated. The membership in and association with the Political Community, including the debates speeches of the observers, have been treated only shortly. As mentioned, my analysis covers the period up until 10 March 1953.

In Chapters 2 and 3, I present the historical context of the politicising moments of supranationalisation and parliamentarisation. I first deal with the rise of pro-European movements during and after the Second World War, culminating in the Hague Congress on Europe in May 1948. Chapter 3 the deals with creation of the Council of Europe as an intergovernmental institution in which the Consultative Assembly followed parliamentary forms, but without parliamentary powers, with certain analogies to the Reichstag of the German Empire.

In the Chapter 4, the point of departure is the Schuman Declaration, on 9 May 1950, which led to the European Coal and Steel Community (ECSC), which vested supranational powers in its High Authority. Its Common Assembly consisted of parliamentarians from the six member countries. They initiated measures to act as a 'first European Parliament', in part, due to the experiences of the Consultative Assembly. The ECSC's Council of Ministers proposed in the first session of the Common Assembly in September 1952, the setup of the Ad Hoc Assembly, including advisory members from Council of Europe countries, for writing a constitutional Draft for the European Political Community.

Chapter 5 deals with the setting up, membership and organisation of the Ad Hoc Assembly until December 1952, including the work of the Constitutional Committee, the Working Party and several Sub-committees. The most important Sub-committee was that of Political Institutions. I left out any analysis of the Counter project of the Gaullist Michel Debré, which rejected supranationalism and marginalised parliamentarism.

Chapters 6 to 9 analyse the debates in plenum, committees and Sub-committees, following to some extent the paragraphs of the final Draft Treaty. The changing range of disagreements will be a topic of detailed analysis, while connecting the chapters to political theories of supranationalism and parliamentarism. The politics of naming (Chapter 6) gives a glimpse into the conceptual and rhetorical controversies that are analysed in detail in the subsequent chapters.

The debates around the interrelated concepts of supranationalism (Chapter 7), parliament (Chapter 8) and government (Chapter 9) are analytically separated and interpreted through different topics of debate as they arose in the Ad Hoc Assembly. The focus is on the break with the past, especially with the Council of Europe and the ECSC, and on repeated debates and changing standpoints of the Ad Hoc Assembly itself. The analyses of the Assembly's debates link politicisation with proposed conceptual innovations, as *Vorgriffe* in the sense of Reinhart Koselleck (1972), as required by the unprecedented character of the proposed supranational parliamentary polity.

In the final Chapter 10 of the book my focus moves beyond the singular momentum of the politicisation, with its link between supranationalism and parliamentarism and its corresponding break with the separation of domestic from foreign politics. I first recapitulate the significance of this momentum, comparing it briefly to two later parliamentarisation projects (the Vedel Report and the Spinelli Project), to the Ad Hoc Assembly's momentum, and in terms of the Assembly as discussing new prospects for parliamentarisation of the EU today.

My interest in EU politics is the result of many years of co-operation in different research projects with Claudia Wiesner, Taru Haapala and Niilo Kauppi, without whom this book would never have been written. I thank Kyösti Pekonen, Niilo and Claudia for their reading and commenting of earlier drafts of this book. I further thank University of Jyväskylä's Department of Social Sciences and Philosophy for the correction of my English.

2 Parliament in post-war European projects

The inclusion of a parliamentary element in international organisations and institutions is a relatively late phenomenon. The Inter-Parliamentary Union (IPU) was founded in 1889 as a peace project in the form of a debating society of parliamentarians. Only after the First World War did it become a forum for debating on and defending parliamentarism and democracy, a feature it lost in part after the Second World War, when countries with façade parliaments, such as the Soviet Union, were accepted as members (see Kissling 2006). Nonetheless, 'representative democracy' remains one of its main activities, in addition to human rights, sustainable development and promoting women in politics (http://archive.ipu.org/iss-e/issues.htm)

The Hague Peace Conferences (1899 and 1907) were hybrid assemblies of diplomats, scholars and parliamentarians, but used parliamentary rules of proceeding as the model for debates in their meetings. The Assembly of the League of Nations and in particular the General Assembly of the United Nations can also be considered quasi-parliamentary institutions in their procedures of deliberating; and many countries have elected parliamentarians to serve as members of their UN delegations, although the government and not the parliamentary delegation decides on the country's vote. Proposals for establishing a parliamentary assembly for the UN been made, but they have still not been realised (see Leinen and Bummel 2017)

2.1 Post-war pro-European projects

The Europe-wide cooperation of the immediate post-war years had its origins in different voluntary Europe-related organisations, which were inspired by ideas from the period of war-time exile (see the documentation *Historical Archives of the European Union*, and *Documents on the History of European Integration*, eds Walter Lipgens and Wilfried Loth, vols III and IV, 1988, 1991 and Loth's introduction to both volumes). These projects could be roughly divided as follows: the federalists à la Altiero Spinelli, who founded the 'Union des Fédéralistes Européens' and the intergovernmental unionists around Winston Churchill and Duncan Sandys with their 'United Europe Movement' as well as Richard Coudenhove-Kalergi's 'Union Parlementaire Européenne' (see Schlochauer 1953/55; Wiesner 2018; for British debates Haapala 2022).

Wilfried Loth mentions four 'basic impulses' for the European integration: 'a desire for a new system of security in a world in which national states could no longer provide effective protection against foreign aggression'; 'the quest for a solution of the "German question" that would provide greater stability than the discredited system of Versailles'; 'attempts to create larger economic areas' and the fact that 'Europeans desired to assert their identity *vis-à-vis* the new world powers' (1991, 1). The main point is that there existed genuine attempts to create political institutions transcending the nation-state. Worth noticing here is the absence of a teleological vision for Europe.

The European projects took place in the context of such events as the formation of the Soviet Bloc, including the Berlin Blockade of 1948–1949 and the forming of the West and East German states, the US policy of the Marshall Plan aid to West European countries, including at first the 1947 Brussels Pact between Britain, France and the Benelux States, and the slow breakup of both the British Commonwealth and the French Union. All this is visible in the debates on a supranational and parliamentary Europe.

The debate on European cooperation in the post-war years and the activities of the European movement were held on a general level. If the documents edited by Lipgens and Lüth offer a representative picture of the movement, it is obvious that parliaments did not play any explicit role in the plans before the Hague Congress of 1948. Even the federalists did not necessarily support parliamentary government (on the different views among British federalists, see Haapala 2022). The supranational and parliamentary stands discussed in this chapter remained minoritarian, and the situation changed only with the Schuman Declaration of 1950.

Why was so little attention dedicated to parliaments? It might have been the case that a parliament was a self-evident part of planning a federation or a confederal union. For example, in the debates on the West German *Grundgesetz* in the *Parlamentarischer Rat* in 1948/49, no real disputes arose on the acceptance of a parliamentary government (see Otto 1971, Feldkamp 2008).

Equally plausible could be that the activists of movement politics were suspicious of parliaments, due to the experiences of parliamentary failures in the inter-war years or the felt need for urgent government action. Public opinion in the early Federal Republic was suspicious of parliamentary government (see Ullrich 2009). Direct participation of citizens, US-style presidential models (as attempted in the Bavarian constitution), and the plebiscitarian practices of Switzerland were present among movement activists and different party groups (see Charles de Gaulle's 'Europe per Referendum', in *Documents* vol. 3, 110–113).

For many in the European movement, political procedures and institutions were regarded as secondary compared to economic interests and cultural values. Only with the Hague Congress for Europe arose the disputes between a parliamentary versus a governmental basis for European institutions as well as between the federalist versus unionist political regimes. For the period after the Hague, the *Documents* of Lipgens and Loth make visible the struggles on the status and the form of parliamentary representation in the European integration.

In this chapter I shall discuss the Hague debates from the viewpoint of the supranational and parliamentary politicisation of Europe. I shall also analyse some less known documents, which, although having no immediate political significance, did contain ideas later discussed in the Ad Hoc Assembly.

2.2 The Hague Congress

The inter-European meeting of parliamentarians and activists was the Congress for Europe in the Hague in May 1948 (see https://archives.eui.eu/en/fonds/158711?item=ME.45.01=). The aim was to bring together federalists and unionists as well as of government representatives. The proceedings followed parliamentary practices.

Different pro-European organisations made remarkable preparations and a huge number of participants came from Western Europe – even a couple of Finnish representatives were present, also emigrants such as Salvador Madriaga from Spain as well as some participants from the Soviet-bloc countries. European unification was on the agenda across the continent. The organising committee consisted of the following organisations: 'Conseil Français pour l'Europe', 'Une Ligne Indépendante de Coopération Européenne', 'Nouvelles Equipes Internationales', 'Union Européenne des Fédéralistes', 'Union Parlementaire Européenne', and 'United Europe Movement' (Document divers, ME–1264.pdf), thus including both federalists and unionists.

In parliamentary committee style, the organisers prepared a 'Political Report' that justified the plans for a new Union. It was a first draft for a constitutional document and was followed by a 'Political Resolution' as a motion to be debated and voted upon in the plenary session of the Congress in a proto-parliamentary manner. I have disregarded the other documents submitted to the Congress.

2.2.1 The 'Political Report' and the 'Political Resolution'

The 'Comité International de Coordination pour l'Unité Européenne' drafted a 'Political Report' to the Congress (Document divers, ME–1264.pdf). Its preamble was based on analysing a common danger:

...increasingly resigned to the possibility, if not the probability, of another war—the peoples of Europe are faced with the prospect of moral and material ruin.

Their peril is great and immediate. But so too is their opportunity.

... Yet all these immense possibilities cannot be realised so long as Europe allows herself to remain enfeebled by internal division.

... it is only by uniting herself that Europe can overcome her immediate difficulties and go forward to fulfill her mission for the future.

The unification of Europe was a move justified by the Cold War. Nothing, however, was said about the art of dealing with the dangers inherent in division. The language of 'mission' gives to the concept of Europe a teleological colour, instead of the transcending of nationalism as a political project. Nonetheless, Article 5 sets 'a political union' as the first of its 'principles and objectives':

> It is impossible to keep problems of economic collaboration and defence separate from those of general political policy. Economic and defence plans having been made, political power is required to implement them. The processes of industrial and military integration, even in the early stages, inevitably give rise to conflicts of national interests. These difficulties can only be resolved and the necessary compromises accepted when the problem is viewed in the light of wider political considerations. If therefore the policy of mutual aid, adopted by the Governments of the Sixteen Nations, is to bear any substantial fruit, it must be accompanied step by step with a parallel policy of closer political union. Sooner or later this must involve the renunciation or, to be more accurate, the joint exercise of certain sovereign powers. (Article 5)

The formulation 'wider political considerations' leaves the impression of rising above a conventional intergovernmental organisation. The words 'a...policy of closer political union' and 'the joint exercise of certain sovereign powers' indicate a break with the system of allegedly sovereign nation-states, although formulated cautiously. Politically, the new European institutions must be based on democracy and human rights, formulated in Article 7: 'The admission of a nation to membership of a European Union must therefore be conditional upon its acceptance of democratic principles and its assurance to its citizens of the fundamental rights of the individual.' Human rights, as contained in the UN declaration from the same year, seems to be the main point and 'democratic principles' concerns only the election criteria of the member states.

The politics of naming deserves attention. The new entity was called in the Political Report 'a European Union'. If we consider the dispute between the two schools, to speak of a Union is here a minimalist solution, as opposed to a European Federation. Article 16 remained explicitly on an intergovernmental basis: 'United Europe would constitute a Regional Group of the kind expressly provided for in the Charter of U.N.O.'. The introduction of a new polity-level is legitimised by maintenance of national traditions: 'One of the aims and advantages of a European Union, achieved by consent, will be to preserve these national traditions and distinctive characteristics which, under forceful totalitarian unification, would assuredly be obliterated' (Article 9). The Nazi and Fascist regimes were not regarded as extreme nationalistic, but rather as anti-national empires.

Article 18 proposed a preliminary institution, 'an Emergency Council of Europe', for which the 'foundations' already existed in the Brussels Treaty between Britain, France and the Benelux States. Although this Council remained intergovernmental, the report also proposed powers which would be making it able to impose its decisions on the member states: 'The Council will, of course, only be effective if Governments are prepared in practice to implement its decisions, even though these should involve sacrifices of national or sectional interests.' The Council could persuade the governments to make 'sacrifices' in favour of a common European policy. For the Council, an 'administrative and planning staff' would be provided (Article 21).

The task of the Political Section was seen as being 'to develop a common European policy; to secure combined action to uphold and strengthen the democratic way of life; and to examine the constitutional problem of bringing about the organic unity of Europe'. The preparation for the European Union's policy was not given to a politically responsible government, but to a group of officials and experts in European matters. To speak of 'the organic unity of Europe' is an attempt to de-politicise the unification, instead of deliberating over alternative policies or negotiating over the powers between the European and national polity-levels.

The agreement on human rights was regarded as a condition for the new Union. 'Governments should, as a condition of membership of the Council, subscribe to a common Declaration guaranteeing the fundamental personal and civic rights essential for the maintenance of democracy, and should recognise the authority of the Council to enforce them' (Article 22). The supervision of the rights was left to an 'independent European Court' (23).

Nonetheless, the Political Report contains a vision of a future in which both the supranational and the parliamentary aspects are included to a certain degree:

Plans must be prepared for the permanent and organic unification of Europe. These should include:

(a) The grant of a Common Citizenship, without loss of original nationality;

(b) The creation of a single European Defence Force;

(c) The development of a unified economic system; and finally

(d) The conclusion of a complete Federation with an elected European Parliament. (Article 26)

The Political Report was perhaps the earliest post-war occasion in which the expression 'European Parliament' was used. The idea and the term were used among the federalists of the European movement, but otherwise it seems not to have been mentioned in the Hague Congress.

The 'Political Resolution' was '[in] accordance with the principles and objectives set out in the Political Report submitted [to the Congress] by the International Committee of the Movements for European Unity' (ibid.). If the Report was a background work for a constitutional draft, the Political Resolution set on the agenda a motion to be debated and voted.

In the first Article of the Resolution, the Congress '[r]ecognises that it is the urgent duty of the nations of Europe to create an economic and political union in order to assure security and social progress'. Again, the vision or philosophy of history expressed here regards the union as a kind of necessity, not a result of political deliberations and choices. The urgency of the situation required, according to the Resolution, further steps towards a union: 'in the present emergency the organisations created are by themselves insufficient to provide any lasting remedy' (Article 2).

The necessity argument was also used for facilitating a partial transfer of sovereignty. The Congress…'Declares that the time has come when the European nations must transfer and merge some portion of their sovereign rights so as to secure common political and economic action for the integration and proper development of their common resources'. This necessity is compatible with retaining the member states as the units that enable common action and integration of resources.

The Article 3 states: [The Congress] 'Considers that any Union or Federation of Europe should be designed to protect the security of its constituent peoples, should be free from outside control, and should not be directed against any other nation'. The disputes between the organisers are left open by the formula 'Union or Federation', the first referring perhaps to a confederation. The very first point in the plenary debate on the resolution draft was a blow against the federalist faction, namely, deleting the words 'union fédérale', and replacing them with a vague voluntary unity of European peoples, 'l'unité volontaire peuples de l'Europe'.

Article 5 contained a parallel between the political and socio-economic parts of the Union: [The Congress] 'Assigns to a United Europe the immediate task of establishing progressively a democratic social system, the aim of which shall be to free men from all types of slavery and economic insecurity, just as political democracy aims at protecting them against the exercise of arbitrary power.' Here we can identify signs of the classical, 'neo-Roman' concept of freedom from dependence, for which slavery and arbitrary power are two sides of the same coin (see Skinner 1998, 2002).

In the Congress plenum, the federalist standpoint was defended by the Swiss personalist philosopher Denis de Rougemont (ME–0388.pdf). For the counter-position spoke Winston Churchill, the Conservative opposition leader (see ME–0421.pdf). For him: 'In the centre of our movement stands a charter of human rights, guarded by freedom and sustained by law'. He interpreted the claims for 'some sacrifice or merger of national sovereignty' in a way that opposes supranationality, as 'that larger sovereignty which can alone protect their [nations'] diverse and distinctive characteristics and national traditions' when they are threatened by totalitarian regimes. Instead of 'drawing rigid constitutions … the leadership must be taken by the ruling Governments'. Nonetheless, he spoke also of the 'voice of Europe as a unified whole', for which 'in one or another form a European Assembly shall be constituted' (ibid). In Churchill's Hague address, the supranational and the parliamentary elements remained very limited.

Although allied to Churchill's Unionists, Richard Coudenhove-Kalergi took a stand for a federalist vision: 'l'Europe doit-elle s'organiser en une Société des Nations Continentale, – ou en une grande nation, régie par une Constitution Fedérale' (ibid.). To speak of Europe as a 'nation' indicates, however, that he had not broken with nationalist thinking. Coudenhove-Kalergi opted for a 'Constituante Continentale', for which he saw his own organisation, 'l'Union Parlementaire Européenne' and its planned meeting in Interlaken in September 1948 as being 'avant-garde'. For him, it was important to get parliamentarians to support the continental federalism of his version.

British Labour MP Bob Edwards said: 'It is important for European socialists to unite with those forces who firstly agree on the economic unification of Europe', indirectly disputing both supranationalism and parliamentarism. French MP Francis Leenhardt (UDSR) turned explicitly against the federalists: 'Il est clair que peuples auraient davantage de raisons d'avoir confiance dans leurs gouvernements plutôt que dans les chefs des mouvements fédéralistes réunis ici'. In the final speech, British Conservative MP and Churchill's son-in-law Duncan Sandys gave parliamentarians a major role in promoting Europe and connected this to Coudenhove-Kalergi's organisation: 'The campaign must be conducted through every channel open to us. Parliamentary action will become increasingly important. The European Parliamentary Union provides an effective instrument for the initiation and a co-ordination of efforts in this vital sphere' (ibid.).

The federalist stand was defended by the French Socialist, former Prime Minister Paul Ramadier, who expressed pro-parliamentary sentiment by opposing the demand for unanimity, favouring instead the use of majority decisions among the European institutions to limit national sovereignty: 'Il faut franchir de nouvelles étapes, établir la loi majoritaire, prendre appui sur l'opinion publique, édifier peu a peu une loi européenne' (ibid.). Italian Liberal Nicolo Carandini wanted to establish a European federation:

> nous la voyons, quant à nous, dans une fédération politique véritable et discipliné des états européens, une fédération qui seule, s'élevant au-dessus de la souveraineté même, en remettant entre les mains des pouvoirs fédéraux la tâche d'obliger chaque nation à accepter les sacrifices initiaux qu'exige l'établissement d'une communauté européenne, non illusoire. (ibid.)

Dutch Socialist and federalist activist Hendrik Brugmans used the term 'supranational': 'le vrai problème', c'est de créer l'organisation supranationale de l'Europe, seule capable de nous offrir un vaste marché intérieur, base d'une prospérité solide' (ibid.). He saw that an organisation of the League of Nations or United Nations type was paralysed by the veto and regarded intergovernmental organisations as having a dependence on nationalism: 'Jamais un rassemblement des Etats souverains ne nous sauvera du nationalisme.' He concludes: 'qu'il faut organiser une volonté politique européenne, qui seule permettra à la démocratie fédérale de fonctionner'. His fellow party member Koos Vorrink supported the idea with a future-oriented justification: 'The accomplishment of the Federative concept should be the nucleus of any constructive and forward-looking policy which is to fill the urgent needs of the moment. In this way alone will European civilisation be able to continue its mission for humanity.' (ibid.)

The parliament hardly played any role in the Hague debates. Even Ramadier saw the use of a parliamentary majority mainly as little more than way to break the nationalistic obstruction to Europeanisation.

The Political Resolution and the plenary debates marked a return to an intergovernmental system with a parliamentary assembly reduced to an advisory position having no legislative powers or powers over the government and administration. European unity was seen in terms of progress, prosperity and human rights instead of as an openly political choice. The titles of the Political Report – European Union, European Parliament and Deliberative Assembly – disappeared from the Political Resolution and from the plenary debates.

2.2.2 'European Deliberative Assembly'

The 'European Union' proposed to the Hague Congress contained, however, a parliamentary aspect called the European Deliberative Assembly, which the Political Report presented as follows:

The success of all these emergency measures will depend upon making the parliaments and general public European-minded. The best way of achieving this would be to create immediately a European Deliberative Assembly through which views could be exchanged and a common European opinion expressed on the problems of the day. This Assembly, whilst it could not in present circumstances exercise legislative powers, would be able to give valuable support and advice to the European Council. The quickest way of bringing such an Assembly into being would be for each parliament to nominate the necessary representatives. Later, a system of popular election should be instituted. (ME-1264.pdf)

In terms of the politics of naming, 'deliberative' was here seen as opposed to a decision-making assembly, that is, it remained an advisory or consultative assembly. In the Westminster language, there is no radical break between deliberation and decision-making, when every motion must contain a resolution to be voted on and voting marks the final move in debate (see Campion 1929, 143). Therefore there would not have been good grounds to call the proposed assembly 'a European Parliament'. The proposed European Deliberative Assembly could only 'exchange views' and 'express opinions' but had no powers to either nominate or dismiss the Council, not to mention controlling the member-state governments. This corresponds to what Weber called a mere *Redeparlament,* lacking the equally necessary qualities of an *Arbeitsparlament* (1918, 234, see Palonen 2014b). While the power to legislate and direct elections of the Deliberative Assembly were seen as future options, the power to elect and dismiss the government was not on the table the Assembly. Nonetheless, the Political Report contained a vision of the future which included certain supranational and parliamentary aspects:

Plans must be prepared for the permanent and organic unification of Europe. These should include:

(a) The grant of a Common Citizenship, without loss of original nationality;

(b) The creation of a single European Defence Force;

(c) The development of a unified economic system; and finally

(d) The conclusion of a complete Federation with an elected European Parliament. (Document divers, ME–1264.pdf, Article 26)

The federalist faction had gained the upper hand in the formulation, although only as applied to the distant future. The vision was, nevertheless, supranational, and included direct election of a 'European Parliament'. Still, the Parliament's standing resembled that of the constitutional regimes of the nineteenth century, without parliamentary responsibility for electing and dismissing government.

Compared to this, the Political Resolution of the Congress gave to what it called the 'European Assembly' very modest advisory objectives:

Demands the convening, as a matter of real urgency, of a European Assembly chosen by the Parliaments of the participating nations, from among their members and others, designed;

(a) to stimulate and give expression to European public opinion;

(b) to advise upon immediate practical measures designed progressively to bring about the necessary economic and political union of Europe;

(c) to examine the juridical and constitutional implications arising out of the creation of such a Union or Federation and their economic and social consequences;

(d) to prepare the necessary plans for the above purposes. (ibid.)

Again, the rhetoric of progress and necessity dominates the language. New is the specification of choosing its own members, as electing other than parliamentarians to the new Assembly would weaken its powers. Missing once more is the political responsibility of the government to the parliament.

In Articles 9 and 10, a European Charter of Human Rights was proposed: 'a Commission should be set up to undertake immediately the double task of drafting such a Charter and of laying down standards to which a State must conform if it is to deserve the name of a democracy'. Compared with the rather natural-law-type view on human rights in the Political Report, the setting up of a Commission marked a recognition of the political quality of the rights, also affirmed by regarding these rights as a necessary condition for a democracy. The competition with the 'people's democracies' of the Soviet bloc is explicit: 'in no circumstances shall a State be entitled to be called a democracy unless it does, in fact as well as in law, guarantee to its citizens liberty of thought, assembly and expression, as well as the right to form a political opposition'. (ibid. Article 11)

2.3 'European Parliamentary Union'

A partial exception to the denigrating of parliaments in the post-war European movement was illustrated by the European Parliamentary Union (EPU), founded by Richard Coudenhove-Kalergi (1894–1972), the author *Pan-Europa* (1923*)*. The EPU collected a great number of parliamentarians across Western Europe and held conferences for them from 1947 to 1950. The parliamentary character of the European polity was not the main point, and the participants were divided between the unionists and the federalists. Nonetheless, the first EPU conference in Gstaad 8–10 September 1947 contained the following paragraph calling for a European Constitution:

To call as soon as possible a Constituent Assembly for Europe, charged to draft a federal constitution; the Assembly shall be elected either by the national Parliaments or directly by the people; its Draft Constitution shall be submitted to the European States, who shall be free to accept or reject it. (Documents 1991, 128)

The parliamentary counterpart of the EPU project was 'a Constituent Assembly for Europe'. The wording indicates that the Draft Constitution was to be submitted to a referendum. The resolution of the second conference (1–5 September 1948 in Interlaken) was shaped by the Hague Congress.

The parliament was presented, above all, as a legislature: 'The legislative powers of the federation should be vested in a parliament which should consist of two Houses, a Senate and a Chamber of Deputies' (ibid. 142). The resolution warned against destroying 'the existing states of Europe', giving instead the Federation the task of providing 'the political machinery which will enable them to attain ends impossible under certain conditions' (ibid.).

The parliament's supranational powers were rather restricted, even if the resolution opted for a federal parliamentary government. 'The executive power of the Federation should be vested in a Federal Council which should elect its Prime Minister. The Federal Council should be elected by both Houses of Parliament and should be collectively responsible to them' (ibid. 143). The language of the resolution corresponds to the Westminster tradition, speaking of Prime Minister and the responsibility of the Federal Council to the Houses of Parliament, probably due to the contribution of the British member Ronald W.G. Mackay (on him, see Haapala 2022). In its later resolutions and recommendations, the EPU can be seen to have adapted itself to the agenda of the Council of Europe and no longer demanded a Federal Council elected by the Parliament.

2.4 A professorial draft for the European Constitution

The *Documents* of Lipgens and Lüth contains a 'Draft for a European Federal Constitution', dated 3 March 1948 and written by the Strasbourg law professors Michel Mouskhely (1903–1964, https://en.wikipedia.org/wiki/Michel_Mouskhely) and Gaston Stefani (see *Documents* 1988, 58–64, and the comment by Wilfried Lüth, ibid. 57–58). The draft was used by the French MRP parliamentary leader François de Menthon at the EPU conference in Interlaken, September 1948.

The Draft legitimised supranationality in following terms:

There is no doubt that this sovereign independence becomes more illusory every day… the economic independence is already no more than a myth. Although the peoples of Europe are more or less aware that there cannot be true political independence without economic independence, they none the less continue to think and act in 'national' terms. No plan for European unity can succeed if it ignores this basic fact. (Documents 1988, 58)

The draft avoids a teleological vision of Europe and sees the root of the problem for building up a European polity by recognising the national sentiments but also the illusory sovereignty of nation-states. It regards nationalism as a vested interest, which the European federation must acknowledge before attempting to transcend it. The two professors acted according to the scheme sketched later by Quentin Skinner (1974) for the figure of the innovative ideologist. They first 'guarantee the political independence and territorial integrity of each state' (*Documents* 1988, 59) and remind that the federal principle would not abolish the states, but construct a new polity-level:

As opposed to national rights, which derive from the constitution of each state, federal rights are those that are conferred or recognised by the federal Constitution and may be exercised within the limits fixed by it. The federal state being an association of individuals and states and may only be exercised within the limits fixed by it'. (ibid.)

Following their view on the illusionary sovereignty of the nation-states, the authors inverted the perspective: instead of a 'delegation' of sovereignty to the federation, they spoke of the sovereignty of the federation, which limits itself by conferring parts of sovereignty to the member states. This was a remarkable legal and political principle which is still rarely acknowledged in the debates on European integration. It is the constitution that would 'delegate' the powers between the polity levels. This was explicitly stated in this article:

(1) Federal law shall take precedence over the national law of member states.
(2) Principle of mediate administration: decisions by all organs of the federal state shall be carried out under the supervision in each member state by agents or officials of that state.
(3) Citizens of the federal state shall have dual nationality: that of the federation and that of the member state to which they belong. As federal citizens they shall enjoy the rights granted by the Constitution in all parts of the federation. In no case they may claim the political rights that a member state grants to its own nationals. (ibid.)

This was a strange compromise. A priority of the federal legislation was declared, but all 'decisions' were set 'under the supervision' of the states, without specifying, whether the parliament, the government or the administration are its 'agents'. The dual nationality was also interpreted in a manner that excluded voting and other political rights in federal elections in the country of residence, while maintaining them in the country of citizenship.

In the organisation of the federation, the separation of powers of the US Constitution served as the model: 'Legislative power resides in a Federal Assembly, consisting of a Federal Chamber and a Chamber of States'. The federal chamber was named the 'House of Representatives' and was intended to represent the people of the federation. It should be elected by direct and universal suffrage, each state having representatives proportionate to its population (ibid. 61). The Chamber of the States was seen as an upper house: 'the Chamber of the States represents member states directly. Each should have the same number of members ... and free to choose its own representatives.' (ibid.)

Despite the closeness to the US model, the Draft supported a version of the parliamentary system. This was visible in the powers of the two chambers: '(i) To pass federal laws on matters of federal concern; (ii) To approve certain treaties concluded by the federal government; (iii) To pass the federal budget; (iv) To elect the members of the federal government'. (ibid.)

The distinctive point was the last one. Not just the prime minister, but the entire government was set to be elected by the parliamentary chambers. It was not said how this would be done, though one paragraph gave mention of 'a provision for a plenary session of both Chambers for certain questions such as the election of the members of the federal government etc.' (ibid.). The government or 'executive organ' was called the Federal Council, as is the Swiss Bundesrat in English.

10 members at most, elected by the Federal Assembly for the same term as members of the House of Representatives...

No more than one representative per state. At least three Council members should belong to countries with a population of over 20 million.

The Council should elect its own President for a term of one year, and should decide the allocation of ministerial duties. (ibid. 62)

A striking difference of the proposed European federation to the Westminster model concerns the head of government, who was not to be called Prime Minister but President, perhaps in the literal sense of the chair who presides over the Council meetings. The Swiss model was also to be followed in electing the President for one year. The federation's fixed-term government for the term of the House and the Chamber of the States deviates from major parliamentary or presidential models. This model would strengthen the cabinet as a collegium over both the parliament and the president. The distinctive characteristic of a parliamentary regime, the power to dismiss the government by a vote of no confidence, was missing from the Draft. The federalists on the European continent largely regarded the United States and Switzerland as their models, and they had difficulty combining that with a parliamentary system, for which the power to dismiss the government is the decisive point.

The analysis of these documents from the late 1940s makes it clear that there was no elective affinity (*Wahlverwandtschaft*) in that context between the federal Europe and the parliamentary form of government. On the contrary, the most successful federalist models at the time were the US separation of powers system and the Swiss semi-plebiscitarian system with a fixed-term government (on a contemporary US interest in seeing a system of federalism in Europe in Europe, see Walton 1952). The key feature of the parliamentary system – the dismissal of government by a vote of no confidence – was, furthermore, regarded in the home country of parliamentary government to be bound up with British national history, and only a few UK parliamentarians were ready to see a trial of a supranational European parliamentary government.

3 The Council of Europe

The political result of the Hague Congress was the creation of the Council of Europe. It was founded, while the struggles between the federalists, unionists and the British Labour government continued, on a compromise close to the British position. On 5 May 1949, ten member states signed the Treaty of London (see Wassenburg 2013, 21–26; Krumrey 2018, 111–116). In this chapter, I shall analyse the text of the Treaty and its federalist criticisms.

The Council of Europe remained an intergovernmental institution, but its Consultative Assembly can be seen as a type of parliamentary institution, though remaining far from fulfilling the criteria for a parliamentary government. Elected by the member states' parliaments, it could, under looser criteria, be seen as the first supranational parliament (as Guerriri 2014 claims; for a critical view, see Forsyth 1964, 12–16).

The politics of naming can serve a rhetorical indicator of the disputes over alternative political choices between Council of Europe participants in its founding years. The name 'Council of Europe' was proposed by Foreign Minister Ernest Bevin (Labour) in a ministerial conference preceding the signing of the Treaty in May 1949. The alternative proposed by French Foreign Minister Robert Schuman (MRP) was 'European Union'. While 'council' refers to an advisory institution where 'European questions' are devolved to the member states' governments, 'union' indicates an entity 'above' the member states and their governments.

Supranational connotations were avoided in the terms 'Committee of Ministers' and 'Consultative Assembly', which were used by the Hague Congress in its resolution on a 'European Assembly' (Wassenburg 2013, 24). 'Committee' refers to a preparatory organ whose results are submitted to the decision-makers, that is, to member state governments. It was to them – and not to their parliaments – that the Consultative Assembly was intended to give advice. A General Affairs Committee, led by French MRP politician Georges Bidault, proposed in 'the Council's first sitting the 'setting up [of] a European Political Authority' (EPA) as a European proto-government; this at least gave recognition to the political weight of the polity at the European level (ibid. 27–30).

I have not analysed the debates of the Consultative Assembly and its attempts to parliamentarise its powers from within. I shall rely instead on the existing literature (see Wassenburg 2013, 26–40; Guerriri 2014; and the thorough study by Taru Haapala and Hanna-Mari Kivistö 2023).

3.1 The Concept of Europe in the Treaty of London

The Statute of the Council of Europe (1949), based on the Treaty of London, formulates extensively the intergovernmental political quality of the Council of Europe with its Consultative Assembly, thus setting clear limits to both supranationalism and parliamentarism. In its margins there are, however, formulations containing the possibility of allowing modifications to these limits. The view on Europe is formulated in the Preamble:

Convinced that the pursuit of peace based upon justice and international cooperation is vital for the preservation of human society and civilisation;
Reaffirming their devotion to the spiritual and moral values which are the common heritage of their peoples and the true source of individual freedom, political liberty and the rule of law, principles which form the basis of all genuine democracy;
Believing that, for the maintenance and further realisation of these ideals and in the interests of economic and social progress, there is need of a closer unity between all likeminded countries of Europe. (The Statute 1949, 104)

The language of the Statute is astonishingly past-oriented. It appeals to 'the preservation of human society and civilisation', to the 'common heritage', to indisputable normative criteria, such as 'spiritual and moral values', to 'principles of genuine democracy' and only then to their 'maintenance and further realisation' and 'economic and social progress'. Of course, in the context we can identify their political point as being against both the experience of Nazism and the threat of the Soviet Bloc. The normative principles, 'individual freedom, political liberty and the rule of law' as well as 'genuine democracy' are clearly directed against both. Compared with federalist declarations from the earlier post-war years, a condemnation of nationalism and an aspiration to transcend the nation-state are completely missing.

The next paragraph gave justifications for the European-level cooperation by invoking a rhetoric of necessity: 'it is necessary forthwith to create an organisation which will bring European States into closer association'. No political vision of a new European polity was presented, merely an 'organisation' that 'associates' the members. Article 1(a) of the Statute declared: 'The aim of the Council of Europe is to achieve a greater unity between its Members' for their common heritage, democratic principles and progress, without any radical break with the past (ibid. 105).

The aims should be 'pursued through the organs of the Council by discussion of questions of common concern and by agreements and common action in economic, social, cultural, scientific, legal and administrative matters and in the maintenance and further realisation of human rights and fundamental freedoms' (ibid. 106). The rhetoric of 'discussion' and 'agreements' marks diplomatic, intergovernmental language, whereas 'political' matters are not mentioned at all. In paragraph 1(d), 'national defence' was excluded from the 'scope of the Council of Europe' (ibid. 107).

A statement of the 'signatories of the Statute' described some political features of the Council as follows:

> The main feature of the statute is the establishment of a Committee of Ministers and of a Consultative Assembly, which together will form the Council of Europe. Of these two bodies, the Committee of Ministers will provide for the development of cooperation between Governments, while the Consultative Assembly will provide a means through which the aspirations of the European peoples may be formulated and expressed, the Governments thus being kept continuously in touch with European public opinion. (ibid.)

The main activity of the Council lies in 'cooperation between Governments', which explicitly limited the Council to intergovernmental 'cooperation'. The Consultative Assembly had to present the 'aspirations of the European peoples', allowing Governments to keep 'in touch with European public opinion'. The mediation of citizens' ideas and opinions resembles Bismarck's view on parliamentary representation: presenting local opinions in the sittings of a parliament (discussed in Palonen 2012; see Goldberg 1998). Both legislation and responsibility of the Committee of Ministers to the Consultative Assembly were excluded.

Article 2 confirmed: 'The Members of the Council of Europe are the Parties to this Statute'. The member states 'must accept the principles of the rule of law and of the enjoyment by all persons within its jurisdiction of human rights and fundamental freedoms' (Article 3), which ruled out authoritarian regimes from membership. As opposed to universal organisations, applying for membership in the Council of Europe remained on a voluntary and invitational basis, as stated in Article 4: 'Any European State, which is deemed to be able and willing to fulfil the provisions of Article 3, may be invited to become a Member of the Council of Europe by the Committee of Ministers'. Article 8 set the criteria for exclusion of a member: 'Any member of the Council of Europe which has seriously violated Article 3 may be suspended from its rights of representation and requested by the Committee of Ministers to withdraw under Article 7' (The Statute 1949, 7–8).

3.2 The Consultative Assembly

Article 13 states: 'The Committee of Ministers is the organ which acts on behalf of the Council of Europe'. The Council contained a minimal supranational dimension: its position enabled it to be part of international agreements, conventions and arrangements. According to Article 16: 'The Committee of

Ministers shall... decide with binding effect all matters relating to the internal organisation and arrangements of the Council of Europe'. The Committee decided on the administrative and financial apparatus of the Council, 'relating to the powers of the Consultative Assembly', that is, hearing its opinion, but not necessarily following it (ibid. 110).

Article 14 specified the Council's intergovernmental practice: 'Each member shall be entitled to one representative on the Committee of Ministers, and each representative shall be entitled to one vote. Representatives on the Committee shall be the Ministers for Foreign Affairs.' (ibid.) The Council was set up to act with a formal equality between the member states, independently of size of their population or political weight. The possibility of voting gave the Committee a minimal parliamentary quality, and the members would be the foreign ministers of member states, only exceptionally allowing 'an alternate' to replace them (ibid. 111). This did not leave much space for debates in the Committee, although no imperative mandate binding them to governments' decisions was required, either.

The Committee's rules of procedure contained three points: 'i. the quorum; ii. the method of appointment and term of office of its President; iii. the procedure for the admission of items to its agenda, including the giving of notice of proposals for resolutions.' (article 18, ibid. 112). The points indicate the possible items to be used in dispute regarding the quorum, presidency and agenda-setting.

A minimal concession to government responsibility to parliament was contained in Article 19: 'At each session of the Consultative Assembly the Committee of Ministers shall furnish the Assembly with statements of its activities, accompanied by appropriate documentation' (ibid). Even if the Assembly could not dismiss or charge the Committee, it could expect the Committee to regularly submit a report for discussion.

The Committee's 'important' recommendations, resolutions and questions (Article 20[a]), 'require the unanimous vote of the representatives casting a vote, and of a majority of the representatives entitled to sit on the Committee'. A simple majority sufficed in 'questions of procedure' and 'financial and administrative regulations', whereas Article 20(c), on adopting full and associate members (Articles 4 and 5), would 'require a two-thirds majority of all the representatives entitled to sit on the Committee', which secures the strong position for the founding members. This was further affirmed in Article 20(d): 'All other resolutions of the Committee, including adoption of the budget, of rules of procedure and of financial and administrative regulations, recommendations for the amendment of articles of this Statute... require a two-thirds majority of the representatives casting a vote and of a majority of the representatives entitled to sit on the Committee' (ibid. 113–114). Although no veto was assumed and regular voting was expected, these articles set high hurdles for the Committee of Ministers to take a stand.

In the style of diplomatic institutions, the Committee was to meet 'privately' (21a) and 'before and during the beginning of every session of the Consultative Assembly' (ibid. 114). For the politics of its time, the Committee had no other regular schedule than the infrequent meetings of the Assembly. The schedule did not give the Committee many options to oppose member governments.

In articles 22 to 37, the Statute dealt extensively with the status and powers of and membership in the Consultative Assembly. Its main purpose was defined in Article 22:

> The Consultative Assembly is the deliberative organ of the Council of Europe. It shall debate matters within its competence under this Statute and present its conclusions, in the form of recommendations, to the Committee of Ministers. (ibid. 115)

'Deliberative' was here again meant to exclude legislation and other binding decisions. In the Westminster language, it would have been more precise to speak of discussion. The debate in the Consultative Assembly could terminate in 'conclusions' to be recommended to the Committee, as in pre-parliamentary advisory assemblies:

> The Consultative Assembly shall discuss, and may make recommendations upon, any matter within the aim and scope of the Council of Europe as defined in Chapter 1, which (i) is referred to it by the Committee of Ministers with a request for its opinion, or (ii) has been approved by the Committee for inclusion in the Agenda of the Assembly on the proposal of the latter. (The Statute, 1949, 115–116)

Items (i) and (ii) show how the agenda-setting of the Consultative Assembly was in its procedure dependent on the Committee and how it granted to the Committee a veto. The inclusion of members' motions arising from debates, was left to the control of the President of the Assembly (23c). The Consultative Assembly could hardly increase its powers from within when it was lacking powers for bringing its own motions to the agenda of debates.

Nor was the mode of selecting members determined by the Assembly, but depended according to Article 25(a) on the member-state governments (and not their parliaments):

> The Consultative Assembly shall consist of representatives of each Member appointed in such a manner as the Government of that Member shall decide. Each representative must be a national of the Member whom he represents but shall not at the same time be a member of the Committee of Ministers. (ibid. 116)

The appointment by government could easily leave out opposition parties, or at least 'extremists', such as the communists. In a supranational assembly, the citizenship of parliamentarians would be irrelevant. The most obvious deviation from parliamentary procedural autonomy concerned the power given to the Committee regarding the summoning of its member to speak in the Assembly: according to the Statute, in principle, the Committee was under no obligation to present its programme or to justify its decisions before the Assembly or before its committees.

Article 28(a) states: 'The Consultative Assembly shall adopt its rules of procedure and shall elect from its members its President, who shall remain in office until the next ordinary session'. The autonomy of the Assembly was granted in its internal matters, including 'the time and manner in which the names of representatives and their substitutes shall be notified'. (28c) 'All resolutions of the Consultative Assembly ... shall require a two-thirds majority of the representatives casting a vote', while other issues were left to a majority vote. We can assume that the institution of the qualified majority rules had the effect of making it difficult for the Consultative Assembly to arrive at any decisions at all, thus weakening its possibilities to oppose the Committee of Ministers or member-state governments (ibid. 118).

Article 31 stated: 'Debates on proposals to be made to the Committee of Ministers that a matter should be placed on the Agenda of the Consultative Assembly shall be confined to an indication of the proposed subject-matter and the reasons for and against its inclusion in the Agenda' (ibid. 119–120). When the debates should be confined to a mere mention of the topic, not allowing the presentation of a full motion, including resolutions, this was another deviation from ordinary parliamentary practice. Extending the debate *pro et contra* in the agenda-setting itself could concern only the weight or the urgency of the item, but to discuss it without a proper motion left the Assembly once again at the mercy of the Committee.

Article 32 indicates an additional weakness of the Assembly in the politics of time:

> The Consultative Assembly shall meet in ordinary session once a year, the date and duration of which shall be determined by the Assembly so as to avoid as far as possible overlapping with parliamentary sessions of Members and with sessions of the General Assembly of the United Nations. In no circumstances shall the duration of an ordinary session exceed one month unless both the Assembly and the Committee of Ministers concur. (ibid. 120)

The powers of parliaments depend on a considerable extent on the length and intensity of their sitting-times. A sufficient time for setting motions as well as amendments onto the agenda are prerequisites for a parliamentary contribution to the decision-making. All this was missing from the Statute of the Council of Europe. Only one session per year lasting one month or less was another sign of its weakness, for it did not require much of a time commitment from members: no European-level parliamentarians could be mentored under such arrangements. For extraordinary sessions, it was the Committee of Ministers that would take the initiative and then seek the agreement of the President of the Consultative Assembly (Article 34, ibid.).

The final article of the chapter reads: 'Unless the Consultative Assembly decides otherwise, its debates shall be conducted in public' (ibid.). Here, if anywhere, parliamentary forms, would have been expected to emerge. The question remains, however, of how much such forms could have strengthened the standing of the Consultative Assembly over the Committee of Ministers and the member-state governments. Nonetheless, the very presence of the Consultative Assembly brought to the Council of Europe a parliamentary element, which also altered the intergovernmental institutions. Scholars of international institutions have recently appreciated the political significance of these Assemblies (see Marshall (2005).

British government representatives, in particular, tried to play down the parliamentary aspects of the Council, reflecting British politicians' and journalists' long-time distrust of continental European countries' ability to conduct efficient parliamentary practices. They tended to assume that parliamentary institutions could only exceptionally be transferred to foreign settings and still less to supranational political entities.

The Statute contained provisions that were practically impossible to overturn from within the Assembly. Still, it was in political disputes in the Consultative Assembly, and in its relationships to the Committee of Ministers and governments, that the actual parliamentary content of the Council of Europe was determined. The parliamentary experiences of its members were sometimes seen as more important than the letter of the Statute (see the discussions in Haapala and Kivistö 2023).

3.3 A federalist critique: André Philip

André Philip (1902–1970, https://fr.wikipedia.org/wiki/André_Philip) was a French politician, scholar and member of the Socialist Party (SFIO) from 1920 to 1957. He represented the federalist wing of the party and was a member of the Consultative Assembly. The *Documents* collection contains a translated extract from his speech in the Assembly on 8 August 1950. Related to both the Korean War and the need for new forms of economic cooperation, Philip insisted that it was 'necessary to appoint competent Ministers with necessary powers at the European level on all these fields' (*Documents* 1988, 122), and continued:

Finally, these organisations must be responsible to a democratically elected body. I think...that...everywhere, parliamentary control is gradually being deprived of its true role because real decisions are been taken where the real problems are arising, whether on the international or on the European level.

The basis of the parliamentary system is being more and more vitiated because our national Parliaments are now in practice no more than large-size county councils, big-scale local organisations competent to deal only with local affairs; the major question on which the future of their countries depend are outside their control because they are negotiated and decided upon another place and at another level. Democracy must be restored in the place where the problem arises. Parliamentary control must be instituted in the place where the negotiations are held, that is to say, here at the European level. (ibid.)

Philip clearly saw that national states were inadequate to the task of resolving the major problems of the time, and he linked this to the national parliaments' diminishing powers. British Labour leaders and some of Philip's Socialist colleagues in France saw in European integration a threat to 'nationalisations'. Philip insisted on the priority of democratic control by parliamentary means and opted for setting up a European-level parliamentary political institution. The main target of Philip's criticism was the Council of Europe itself:

Are we going to be able to increase our power? Shall we be able to get beyond our advisory role and at last persuade the Committee of Ministers to grant the Assembly, as we proposed last year, certain limited but real powers within the framework of the functions assigned to us? If we do not do this, my friends, another Assembly will do it. (ibid.)

In this speech, Philip still set his hopes on the Consultative Assembly as a parliamentary institution able to operate on a broad European basis. 'Here and now, we must take decisions and try to save Europe by trying to agree unanimously if possible, or, if that is not possible, to persuade those who want to create a unified Europe to press forward, trusting that our other colleagues will join us in their turn little later' (ibid.). Knowing the Schuman plan for the Europe of the Six, Philip wanted the Common Assembly of the ECSC with parliamentary responsibility to end the 'endless discussions'; he also wished to dispense with the unanimity rule of the Council of Europe, for due to it, he explained, 'nothing is achieved...We shall make this authority responsible to a parliamentary Assembly; we very much hope that it will be ours' (ibid.). Philip deemed that the result of this would be the 'set up [of] various European Ministries, which will be responsible towards what will become a European Parliament' (ibid. 123). This was an optimistic view inspired by the 'functional method' of Jean Monnet, and Philip regarded as realistic the creation of sectoral European ministers which would be responsible to a common European Parliament.

André Philip saw how intergovernmental institutions were lacking both supranational and parliamentary responsibility, but he regarded the institutions of the Schuman Plan as also too narrow. Despite his disappointment with the Council of Europe, he still entertained hopes for its parliamentarisation from within. For this project, however, he failed to gain the majority support of the Consultative Assembly.

Equally important was Philip's judgement on the weakness of parliamentary institutions in post-war Europe. His critique targeted the insidious growth of the powers of the planning apparatus, which strengthened the bureaucratic part of the government at the cost of politicians, be they parliamentarians or ministers responsible to the parliament. This critique was also directed at the by-products of the 'welfare state' policies of the Social Democratic and Labour parties in Europe as they were proliferating beyond the parliamentary and democratic control of the administration. Philip's criticism resembles Max Weber's *Parlament* pamphlet (1918, 235–248) and was exceptional among both the European federalists and the Socialist parties of the time.

3.4 Committee plans for supranationalism

Despite its strong demarcation from both supranationalism and parliamentarism in the Treaty, the Consultative Assembly also undertook attempts to advance in both of these directions. Numerous Consultative Assembly members were later members of the Common Assembly of the ECSC and of the Ad Hoc Assembly. Many of the latter did not want a definite break with the Council, proposing instead a joint membership in the Senate of the European Political Community and in the Consultative Assembly, with membership in both bodies being elected by the parliaments of the member states (see Chapter 8).

The proposals of the Council's Committee on General Affairs 'for the strengthening of the political role of the Consultative Assembly vis-à-vis the Committee of Ministers' has now been studied in detail by Taru Haapala and Hanna-Mari Kivistö (2023), based on the Digital Archives of the Council of Europe (https://www.coe.int/en/web/documents-records-archives-information/search1). Although their focus is not related to the work of the Ad Hoc Assembly, both supranational and parliamentary topics are central to their study. I decided to rely on this article of my former students and not analyse the Council debates directly myself.

Haapala and Kivistö mention an amendment moved by the Conservative Harold Macmillan, later British Prime Minister, for giving the Committee of Ministers 'supranational powers with its own permanent Secretariat comprised of European officials' (17 August 1949, quoted in Haapala and Kivistö 2023, 312). The proposal shows that not all British Conservatives were against supranationalism *per se*, as in this context, when the Labour government had given up its federalist sympathies; it was more that they were afraid of parliamentarisation of the supranational level. This view has later been called 'executive federalism' (see e.g Tiilikainen 2011).

The Committee for General Affairs did not support Macmillan's proposal. Its rapporteur was French Socialist leader Guy Mollet, later a member of the Ad Hoc Assembly and Prime Minister in the Fourth Republic. The committee had three alternatives '(1) a federal pact, (2) a European confederation [, or (3)] periodical revision of the Statute of the Council of Europe', the latter called by Mollet 'a functional approach'. The Committee opted for the last one, justified by the unanimity of the members (17 August 1950, quoted from Haapala and Kivistö 2023, 313–314). This left the intergovernmental basis of the Council of Europe untouched. The British federalist and Labour backbencher Ronald Mackay had an interesting proposal to render the Committee of Ministers into a second Chamber of the Council, which would strengthen the parliamentary quality of the Consultative Assembly (quoted in ibid. 314–315; on Mackay's federalism, see Haapala 2022).

The Committee proposed the 'creation of European Political Authority' with 'an effective parliamentary control at the European level' (quoted from Haapala and Kivistö 2023, 316). The proposal was a further attempt to set up a Europe-level executive institution that would be more than the Committee of Ministers, although the form of the parliamentary control was not specified.

The Committee managed to change the Statute in May 1951 'so that representatives were elected by their parliament or appointed from among the members of parliaments' (quoted from ibid. 317). Thus, the Committee strived for parliamentarisation of the Consultative Assembly's mode of election and to provide it with autonomy in agenda-setting, but motions for its direct election were rejected.

The proposals for increasing the powers of the Consultative Assembly might have marked a real step towards European-level parliamentary politics. Despite its weakness, the Consultative Assembly offered to numerous West European parliamentarians the first regular non-national venue for debating in the parliamentary manner. The parliamentarisation of powers in Europe frequently arose out of concrete controversial debates, which were only later confirmed by constitutions or procedural commentaries. West European parliamentarians in the Consultative Assembly exchanged their experiences and put forward various proposals to strengthen the parliamentary aspects of the Council of Europe. Knowing what parliaments can do, they floated various ideas for making the Consultative Assembly more like a European Parliament. The members serving on the Ad Hoc Assembly frequently allude to the practices of the Consultative Assembly.

It seems, however, that those wanting to extend Common Assembly's powers would have been content with efficient control and oversight over a European Executive. While election of the Committee by the Common Assembly was proposed, no idea of dismissing it through a vote of no confidence seems to have been forthcoming. In this respect, the Common Assembly of the European Coal and Steel Community was a novelty.

4 European Coal and Steel Community (ECSC)

The histories of the European Union commonly begin with the European Coal and Steel Community (ECSC). Relative to the Council of Europe, the ECSC marks two steps backwards. It was limited to six West European countries (Belgium, France, [West]Germany, Italy, Luxembourg and the Netherlands) and thematically restricted to the field of two major industries. The point is that it was politically possible to create supranational institutions, if only within these parameters. Franz Schorkopf judges that 'die institutionelle Architektur der Montanunion einen Maßstab setzte, von dem aus weitere Schritte gedacht werden konnten' (2023, 36). Thus, it makes sense to celebrate Europe Day on 9 May, the date of the Schuman Declaration in 1950 can be regarded as marking the origins of supranational Europe.

Robert Schuman (1886–1963), the French Foreign Minister, and Jean Monnet (1888–1979), a planning official of the French government, did not intend to create a momentum for a parliamentary Europe. In planning the new organisation, the Common Assembly for parliamentarians of the member countries was instituted, and the Treaty of Paris included the possibility for the Assembly to dismiss the executive High Authority, although under highly restricted conditions. This was part of the process of legitimising supra-nationality among the member states. In its first session in September 1952, at the initiative of ECSC Council of Ministers, the Common Assembly set up the Ad Hoc Assembly for drafting a constitution for the planned European Political Community. Combining these two moves, together with the willingness of the Common Assembly members to act as if they were members of a European Parliament, we can speak of the ECSC's Common Assembly as one of the points of origin of a parliamentary and supranational Europe.

4.1 From the Schuman Declaration to the ECSC

French Foreign Minister Robert Schuman, of the Christian-Democratic party Mouvement Républicain Populaire (MRP), defended supranationalism as a 'demand of the time' already on 16 May 1949 in the context of the founding of the Council of Europe:

> Our century, that has witnessed the catastrophes resulting in the unending clash of nationalities and nationalisms, must attempt and succeed in reconciling nations in a supranational association. This would safeguard the diversities and aspirations of each nation while coordinating them in the same manner as the regions are coordinated within the unity of the nation. (https://www.schuman.info/Strasbourg549.htm)

On 9 May 1950 the Schuman Declaration was published. It begins as follows:

Il n'est plus question de vaines paroles, mais d'un acte, d'un acte hardi, d'un acte constructif. La France a agi et les conséquences de son action peuvent être immenses. Nous espérons qu'elles le seront. (https://www.robert-schuman.eu/fr/declaration-du-9-mai-1950)

The opening paragraph's anti-rhetorical salvos are directed against the Council of Europe as a discussion forum, which the Declaration wanted to overcome by the 'constructive act' of initiating an integration from below. The next point, the peace project, marked a change in the French policy towards the Germany of the Allied rule of the first post-war years:

Elle a agi essentiellement pour la paix. Pour que la paix puisse vraiment courir sa chance, il faut, d'abord, qu'il y ait une Europe. Cinq ans, presque jour pour jour, après la capitulation sans conditions de l'Allemagne, la France accomplit le premier acte décisif de la construction européenne et y associe l'Allemagne. Les conditions européennes doivent s'en trouver entièrement transformées. (ibid.)

The Cold War, the founding of the two German states and the beginning of the *Wirtschaftswunder* after minister Ludwig Erhard's currency reform which introduced the D-Mark in 1948 contributed to France's new willingness to accept the Federal Republic as an equal partner:

Cette transformation rendra possibles d'autres actions communes impossibles jusqu'à ce jour. L'Europe naîtra de tout cela, une Europe solidement unie et fortement charpentée. Une Europe où le niveau de vie s'élèvera grâce au groupement des productions et à l'extension des marchés qui provoqueront l'abaissement des prix. (ibid.)

The next paragraph of the Schuman Declaration formed a new cross-border alliance within a definite policy area: 'Une Europe où la Ruhr, la Sarre et les bassins français travailleront de concert et feront profiter de leur travail pacifique…'(ibid.). Building European integration from below replaced the historical Franco-German rivalry with a tight economic unity:

L'Europe ne se fera pas d'un coup, ni dans une construction d'ensemble: elle se fera par des réalisations concrètes, créant d'abord une solidarité de fait. Le rassemblement des nations européennes exige que l'opposition séculaire de la France et de l'Allemagne soit éliminée: l'action entreprise doit toucher au premier chef la France et l'Allemagne. (ibid.)

The Declaration projected a merging of French and the German coal and steel industries around their common interests. The unity from below was, however, seen as the first step and as a model that allowed other European states to join the new 'European federation':

Le Gouvernement français propose de placer l'ensemble de la production franco-allemande du charbon et d'acier sous une Haute Autorité commune, dans une organisation ouverte à la participation des autres pays d'Europe. La mise en commun des productions de charbon et d'acier assurera immédiatement l'établissement de bases communes de développement économique, première étape de la Fédération européenne, et changera le destin des régions longtemps vouées à la fabrication des armes de guerre dont elles ont été les plus constantes victimes. (ibid.)

The coal and steel industries as the focus relates to the historical rivalries over the geographically adjacent industrial areas, which, if organised in common, promised economic growth. The core of the organisation was the 'High Authority', a title in the French administrative tradition to which Jean Monnet belonged. It is remarkable to see the first stage of the 'European Federation' in the ECSC, indicating a supranational element missing from the Council of Europe. A union of the producers would render a war between France and Germany 'matériellement impossible'. On this basis a federation could be created:

Par la mise en commun de production de base et l'institution d'une Haute Autorité nouvelle, dont les décisions lieront la France, l'Allemagne et les pays qui y adhéreront, cette proposition réalisera les premières assises concrètes d'une Fédération européenne indispensable à la préservation de la paix. (ibid.)

The only institution mentioned in the Declaration is the supranational High Authority, composed of independent persons, selected on the basis of equality between the member governments:

La Haute Autorité commune chargée du fonctionnement de tout le régime sera composée de personnalités indépendantes désignées sur une base paritaire par les Gouvernements; un Président sera choisi d'un commun accord par les autres pays adhérents. Des dispositions appropriées assureront les voies de recours nécessaires contre les décisions de la Haute Autorité. (ibid.)

Besides the power of the governments to appoint members of the High Authority, the declaration proposed a controlling 'arbitre', a court of justice, as another supranational institution to decide disputes: 'd'un arbitre désigné d'un commun accord: celui-ci aura chargé de veiller à ce que les accords soient conformes aux principes et, en cas d'opposition irréductible, fixera la solution qui sera adoptée' (ibid.). In addition, supervision by the UN is referred to as a guaranty for maintaining the peace (ibid.).

As presented in the Declaration, the new unit might have been like a European section of an UN special organisation consisting of experts in the field. In the planning stages, corporative models of cooperation with the High Authority were discussed, corresponding to the French term *communauté* (see Schorkopf 2023, 50–53). The Declaration, however, mentions that the specific content of the new institution is to be negotiated between the parties.

The plan was considerably modified in the course of the negotiations. Bernard Rittberger assessed their significance as follows: 'The Schuman Plan negotiations can be considered a constitutional "founding moment", which led to the creation of an entire novel system of "rules about rules", and a set of "higher level" institutions which framed political processes' (2005, 81).

The chief of delegations wrote in a memorandum that it was impossible to set up a High Authority that lacked political responsibility: 'Il a donc semble normal d'instituer une Assemblée comme, formée de délégations des divers Parlements.' (*Plan Schuman. Rapport sur les travaux 20 juin 10 août 1950*; quoted from Kapteyn 1962, 19).

Jean Monnet wrote in his *Memoirs:* 'Other ideas that emerged that day were the Consultative Committee and the name of the parliamentary body, the Common Assembly. Little by little, the whole structure was taking shape.' (Monnet 1978, 323) He also noted how the 'right to democratic control' (ibid. 382) of both government's *arcana imperii* as well as of business confidences would be stronger by including a debating parliamentary assembly in the decision-making.

Those agreeing to set up the ECSC saw in the Common Assembly a link to the member-state parliaments, a controlling institution that would prevent the High Authority from causing disaffection in the public opinion of the member countries. The point was for the parliament to exercise control over a supranational institution rather than to regard the Common Assembly as itself a supranational parliamentary assembly. As we have seen from the Council of Europe, parliamentarians elected to this new institution were not slow to attempt to make it at least look like a proper parliament.

4.2 The Paris Treaty

The *Treaty establishing the European Coal and Steel Community* was signed in Paris on 18 April 1951 between Italy, France, West Germany, Belgium, and the Netherlands (https://eur-lex.europa.eu/legal-content/FR/TXT/PDF/?uri=CELEX:11951K/TXT&from=LV) and it began its activities on 23 July 1952. I shall quote the Treaty mainly from the English version (http://aei.pitt.edu/37145/1/ECSC_Treaty_1951.pdf). The text avoids using pathos in its declarations. Its Preamble repeats the emphasis on peace and progress known from the Council of Europe and appeals to a 'solidarité de fait' and to establishing a common basis for economic development for the sake of peace and the standard of living (*niveau de vie*). The first paragraph combines an appeal to the common interest with a reminder of the past rivalries and bloody divisions that need to be overcome:

RESOLVED to substitute for age-old rivalries the merging of their essential interests; to create, by establishing an economic community, the basis for a broader and deeper community among peoples long divided by bloody conflicts; and to lay the foundations for institutions which will give direction to a destiny henceforward shared.

The paragraph contains the vision of broadening and deepening the community in the future. Article 2 sets the task of improving the standard of living by economic expansion, 'to economic expansion, growth of employment and a rising standard of living in the Member States'. Classical free-market economics was judged able to create a new division of labour within the ECSC: 'the most rational distribution of production at the highest possible level of productivity', while saving jobs and avoiding recurring 'troubles'. The ECSC strategy of a new beginning assumed that interests 'are most easily dealt with by finding common ground' while retaining a general economic policy a broader vision of the European 'community'.

4.2.1 The High Authority

Article 6 declares that the Community has a juridical personality, an explicit recognition of its supranational character. It has also certain rights towards its member states. Article 7 then enumerates the institutions of the ECSC as a polity:

a High Authority, assisted by a Consultative Committee;
a Common Assembly (hereinafter called the "Assembly");
a Special Council of Ministers (hereinafter called the "Council");
a Court of Justice (hereinafter called the "Court".

Nonetheless, as J.P.G. Kapteyn writes, '[t]out le traité est construit autour de la Haute Autorité' (1962, 18) as the original supranational institution drafted by Monnet (1978, 297–298). Article 8 declared: 'It shall be the duty of the High Authority to ensure that the objectives set out in this Treaty are attained in accordance with the provisions thereof.' In other words, the High Authority forms, above all, the executive power of the ECSC.

The nine High Authority members were selected for six years and elected 'en raison de leur compétence générale' (Article 9:1). The long and fixed tenure of the members is directed against the notoriously short-lived governments in the French Third and Fourth Republic.

Supranationalism is characterised by the general competence of members as opposed to their party affiliation or dependence on imperative mandates from the national level. Whether 'general competence' is restricted to the scope of the coal and steel matters or to the competence of experienced politicians, that is, whether the High Authority would be a board of economic and administrative experts or a cabinet of politicians, was left open.

The members were re-eligible for appointment and their numbers might be reduced by unanimous decision of the Council of Ministers (9:2). The members must nationals of the member states (9:3), likely referring to citizens rather than to long-term resident non-citizens. However, only two citizens of a single state could simultaneously be members of the High Authority (9:4), reflecting the vulnerability of the Benelux States to Franco-German domination. In Article 9:5, supranationality (*supranationalité*) is explicitly mentioned:

> The members of the High Authority shall, in the general interest of the Community, be completely independent in the performance of their duties. In the performance of these duties, they shall neither seek nor take instructions from any Government or from any other body. They shall refrain from any action incompatible with the supranational character of their duties.

In parliamentary terms, supranationalism forbade members of the High Authority to be bound to any imperative mandate from the member-state governments. It required a dedication to the general interest of the Community, incompatible with any dependencies on specific or special interests. The member states were required to respect and guarantee the independence of their citizens serving in the High Authority (9:6):

> The Members of the High Authority may not engage in any other occupation, whether gainful or not, nor may they acquire or hold, directly or indirectly, any interest in any business related to coal and steel during their term of office and for three years after ceasing to hold office.

The incompatibility mentioned also involved the full-time nature of the work of High Authority members and prohibited having any paid or unpaid side-businesses in the coal or steel industry during and up to three years after serving in office. This was a strong obstacle against the temptation to move the service into the hands of the corporate interests. To preserve their independence, members were appointed by parliaments or by a lottery among a number of candidates, rather than by governments, as the latter might have resulted in indirect dependencies.

The co-optation of the ninth member by the High Authority itself was perhaps intended to counter this danger by electing a person internationally known as competent but without the support of any government. Why merely one member would be chosen in this manner was not further explained in the Treaty. Appointing the President and the Vice-President of the High Authority was also left to the governments, instead of the collegial principle of choosing them among themselves, although the Authority was 'heard' in this process. Their two-year term, instead of for the duration of membership, resembled the Swiss practice (Article 11).

Article 13 affirmed that 'deliberations' of the High Authority were followed by a majority vote, but a quorum of at least half of the members was also mentioned. Here, elements of a collegial parliamentary cabinet can be identified, instead of vesting individual members with veto powers. The High Authority followed the common principle that the President had the deciding vote in a draw.

Article 14 qualified the resolutions of the Authority according to their degree of binding: to make decisions, to present recommendations or to deliver opinions (in French 'la Haute Autorité prends décisions, formule des recommandations ou émet des avis'). 'Decisions' were 'obligatory' for the targeted audience, while 'recommendations' left them free to choose the means to realise them, and 'opinions' were not binding. The Authority had to justify (*motivér*) decisions and recommendations, and their promulgation must be notified or published (Article 15). Disputes about the character of resolutions and the content of the justifications were expected. The High Authority had the power to set up study committees, especially for economic matters (Article 16).

Article 17 looks at first rather harmless: 'The High Authority shall publish annually ... a general report on the activities and the administrative expenditure of the Community.' This resembles any organisation's report to their annual meeting, but the parliamentary point can be seen only when looking also at Article 24 and the possibility of the Vote of Censure implied there (see below).

The Consultative Committee of the High Authority was presented in Article 18:

A Consultative Committee shall be attached to the High Authority. It shall consist of not less than thirty and not more than fifty-one members and shall comprise equal numbers of producers, of workers, and of consumers and dealers. The members of the Consultative Committee shall be appointed by the Council.

This committee formed a corporative element, based on trade unions and employers', consumers' and commerce organisations. The members would be elected for two years, but there was no mention of how, by whom or how regularly it would convene. The Ad Hoc Assembly proposed funding an Economic and Social Council on a similar basis (see below), continuing the practices of the interwar era, although without major political significance.

4.2.2 The Common Assembly

The Common Assembly was dealt with in six articles of the Treaty. Article 20 describes its role: 'The Assembly, which shall consist of representatives of the peoples of the States brought together in the Community, shall exercise the supervisory powers which are conferred upon it by this Treaty.'

The Assembly had in this sense both representative and controlling powers. 'Representing the peoples of the states' refers to popular sovereignty as a legitimising representation, in contrast to representing the states as in an intergovernmental organisation. The supervision aspect here might be seen as alluding to the range of parliamentary tools for controlling government that are available in a parliamentary regime. The formula seems, however, to ignore the possibility of a Westminster-style of parliamentary sovereignty (see Dicey 1885) with its emphasis on the debating aspects of the parliament. 'Peoples' in the plural instead of the singular reminds us that the Community still does not have a single people that would legitimise the Assembly.

The mode of electing the Assembly was presented in Article 21: 'The Assembly shall consist of delegates who shall be designated by the respective Parliaments once a year from among their members in accordance with the procedure laid down by each Member State.' The term delegates (*délégués*) might give the impression of an imperative mandate, which the German *Abgeordnete* does not. The members, if elected among the parliamentarians of member countries, would hardly accept a reduction of their powers by an imperative mandate, and still less if concerning the directly elected members of the Common Assembly.

The Treaty gave no justifications for restricting the term of Assembly members to one year, as compared to the six-year term of High Authority members. Such restriction was likely to weaken the Assembly's ability to exercise efficient parliamentary control. The Assembly's politics of time in relation to the other institutions of the ECSC was dealt with in Article 22:

The Assembly shall hold an annual session. It shall meet, without requiring to be convened, on the second Tuesday in May. The session may not last beyond the end of the current financial year.

The Assembly may be convened in extraordinary session at the request of the Council in order to deliver an opinion (*avis*) on such questions as may be put to it by the Council.

It may also meet in extraordinary session at the request of a majority of its members or of the High Authority.

The length of the sitting time is a rough indicator of the powers of an institution. The sitting period given to the Common Assembly corresponded to the time needed for dealing with the Annual Report of the High Authority, that is, a few weeks from May to June. It was far shorter than that of ordinary parliaments but longer than the few days given in the Soviet Union for Supreme Soviet sessions. Provisions were given for extraordinary sittings, at the convocation of the Council of Ministers, the High Authority or a majority of the Assembly, which could be an important means of extending the powers of the Assembly.

The ESCS Common Assembly had power over its rules of procedure, in contrast to the limited power of the Council of Europe's Consultative Assembly. Article 25 stated: 'The Assembly shall adopt its rules of procedure, acting by a majority of its members'. The presence of both the High Authority and the Council of Ministers (Article 23) roughly resembled the practices of executive institutions in a parliamentary sitting, but it was not the Common Assembly that invited these institutions to speak, but the executive institutions who could ask to be heard. Nonetheless, the Assembly members had the right to put oral and written questions to the High Authority, which looks to be a more important means of control than hearing them at their own request.

The most important rule for the Common Assembly was, however, Article 24:

The Assembly shall discuss in open session the general report submitted to it by the High Authority.

If a motion of censure on the report is tabled before it, the Assembly shall not vote thereon until at least three days after the motion has been tabled and only by open vote.

If the motion of censure is carried by a two-thirds majority of the votes cast, representing a majority of the Members of the Assembly, the members of the High Authority shall resign as a body. They shall continue to deal with current business until they are replaced in accordance with Article 10.

This article gave to the Common Assembly a strong parliamentary quality by investing it with a 'vote of censure'. A vote of no confidence was raised for the first time in the British House of Commons by Samuel Sandys in 1741 (see Turkka 2007) and established as a House principle in 1835, after the Parliamentary Reform of 1832 (see Andrén 1947). For this reason, the Common Assembly was not merely 'consultative' or 'advisory' but contained genuine parliamentary aspects according to the contemporary scholarship in political science and constitutional law. Kapteyn highlights the point: 'Sans le droit de pouvoir obliger la Haute Autorité à démissionner la fonction de l'Assemblée aurait peu différé pour l'essentiel du rôle de nombreuses institutions internationales' (1962, 180).

Of course, the hurdles for dismissing the High Authority were high, as compared to member-state parliaments. The vote of censure was bound to the Authority's Annual Report and required a two thirds majority of the members, a requirement being obviously borrowed from the German Federal Republic's *Grundgesetz*. Nonetheless, the very institution of the vote of censure served as the basis on which the Common Assembly had chances to increase its parliamentary powers in the ECSC beyond those directly given in the Treaty.

If judged solely in terms of the ECSC Treaty, the Common Assembly was far from being a parliament. It could not elect the High Authority, it had practically no powers over the Council of Ministers, and it had no legislative or budgetary powers, the latter being an important means by which early parliaments could empower themselves. The Assembly's range of activities was limited to coal and steel policies, although the Treaty mentioned a possibility of extending the competence. The Assembly's sitting time was limited, and its members were part-time parliamentarians whose main arena for doing politics was their national parliament. The Treaty contained nothing about parliamentary committees that could debate on the motions on its agenda in detail.

For these reasons, it has been easy for European integration scholars to be dismissive of the Common Assembly as a political institution.

Nonetheless, studies on the increase of parliamentary powers within the EU have good reason to start with a detailed discussion of the Common Assembly (see Forsyth 1964; Rittberger 2005; Krumrey 2018). Typological studies of parliamentary systems would regard the possibility to dismiss the High Authority by means of a vote of censure as a minimal, but decisive condition for a qualification as a parliamentary regime, even if that instrument was never used by the Assembly.

The Assembly's right to determine its own rules of procedures allowed it to follow well-known parliamentary principles and practices. The members who were experienced parliamentarians were not willing to regard the Common Assembly as another intergovernmental meeting but treated it as far as possible as if it were a proper parliament.

The members adopted the principle that everything that was not explicitly forbidden in the Treaty was allowed, as noted, for example, in Assembly member Pierre Wigny's report (1958, 33). With this principle, they set up committees that had sittings outside of Assembly sessions, later installing party groups and setting limits to co-operation with the Council of Europe's Consultative Assembly (see Krumrey 2018, 118). Wigny pointed out the difference that in a deliberative assembly, the vote is a part of the debate: 'Dans une Assemblée deliberative il est artificiel de distinguer la discussion et le vote car, par hypothèse, l'exchange de vues a une influence sur le résultat du scrutin' (Wigny 1958, 28).

How far the drafters of the ECSC Treaty understood the power to dismiss the High Authority with a qualified vote of censure as a decisive distinction between parliamentary and proto-parliamentary European institutions does not matter here. What does matter is that this modest formula allowed the Common Assembly parliamentarians to expand the Assembly's parliamentary quality well beyond what the Council of Europe's supranational-minded minority was able or willing to do.

4.2.3 The Council of Ministers

The High Authority had, according to the Treaty, the legislative initiative in the ECSC; however, this was under control of the Council of Ministers. Paragraph 26:1 determined its objectives:

> The Council shall exercise its powers in the cases provided for and in the manner set out in this Treaty, in particular in order to harmonise the action of the High Authority and that of the Governments, which are responsible for the general economic policies of their countries.

The 'harmonisation' made of the Council a kind of mediator between the supranational High Authority and the member state governments. Paragraph 26:2 on exchanging consultations and information with the High Authority could have bound the Council closer to the ECSC than to the member-state governments. Paragraph 26:3 gave the Council an indirect power of initiative in relation to the High Authority by giving the Council the ability to ask for a study of matters it thinks appropriate: 'The Council may request the High Authority to examine any proposals or measures which the Council may consider appropriate or necessary for the attainment of the common objectives.'

The composition of the Council was presented in Paragraph 27:1: 'The Council shall consist of representatives of the Member States. Each State shall delegate to it one of the members of its Government.' Again, the concepts of both representation and delegation were mentioned, but this was by no means an imperative mandate for the minister as member of the Council, as is visible in the French title, the *Conseil de Ministres*, not *Conseil des Ministres* (noted by Wigny 1958, 53).

The powers of the Council and the consultative character of its decision-making were explained in paragraph 28:2: 'When the Council is consulted by the High Authority, it shall consider the matter without necessarily taking a *vote*. The minutes of its proceedings shall be forwarded to the High Authority.' The vote refers to deliberation and not to negotiation and is therefore indication of a parliamentary rather than an intergovernmental way of doing politics.

Although there might in point of fact be instructions from the 'home government' for the minister as a member of the Council, the very possibility to alter the stand after the debate among the member's colleagues gave to the Council a proto-parliamentary character as a minimal 'second chamber' of the ECSC. When linked directly to the High Authority, the Council had an executive role, like a cabinet collegium possessing the power to veto or revise High Authority decisions.

A major question in the ECSC was the delicate balance between the bigger and the smaller member states. The article enabled the Benelux Countries to form a majority by allying with one of the bigger states. Still, the Council could not decide by a simple majority, as the rate of producing coal and steel was factored into the count. This could alter the voting powers as compared to determining them based on a counting of the total population. There were also issues requiring unanimity, which might give a veto power to one of the ministers. 'Wherever this Treaty requires a unanimous decision or unanimous assent, such decision or assent shall be duly given if all the members of the Council vote in favour' (28:4).

It might be assumed that use of the veto was agreed with the member states' government. It was, however, possible for a representative in the Council to abstain from the veto after deliberations, despite a threat from their government to use it. In this respect, paragraph 28:7 is important: 'Wherever this Treaty requires a unanimous decision or unanimous assent, such decision or assent shall be duly given if all the members of the Council vote in favour'. The representing minister was not required to explain the vote to their own government but could leave that to the Council president.

Article 29 gave the Council certain powers over the High Authority. Its financial powers prevented the High Authority and the Court members from determining their own salaries and other benefits. The question arises: Why did the Council and not the Common Assembly have this power?

To sum up, the political character of the Council of Ministers was ambiguous. As a supplement to the High Authority, it was part of the executive, and it possessed supranational legislative powers to modify the High Authority's proposals. When unanimity was required, the Council possessed in practice a veto power against the decisions of the High Authority. In its internal decision-making, however, it followed a parliamentary style of deliberation and vote, while qualified majorities gave it also the power to conduct diplomatic-style negotiations.

There was no direct link between the Council of Ministers and the Common Assembly, which could have made them compete over which would have more 'influence' on the High Authority. This absence of mediation between the Council and the Assembly could guarantee the priority of the supra-national level, as represented by the High Authority, in the decision-making.

The weakness of the Common Assembly, as well as the position of the Council of Ministers as both an executive and a proto-parliamentary institution, were questionable constructions of the Treaty, which have left their shadow on the later European institutions. For how this combination of supranational with parliamentary momentum worked in practice, the first session of the Common Assembly deserves a closer look.

4.3 The Common Assembly plenum in September 1952

The political composition of the Common Assembly was based on quotas of the member states in article 21 of the Treaty: 'Of a total of 78 parliamentarians, France, Germany and Italy sent 18 each, Belgium and the Netherlands sent 10 each and Luxembourg sent four' (Piodi 2017, 3). Among the members, there was only one woman, Marga Klompé from the Catholic party in the Netherlands. There was a high proportion of lawyers and university professors, also as compared with the composition of the member-state parliaments of the time.

In this section, I shall discuss how the Common Assembly's parliamentary quality was judged by its members. This will begin with a look at the speeches of Jean Monnet and Konrad Adenauer in the Assembly's first session in

September 1952. Although party groups were officially formed only in the June 1953 session, I shall identify the speakers in terms of their later Common Assembly party groups, i.e. Christian Democrats (CD), Socialists (Soc) and Liberals (Lib). Among the Liberals, several national parties were included. Only occasionally shall I mention a member's nationality and party affiliation in their home country. Outside the party groups, the Gaullist Michel Debré was the most prominent member.

4.3.1 Opening declarations

The first meeting of the Common Assembly on 10 September 1952 (quoted from Journal official 1952/53, http://aei.pitt.edu/64508/1/A6595.pdf) was opened by the oldest member, the Italian law professor Antonio Boggiano-Pico (CD). He first pointed to a federalist interpretation of European unification, to 'la grande idée de l'Europe fédérée'. Thanking Jean Monnet as the *primus motor* of the Europeanisation, Boggiano-Pico regarded the Assembly as representative and deliberative in its character as well as open to new members: 'à l'ouverture de cette Assemblée représentative et délibérante de six nations centrales de l'Europe libre et démocratique', by which he already opposed negotiation-based intergovernmental organisations.

For Boggiano-Pico, the delegation of sovereignty from member states was a common practice: 'de même le principe de la souveraineté n'est nullement entamé par le fait que l'on délègue, suivant accord entre certains Etats déterminés, l'exercice des activités qui, *strictu sensu,* rentreraient dans les prérogatives souveraines'. He continued by reminding his listeners of the Assembly's double links to the High Authority: although the High Authority is the initiator of policies, it is also subject to the Assembly's vote of censure: 'l'Assemblée dépendent l'approbation ou le refus des rapports et des propositions que la Haute Autorité devra lui soumettre et le pouvoir implicite de provoquer, par la désapprobation, la démission des membres de la Haute Autorité'. (ibid.) He regarded the Common Assembly as comparable to other parliaments and their controlling power as an instrument which governments in democratic organisations may profit from: 'Il s'agit donc de ce pouvoir effectif, raisonnablement requis pour que tout parlement puisse être un instrument utile de gouvernement dans n'importe quelle organisation démocratique'.

Boggiano-Pico saw in the ECSC the origin of the project of European unification, 'foyer et embryon de cette plus vaste fédération des Etats libres de vieux continent'. Jacob Krumrey commented that '[this is] most remarkable for what he did not mention: coal and steel'. He did not regard the Assembly as 'something akin to an inter-parliamentary economic committee' (2018, 117).

In the Common Assembly sitting of 11 September 1952, Jean Monnet, the Chair of the High Authority, and Konrad Adenauer (1876–1967), the West

German Federal Chancellor and Foreign Minister as well as the rotating Chair of the Committee of Ministers of the ECSC, presented their view on the Common Assembly. Monnet first stated the parliamentary responsibility of the High Authority, which he now accepted as highly valuable. 'C'est devant vous seuls que la Haute Autorité est responsible'. He then characterised the Common Assembly as the first supranational assembly with decision-making powers:

> Ainsi, dans les limites de sa compétence, votre Assemblée est souveraine. C'est la première Assemblée européenne qui soit investie d'un pouvoir de décision. Ces responsabilités font de vous et de nous les mandataires de la Communauté tout entière, et ensemble, les serviteurs de ses Institutions. (Journal official, 11 September 1952)

Monnet emphasised that the Assembly shared its supranational quality with the High Authority. He also stressed the exclusion of an imperative mandate or any equivalent that would have saddled the Assembly with dependence on its electors, parties or professional groups. His words resembled Edmond Burke's famous speech to the Bristol electors opposing a 'deliberative assembly' to a 'congress of ambassadors' (Burke 1774):

> Dans l'exercice de leurs fonctions, les membres de la Haute Autorité ont pris l'engagement solennel de ne solliciter ni accepter aucune instruction et de s'abstenir de toute action incompatible avec le caractère supranational de leur mandat. Votre mission participe de la même nature. Dans l'exercice de votre mandat, vous êtes les représentants de la Communauté tout entière. (Journal official, 11 September 1952)

Monnet proposed that the Assembly elect in its September sittings a large committee to act between the sitting periods. It should have the objective 'pour …à voir les problèmes de la Communauté dans leur ensemble et nous obliger nous, la Haute Autorité, à nous expliquer avec vous largement sur la poursuite de la politique dont le traité nous donne la charge'. With this parliamentary committee, the political relationships between the High Authority and the Common Assembly could transcend the vote of censure outside the final report, and a considerable portion of Assembly members would be regularly engaged in the committee's sittings. Monnet concluded:

> La grande révolution européenne de notre époque, celle qui vise à substituer sur notre continent, aux rivalités nationales, l'union des peuples dans la liberté et dans la diversité, la révolution qui veut rendre possible un nouvel épanouissement de notre civilisation et lui permettre une nouvelle renaissance, commence dans ces jours où se constituent les premières institutions supranationales de l'Europe. (ibid.)

By speaking of revolution and renaissance, Monnet opened a wide supranational and parliamentary perspective on European unification, connecting this to a progressivist philosophy of history, albeit recognising: 'Nos institutions communes supranationales sont encore faibles et fragiles'. (ibid.) Unlike what could perhaps have been expected, Monnet did not covet controlling power for the Common Assembly but saw it as a parliamentary ally allowing for supranational politics as opposed to the national interests.

Chancellor Konrad Adenauer gave his judgement on the mutual solidarity of the ECSC institutions and the historical novelty of the Common Assembly as a sovereign supranational parliament:

> Vous êtes en Europe le premier Parlement souverain établi sur une base supranationale. La formation de votre Assemblée fait accomplir un nouveau grand progrès à nos projets de création d'une nouvelle Europe. Le Conseil de ministres ressent très profondément la solidarité qui unit tous les organes de la Communauté. (ibid.)

To characterise the Common Assembly as a parliament was a bold move, encouraging the members to think and act like a parliament and not merely as a controlling assembly with restricted powers. Adenauer also saw the Common Assembly as part of the project of creating 'a new Europe'.

He further characterised the Council of Ministers as a supranational institution: 'Le Conseil de ministres n'est pas un Conseil des ministres tel que nous en connaissons dans les conférences et organisations internationales. C'est un élément organiquement inséré dans la nouvelle communauté supranationale européenne'. (ibid.) As I already noted, the point lies in the distinction between 'de ministres' and 'des ministres', or in German, 'der Rat der Minister ist kein Ministerrat' (ibid.). Adenauer also emphasised the absence of an imperative mandate of the Council members to their governments, which do not have a veto power over the decisions of the Council.

Adenauer interpreted the institutions of the ECSC in the federalist sense, as re-established in the *Grundgesetz* of the Federal Republic in 1949. 'La position du Conseil et de l'Assemblée est peut-être à certains égards comparable aux rapports entre deux Chambres dans la vie constitutionnelle d'un Etat.' (ibid.) In German he did not speak of *Staat,* but of constitutional life (*Verfassungsleben*). Despite his reservations, Adenauer was willing to consider the nine-member Council as a rudimentary upper house of the ECSC, analogous to Mackay's views in the Consultative Assembly of the Council of Europe. Adenauer did not see Council and the Assembly in the Treaty as solely institutions to control the political initiatives of the High Authority.

Adenauer judged the powers of the ECSC institutions in an original way, one allowed by the ambiguities of the Treaty. For him, the vote of censure made the Assembly resemble a parliamentary opposition: 'A vous, l'Assemblée, appartient le droit opposé: par votre décision, vous pouvez provoquer la démission de la Haute Autorité'. The Council of Ministers was a more conservative force: 'Il est dans la nature des choses que, dans le Conseil de ministres, les forces de conservation (*die bewährenden Kräfte*) exercent peut-être plus d'influence que dans l'Assemblée' (ibid.).

This corresponds to the historical role of the lower and upper houses of parliaments: the Council could, according to the Treaty, amend the policy of the

High Authority, whereas the Common Assembly only could dismiss it retroactively. Adenauer seemed, unlike Monnet, to expect the Common Assembly of parliamentarians would act in opposition to both the High Authority and the Council.

La nature même du Parlement comporte en général un plus fort dynamisme. Dans votre Assemblée, il arrivera souvent, et cela tient à la nature même de la vie parlementaire, qu'agiront les forces qui poussent vigoureusement en avant. Permettez-moi de dire au nom du Conseil que nous apprécions pleinement le caractère particulier de votre travail parlementaire, et même que nous considérons comme nécessaire le dynamisme qui émane de vous. (ibid.)

Speaking on behalf of the Council of Ministers, Konrad Adenauer used a federalist language when he praised parliamentary dynamism against the conservative tendencies of the Council. This speech casts him as a politician in a different light than the common view on Adenauer as a proponent of *Kanzlerdemokratie*, which left little power to parliament (see e.g. Recker 2018).

The support for the Common Assembly by Monnet and Adenauer was at a marked distance from the mood in the Council of Europe. Both Monnet and Adenauer were proud of launching the first 'European Parliament' worthy of the name, and both regarded the ECSC as a training ground for a supranational parliament with powers and competence comparable to the parliaments of the member states.

4.3.2 The Rules of procedure

The Common Assembly began to organise itself on 11 September 1952 with a debate on its Rules of procedure (*Réglement*). The rapporteur of the committee for the preliminary draft, the President of the Belgian Senate, Paul Struye, (CD), opened the debate. The debates of the Assembly in the first session strongly affirmed the parliamentary character of the Assembly, to judge by the work of the committee that drafted the first sitting of the Assembly, as the Treaty itself did not mention any Assembly committees at all.

Struye emphasised the supranationality of the Assembly in its personal decisions. '[L]a commission a estimé que, tout en soulignant que, dans une assemblée supranationale comme la nôtre, c'est aux titres des candidats et non à leur nationalité qu'il convenait d'avoir l'égard' (Journal official, 11 September 1952). Despite this, he agreed that each member state should be represented in the presidency (*bureau*) of the Assembly. He referred to the available 'sound parliamentary methods' for the rules of procedure: 'Nous devons nous constituer de manière définitive conformément aux saines méthodes parlementaires et, toute affaire cessante, préparer le règlement' (ibid.). The rules of procedure were an indispensable part of the Common Assembly's parliamentary identity.

Member-state quotas in the presidency were rejected by P.A. Blaisse (CD) as nationalistic: 'L'on introduit de ce fait une tendance nationale, un élément national, dans la structure de cette Assemblée' (ibid.), although he proposed no amendment to the draft. He compared the degree of supranationality in the ECSC's different political institutions:

> La communauté... comporte, vous les savez tous, quatre organes qui possèdent manifestement un caractère supranational. Cela ressort de façon très nette, non seulement du texte du Traité, mais également des autres actes, et en particulier des débats parlementaires dans les six pays. Je songe tout d'abord à l'Haute Autorité, puis à la Cour et à l'Assemblée. Un peu moins net est le caractère supranational du Conseil de Ministres, et c'est consciemment qu'il ainsi est prévu dans le Traite. (ibid.)

The supranationality of the Common Assembly was, however, not evident in the Treaty, which rather gave the impression that the Assembly, the Council and the Court were types of checks and balances to prevent the High Authority from going too far in its supranational policies. Blaisse situated the Assembly on the side of the High Authority within the ECSC, while regarding the Council with certain suspicion for its willingness to follow the biddings of the governments.

On 12 September, Chair Paul Struye presented the work of the preliminary committee. The committee explicitly supported empowering the Assembly, in contrast to the 'too restrictive' wording of the Treaty: 'la commission s'est préoccupée de sauvegarder et, dans toute la mesure du possible, ... de préciser ou même de renforcer les prérogatives de votre Assemblée' (12 September 1952). This concerned above all the procedures for dealing with members' and parliamentary groups' questions to the High Authority: 'Nous avons tenu notamment à organiser, ... la façon dont, tant les représentants à titre individuel que l'Assemblée en tant que corps, pourraient poser des questions à la Haute Autorité et les conditions dans lesquelles les réponses devraient être faites et publiées.'(ibid.) In other words, parliamentary questions should be regarded as ordinary praxis in the ECSC.

The preliminary rules committee proposed that common parliamentary practices – 'ce qui se fait, en pratique, dans toutes les assemblées parlementaires'(ibid.) – should serve as the model for the rules of procedure of the Common Assembly. Accordingly, the President of the Assembly would present the agenda for the next sitting at the end of a sitting, to serve as an example. This is a further sign of identifying the Assembly with parliaments and not with international organisations.

Variations in parliamentary practice were indicated in Article 31 of the draft: 'Sauf décision contraire de l'Assemblée, l'examen en commission précède toute discussion générale'. Hence, the Assembly would follow the Francophone tradition, as opposed to Westminster practice, in that the plenum's first reading would precede the committing of items, although the latter, as Struye said, followed the practices of the Consultative Assembly of the Council of Europe. He did not regard the choice as important, as the Assembly could in any case change the procedure: 'puisqu'en fait, chaque fois ... l'Assemblée pourra décider dans tel ou tel sens'. (12 September 1952)

Struve underrated here the historical differences in procedural styles. The committees do play a different political role in parliamentary debates. Francophone committees are preparatory organs for facilitating and simplifying the terms for plenary debates, whereas in Westminster, the first reading debate in the plenum concerns the general principles and then the committees deal with the details of the motions. In plenum, a member can as a rule speak only once, whereas in the committee replies are automatically part of the debate (see Palonen 2014a and the literature discussed there). The European Parliament still follows the Francophone procedure, and the possibility to open the debate in plenum is no longer mentioned in its procedural documents. Eventually this might have been one reason for the relative weakness of the European Parliament.

Another deviation from the Westminster practice lay in Article 31: 'Les représentants qui demandent la parole sont inscrits suivant l'ordre de leur demande' (Journal official, 12 September 1952). Instead of letting the President of the Assembly rotate between the expected *pro* and *contra* speeches, a list of speakers in order of requests was formed, as in many continental parliaments. This practice diminishes the role of debate as distinctive for parliamentary speaking. The parliamentary character was, however, strengthened when Struye disallowed experts and functionaries from speaking in the Common Assembly 'ne pouvait être admise dans une assemblée comme la nôtre'(ibid.).

Creating committees of the Common Assembly was in the opening session regarded as a major measure to affirm the Assembly's powers. The Assembly did not agree to restrict its proceedings in the debate to the annual report of the High Authority. Struye regarded the committees, in particular, as being an inherent part of parliamentary politics: 'Il faut...que notre Assemblée commence sa véritable tâche et elle ne pourra le faire, semble-t-il, que s'il y a déjà quelque chose d'organisé en matière de commissions' (ibid.).

In the debate, Herbert Wehner (Soc) supported a strategy of maximising powers if they were not explicitly forbidden in the Treaty: 'Es muß das Interesse dieser Versammlung sein, diese Bestimmungen, soweit es um die Kompetenzen dieser Versammlung angeht, bis zum äußersten, eben bis zur äußersten Grenze auszuschöpfen' (12 September 1952). Antonio Azara (CD), for his part, warned against using committees at the cost of the Assembly itself: 'que la commission des affaires générales ... puissent s'attribuer un rôle de "substituts" ... de l'Assemblée.' (ibid.)

The final formulation of article 39 was suggested by the President of the Assembly, Paul-Henri Spaak (Soc): 'L'Assemblée constitue des commissions permanentes ou temporaires, générales ou spéciales, et fixe leurs attributions' (ibid.). Struye proposed to call the 'general affairs committee' of the draft the 'commission d'organisation'. The Assembly was already prepared to set up different types of committees, but it postponed their nomination.

The willingness of members to emphasise the parliamentary quality of the Assembly was shown in the procedural rules they devised. Regarding the status of the committees, there were tactical differences between those who wanted to maintain the priority of the plenary sessions and those who put their trust in the committees as the means of controlling and maintaining connections with the High Authority.

The members elected from national parliaments had no doubts about the parliamentary quality of the Common Assembly. It was not just a seldom-meeting joint coal-and-steel committee of the member state parliaments. They opted for a contrafactual vision of acting as much as possible as a full-fledged parliament, following what they had learnt to do in their own parliaments. In other words, they saw an extraordinary *Chance* to combine their European vision with their parliamentary competence and experience for creating a supranational parliament, which later could expand its range of competence. The recommendation for founding the Ad Hoc Assembly encouraged such a combination of parliamentary and supranational forms as a way towards Europeanisation.

4.3.3 Parliamentary powers of the Common Assembly

The initial session of the Common Assembly, in September 1952, illustrated the mood in favour of Europeanisation and politicisation of the West European order by a double means of supranationalisation and parliamentarisation. In the Arendtian (1982) sense, an *erweiterte Denkungsart* – a willingness to think something new which transcends the existing rules and conventions – prevailed among the majority of the Common Assembly's members. They were open to include a European polity level above their own member states as well as to apply the parliamentary style of politics to this supranational polity (see Chapter 10.3).

In contrast to the Council of Europe and other post-war Europeanisation projects, the ECSC assumed supranationalism from the beginning, and the Common Assembly saw it as a platform for Europeanising additional topics. Although its parliamentary power of a vote of censure against the High Authority had strict conditions attached, its debates showed that the parliamentary powers of the Common Assembly were 'real'. Its powers to develop the rules of procedure and to set up an extensive committee system (enlarging the sitting time for parliamentarians as well as the *de facto* alliance with the High Authority, alluded by Monnet, as a second supranational pillar of the ECSC) were realistic possibilities for expanding the parliamentary politicisation of the

ECSC. Its setting up of the Ad Hoc Assembly was a milestone for the double momentum linking supranationalism with parliamentarism as constitutive principles of a European polity.

I shall not follow in detail the history of the parliamentarisation of the Common Assembly and the ECSC. The members constructed different procedures, such as replacing the sitting order according to nationality and party group in summer 1953. They invented indirect procedures for controlling the ECSC budget, turned the right to put forward parliamentary questions into oblique ways of putting forward parliamentary initiatives, and introduced measures to control the Council of Ministers. Most important was their extension of the annual sitting time by introducing extraordinary sessions and their possibility to raise the question of no confidence on items other than the annual report of the High Authority (see the report of Assembly member Pierre Wigny 1958 and my discussion in Palonen 2021a).

The decisive difference to the attempts by the Council of Europe's Consultative Assembly to promote parliamentarisation consisted in the Common Assembly's willingness to interpret the Treaty of Paris by the principle that anything not explicitly forbidden was allowed. The Common Assembly applied well-established parliamentary procedures and practices as a regulative principle to gauge its parliamentary powers and extend them boldly to the supranational level. Here the nearly identical membership of the Common Assembly compared to the Ad Hoc Assembly also led to fruitful exchange of experiences on both parliamentary fora.

5 Setting up the Ad Hoc Assembly

The preceding chapters have offered a political context for understanding the singularity and political significance of the Ad Hoc Assembly and its debates on a constitutional Draft for the planned European Political Community. This context is necessary for understanding the specific debates, proposals and thought experiments of the assembly, while a longer historical perspective is needed for the discussion of the parliamentary-government aspects of the Ad Hoc Assembly.

5.1 The political impulse

Although the members of the Ad Hoc Assembly were mainly the parliamentarians of the ECSC's Common Assembly, the origins of the Assembly lay in an initiative by its rival the Consultative Assembly of the Council of Europe. Its resolution from 10 December 1951

> advised the Committee of Ministers to encourage the early conclusion...of an agreement setting up a Political Authority, subject to the democratic control of a Parliamentary Assembly and having a competence limited *to the domains of defence and external affairs,* in which the exercise of sovereignty in common becomes necessary through the organization of a European army and its employment within the orbit of the Atlantic Treaty. (Ad hoc-Assembly, 1953, 7).

The plan was limited to foreign and defence policy, topics which traditionally belonged to the *arcana imperii* of the states, although strivings for parliamentary control of foreign policy were initiated after First World War in the League of Nations and elsewhere.

A British response to the Council's resolution was the Eden Plan, named after Foreign Minister Anthony Eden (1897–1977), who was its initiator. The British government submitted the plan to the ECSC and the Council of Europe on 19 March 1952. In Eden's statement, we can read of his support for European unity and 'how the Council of Europe can fulfil the useful and vital role it has to play in these developments' (Statement by Anthony Eden, 19 March 1952)

Eden was worried about the Consultative Assembly's recently adopted Draft Statute, of 'its aim of transformation of what is now a purely consultative body into a quasi-federal institution with legislative and executive powers and the right to be consulted by Member Governments on certain matters within its competence'. With the cooperation plan, Eden aimed at preserving 'the Council of Europe...as an organisation for intergovernmental cooperation in Western

Europe'. He was, accordingly, looking for ways in which 'countries, like the United Kingdom...could be associated in an appropriate way, with the parliamentary and ministerial institutions of the Community' (ibid.).

The statement shows that while British Conservative government was supporting European unification, it still excluded membership in federal and supranational institutions and opposed the steps towards giving full parliamentary powers to the Consultative Assembly of the Council of Europe. The government's aim was only to become 'associated' with the supranational institutions such as the ECSC (called the 'Schuman pool' by Eden), and the plan aimed at creating the forms for such an association.

Another pillar of the Ad Hoc Assembly was the European Defence Community, which French Prime Minister René Pleven proposed in 1950. It was seen as an alternative to the US plans for West German re-armament, including offering it membership in NATO (Schorkopf 2023, 54). On 27 May 1952, the six West European ECSC member states agreed on another Treaty of Paris (see *Treaty Establishing the European Defence Community*). Article 8 defines its institutions:

The institutions of the Community shall be:

- A Council of Ministers, hereinafter called the Council.
- A Common Assembly, hereinafter called the Assembly.
- A Commissariat of the European Defense Community, hereinafter called the Commissariat.
- A court of Justice, hereinafter called the Court.
(unofficial English version, https://aei.pitt.edu/5201/1/5201.pdf)

The language of the Treaty follows the ECSC, except replacing 'High Authority' with 'Commissariat', which might better have suited an organisation with competence in foreign and defence policy. The competence was not defined in the Treaty but was left to the Assembly to draft.

The responses to the Eden plan by the ECSC's Council of Ministers and the Consultative Assembly of the Council of Europe changed the situation. The Italian government, advised by European Movement federalists around Altiero Spinelli, including the Belgian socialists Paul-Henri Spaak and Fernand Dehousse, took the initiative at a meeting of the Council of Ministers of the ECSC (see Griffiths 2000, 63–70; Schorkopf 2023, 55–58). The Council of Ministers addressed the Common Assembly, proposing that they act together with representatives of the Council of Europe as a kind of constituent assembly to provide the political backup for the European Defence Community.

On 30 May 1952, the Consultative Assembly responded to Eden and proposed the creation of a supranational Political Authority, 'considering that several Governments and Parliaments have held it essential that the setting up of the European Defence Community should be accompanied by the constitution of a supranational political authority' (Ad Hoc Assembly, 8). It recommended that 'the Governments concerned should charge either the Coal and Steel Assembly, or the Assembly of the Council of Europe sitting with a restricted membership to draft the Statute of a supranational political community'. It also expanded the range of the new political authority: 'that the institution to which this mandate had been given would not confine itself to studying the permanent organization of the E. D. C. [which was the particular mission given to the Assembly of the European Defence Community by article 38] but should proceed to draft a statute for a supranational European political community' (ibid.). Article 38 gave relatively detailed objectives to this preparatory Assembly:

1. Within the period provided for in Section 2 of this Article, the Assembly shall study:

(a) the creation of an Assembly of the European Defence Community elected on a democratic basis;

(b) the powers which might be granted to such an Assembly; and

(c) the modifications which should be made in the provisions of the present Treaty relating to the other institutions of the Community, particularly with a view to safeguarding an appropriate representation of the States. (ibid.)

Indeed, the European Political Community arose from what was initially a joint project of the ECSC, the Council of Europe and the planned EDC. These gave the above tasks to that what was to become Ad Hoc Assembly. The political backup for the European Defence Community was to be an institution based on a separation of powers and a bicameral parliament, leaving open the choice between a federal or a confederal organisation, that is, its degree of supranationalism.

In its work, the Assembly will particularly bear in mind the following principles:
The definitive organization which will take the place of the present transitional organization should be conceived so as to be capable of constituting one of the elements of an ultimate Federal or Confederal structure, based upon the principle of the separation of powers and including, particularly, a bicameral representative system. (ibid.)

The EDC should co-operate with 'different organizations for European cooperation, now in being or to be created in the future'. The Ad Hoc Assembly was given six months to write the draft, which was to be 'submitted to the Council'.

5.2 Remarks on studies on the Ad Hoc Assembly

Why have the Ad Hoc Assembly and its Draft Treaty for the European Political Community (EPC) received such scant attention among European integration and parliamentary scholars? An obvious reason is the tendency towards writing histories of the winners. For example, Franco Piodi's quasi-official study, *Towards a Single Parliament* (2007, 14), takes the ECSC Common Assembly as its point of departure, mentioning only briefly the 'setback' of the planned EDC, and not at all the Ad Hoc Assembly and its work for the Constitution of the European Political Community.

With his article entitled 'The start of European integration and the parliamentary dimension: the Common Assembly of the ECSC (1952–1958)', Sandro Guerriri (2008) is not wrong in focusing on the internal moves for empowering the Common Assembly, but he, too, fails to mention the Ad Hoc Assembly at all. Guerriri also unduly extends the definition of what, to him, qualifies as a parliamentary assembly. Teija Tiilikainen and Claudia Wiesner refer to the '1952 and 1953 debates on a European Community of Defence and a European Political Community' with the plan for a bicameral parliament as well as 'a draft constitution' without going into the details (2016, 293–294).

In the older literature, a Murray Forsyth ironically characterised the period as one of naïve enthusiasm für Europe, 'dass die Jahre 1952 und 1953 den Höhepunkt der idealistischen Begeisterungswelle für die europäische Einigung brachten' (1964, 22). He nonetheless describes the Ad Hoc Assembly's proposed powers for the Parliament in some detail, calls the European Executive Council 'the government' of the Community and notes that the proposals presented 'sehr genau den zu errichtenden politischen Apparat'. He does not mention, however, that the political apparatus remained vague in its policies, except in the fields of the ECSC and EDC (ibid. 24).

The contemporaneous journal articles manifest a greater openness towards the new. Herbert W. Briggs quotes Heinrich v. Brentano, Chair of the Ad Hoc Assembly's Constitutional Committee: 'A supra-national executive organ is envisaged in the form of a European Executive Council, whose formation, composition and activity will, in accordance with the principles of parliamentary democracy, require the confidence of Parliament' (1954, 112). For Briggs it 'appears that most of the decisions which the Parliament, the European Executive Council, the High Authority and the Court of Justice will be called upon to make will be of a supra-national character' (ibid. 121).

Basil Karp points out that the Constitutional Draft 'represents the thinking of an imposing group of parliamentarians as to the scope and character of political union that is workable and attainable today' (1954, 181). He further notes: 'The Ad Hoc Assembly was composed largely of individuals who were already favorable toward the idea of "Europe" and who wanted to build a political authority that would enjoy the maximum independence' (ibid.).

Hans-Jürgen Schlochauer, in the pacifist Friedens-Warte, highlights the supranational aspect: 'Der an den Verträgen über die EGKS und die EVG entwickelte Begriff einer "supranationalen Gemeinschaft" findet in den Vertragstext der EG Eingang durch Art. 1: "Mit diesem Vertrag wird eine Europäische Gemeinschaft übernationalen Charakters errichtet"' (1954/1955, 18). He notes, however, that its competence remained vague and was interpreted restrictively (ibid.). His contemporaries receptive to the new in the European Political Community, but parliamentary government on supranational level was not discussed.

Richard T. Griffiths' *Europe's First Constitution. The European Political Community, 1952–1954* (2000) is the only monograph on the Ad Hoc Assembly and its Draft Treaty. It is a historian's work on the Community from the planning stages in the Council of Europe and European Defence Community through the setting up of the Ad Hoc Assembly, and it describes its Draft Treaty and summarised the work of the Assembly with 24 pages. Griffiths follows the subsequent fate of the Community in the member countries, including its non-ratification by the Assemblée Nationale.

His point of comparison is German Foreign Minister Joschka Fischer's (of the Greens) well-known speech at the fiftieth anniversary of the Schuman Declaration in May 2000 (Fischer 2000).

A re-examination of the discussion on the EPC, the intellectual and political climate in which it took shape, and the nature of the problems then confronting European policy-makers provide uncanny echoes with the situation of today. Let it not be the lack of knowledge that prevents us from learning from the past. The fundamental logic for wanting a federal constituent assembly has little changed over past fifty years and many of the specific choices that will have to be made for a federal constitution defining the distribution of power between the European and the national (and regional) levels remain the same. (Griffiths 2000, 21)

I share Griffiths' view on the contemporary relevance of the EPC plans, and I have learnt details from him on the background and the work of the Ad Hoc Assembly. His approach focuses on the events, facts, parties and persons, but he does not analyse the debates as such or regard the documents as being the results of them. Although he discusses the 'democratic deficit' claim in the EU debates (ibid. 176–179), he fails to appreciate parliamentary government as the main innovation of the EPC Draft Treaty, as compared to the Council of Europe and the ECSC.

Griffiths has noted a turning point in the debates, namely the plenum of January 1953, when the Ad Hoc Assembly altered the election of the President of the European Executive Council, from the Council of Ministers to be decided by the Senate, the second chamber of the Parliament, by a vote of 22 to 21 (see also Werdegang 1954, 81). He traces this decision back to the standpoint of the

European Movement's members in the Ad Hoc Assembly (Griffiths 2000, 78). Griffiths does not say that by this decision, which was affirmed in the committees, in the plenum and finally in the Draft Treaty, the Ad Hoc Assembly combined supranationalism and parliamentary government in a unique way.

Linda Risso's conference paper, *The "Forgotten" European Political Community 1952–1954* highlights its certain similarities with the 2004 debates on the European Constitution. Although only few participants

> had made any reference to it; indeed, one might conclude from their silence that many of them hardly remembered it. Hence the need to investigate and comprehend nature and limits of the EPC: an insight into the history – and particularly to the failure – of the Political Community would offer a better understanding of the obstacles on the way of the 'Constitution for Europe'. (Risso 2004, 1)

Risso saw the obstacles to a supranational European Constitution as persisting fifty years after the first attempt. Her interpretation of the Ad Hoc Assembly betrays a certain nation-centredness, and she assessed the results: 'The Constitutional Committee focused more on the need to provide the European Institution with sufficient democratic control than it did on the enlarging the capacities of the Community' (ibid. 4). As an International Relations scholar, she was not interested in the novelty of applying parliamentary government to a supranational polity.

Risso sees the European Defence Community as the primary project and the European Political Community as a by-product. For her, the failure of the EPC was mediated by the hope for a *détente* with the Soviet Union post-Stalin and the shift from the Antonin Pinay to the René Mayer government in France, which, needing the support of the Gaullists, replaced Robert Schuman with Georges Bidault as foreign minister (ibid. 6–7).

In a subtitle, Risso nonetheless asks: 'The EPC: a missed opportunity or a misunderstanding?' For the former view, she argues: 'The EPC provided democratic control, the lack of which was to be criticized the following fifty years. Moreover, the Draft Treaty established the superiority of the community over national law. Finally, by directly addressing the need to establish a common market, the EPC Treaty paved the way for the further European integration' (ibid. 7). Still, her overall judgement is that the EPC had no chance: 'The EPC would hardly have been able to have effective and independent foreign and fiscal capacities and national vetoes could have easily impeded, if not paralysed, its functioning' (ibid).

This argument misjudges the inter-institutional powers in the Draft Treaty: 'The supranational features of the EPC should not make us forget that the Council of Ministers was still the central body of the new Community and preserved the clear intention to protecting the will of each of its member' (ibid.). The Ad Hoc Assembly decision in January 1953 for the Senate to appoint the President of the European Executive Council undermines her interpretation (see

Chapter 9). Linda Risso seems to assume that the losers of history deserve their fate.

Franz Schorkopf's *Die unentschiedene Macht* (2023) is a comprehensive constitutional history of the European Union. He formulated the problematic as follows:

> Mein Augenmerk liegt jedoch auf den erwähnten verfassunghistorischen Leitfragen, das heißt konkret auf Vertragsverhandlungen, Organen und Einrichtungen, Abstimmungmodi, Stimmgewichtung, auf Kompetenzen, Grundrechten und der Legitimation europäischer Hoheitsgewalt, pointiert formuliert auf der Machtarchitektur der Europäischen Union. (2023, 19).

Thematically, this concentration on the 'power architecture' is close to mine, although Schorkopf only devotes 18 pages to the *Verfassungsversuch* of the European Political Community. He does not discuss conceptual history or the political theory of parliamentarism, nor does he analyse the debates of the Ad Hoc Assembly. He does acknowledge that the project 'zu Unrecht nicht zum Erinnerungskanon gehört und mehr Aufmerksamkeit verdient' (2023, 54). For information on the later constitutional history of the EU, I have profited much from Schorkopf's study.

For my purposes, the state of the art of Ad Hoc Assembly studies means that I seldom can rely on them, and I am therefore under no obligation to engage in disputes with previous research. So, I am free to follow my own research agenda for both European and parliamentary studies.

5.3 The Ad Hoc Assembly debate in the Common Assembly

In his speech on 11 September 1952 to the ECSC Common Assembly, West German Chancellor and Foreign Minister Konrad Adenauer reported from the ECSC Council of Ministers meeting of the previous day. Whereas the ECSC had a definite and seemingly narrow competence, the Council's ministers had sent an invitation to the Common Assembly to elaborate, together with advisory members from the Consultative Assembly, the Draft Treaty for the new European Political Community: 'à élaborer le projet d'un traité instituant une communauté politique européenne'. Adenauer regarded the project for a European Constitution as a truly historical objective. He explained that the task of drafting the Constitution was assigned to the ECSC Common Assembly as a European Defence Community Assembly did not yet exist, and as the Consultative Assembly could not provide a basis for a supranational Constitution (11 September 1952).

On 12 September 1952, the Common Assembly began to debate the ECSC Foreign Ministers' proposal, which Adenauer presented. President Paul-Henri

Spaak (Soc) reported that the proposal did not concern the Common Assembly as such, but rather its members, to be complemented with three additional members from the largest European states. They were together invited to form, assisted by selected members of the Consultative Assembly, an *Ad Hoc Assembly* to accomplish the resolution of the ministers, 'une Assemblée spéciale *ad hoc* qui serait chargée d'examiner et d'exécuter les propositions contenues dans la résolution des Six' (12 September 1952).

The members of the Common Assembly were not fully prepared for this proposal, although the first speaker, Luxembourgian professor Nicolas Margue (CD), who had been rapporteur in the Consultative Assembly, supported it. Paul Struye (CD) remarked that, for a parliamentary assembly, the expression of dissent was essential and that also concerned this proposal: 'nous sommes, je pense, une assemblée parlementaire dont c'est l'essence même de permettre aux diverses opinions de s'exprimer en toute liberté' (ibid.). The initiative of the ministers did not correspond to the golden rule of the relationship between a sovereign parliament and an executive, 'ne me paraît pas la règle d'or qui doit déterminer les rapports entre le Parlement et l'exécutif' (ibid.).

Struye considered the words of the ministers' resolution, from a constitutional, legal and parliamentary-prerogative point of view, as an assault (*atteinte*) on the parliaments of the member states. He did not oppose the proposal but would have preferred it to have been a joint initiative of member state parliaments. Whether they would have been willing at this stage to such a motion, we cannot know. Struye was not against the supranationality of the ECSC, but rather gave a reminder of its specific objectives: 'nous étions, nous…le premier pouvoir agissant au nom des peuples dans un cadre ou dans un intérêt supranational bien déterminé'. He would have rather supported extending the ECSC into a proper European Community: 'l'élargissement de notre Europe à six que nous espérons voir devenir un jour la véritable Europe' (ibid.).

The Gaullist Michel Debré expressed major reservations about European political authority: 'La première est la suivante: cette autorité politique doit avoir un caractère confédéral; la seconde…est que la France doit y entrer avec la totalité de l'Union française' (ibid.). In other words, Debré opposed supranational Europe, wanted to include the French overseas departments and declared himself as a 'resolute adversary' of both the European Defence Community and the Ad Hoc Assembly.

Pierre-Henri Teitgen (CD) mentioned the possibility that the ministers could have elaborated the draft themselves: 'Ces six ministres pourraient parfaitement préparer seuls, entre eux, un projet de traité instituant une autorité politique commune pour nos six'. The proposal, however, marked the support that existed for a parliamentary dimension to Europeanisation. Antonio Azara (CD) also remarked that the Council of Ministers had invited and not ordered the parliaments, and that '[l]a décision appartient aux Parlements'. Herbert Wehner

(Soc) warned the Common Assembly against overloading its activities, that 'es wird...vernünftig sein, unsere Kräfte nicht zu überladen', whereas Hans-Joachim v. Merkatz (Lib), referring to the Treaty, claimed that 'Durch die Errichtung einer wirtschaftlichen Gemeinschaft den ersten Grundstein für eine weitere und tiefere Gemeinschaft unter den Völkern legen'. Heinrich v. Brentano (CD) said that the members, if they wanted to create a federal Europe ('wenn wir eine europäische Föderation erreichen wollen') have the Council of Foreign Ministers to thank for it (ibid.).

E.M.J.A. (Maan) Sassen (CD) agreed with 'l'élément démocratique, et spécialement l'élément parlementaire' in planning the treaties for a future Europe'. Law professor Fernand Dehousse (Soc) declared himself to be a 'militant de la cause européenne depuis de longues années', supporting both the supranational and the parliamentary aspects of Europeanisation: 'Nous sommes, dans l'histoire, le premier parlement international véritablement digne de ce nom. Prouvons-le en agissant comme un parlement et en prenant toutes nos responsabilité'. (12 September 1952) He thus regarded the Common Assembly as a parliament, although qualifying as international rather than supranational. On the next day, Théodore Lefevre (CD), became the first member to speak explicitly of the Common Assembly as a European Parliament: 'notre Assemblée qui est la première à mériter le nom de "Parlement européen"' (13 September 1952).

Giovanni Persico (Soc) shared the federalist vision of Adenauer's address, regarding the Council of Ministers as the Senate of the ECSC:

[le] Conseil qui n'est pas l'habituel conseil des ministres, mais qui est notre conseil des ministres, celui de la Communauté du charbon et de l'acier, et qui a, dans le cadre de la Communauté, une fonction semblable à celle d'une des Chambres, dans le cadre parlementaire des divers pays. Ainsi, le Gouvernement serait la Haute Autorité, nous serions la Chambre et le Conseil de ministres représenterait le Sénat. (ibid)

Persico, in line with the older federalist thinking, called the new entity a 'state' and supported creating 'l'Etat de la Communauté européenne' as soon as possible. Alberto Giovannini (Lib) referred to supranationalism when stating that in the Common Assembly, party divisions are more important than nationalities. This was for him 'un grand pas vers l'unité européenne'. (ibid.)

Among the warning voices was Jean Maroger (Lib), who regarded those who wanted to rapidly construct the political community ('de se lancer dans une construction politique générale de l'Europe', ibid.) as having their head in the clouds. Peter A. Blaisse (CD) considered economic unification a precondition for political unification, thus setting an agenda for the economic integration well beyond that of the ECSC.

Une fédération politique sans l'existence d'un marché unique, sans une politique commune dans le domaine commercial et sans une politique progressive sur le terrain de la main-d'oeuvre, sans un libre mouvement des capitaux, sans une harmonisation, une politique commune en ce qui concerne les impôts et la stabilité financière intérieure, n'est ni concevable ni réalisable. (ibid.)

François de Menthon (CD) saw, in contrast, the political community as a condition for the functioning of the ECSC and for a common economic policy in general, which called for rapid realisation of the Council of Ministers' proposal: 'Tout retard nouveau compromettrait, à mon avis, l'efficacité de la Communauté du charbon et de l'acier'. (ibid.)

Michel Debré welcomed the parliamentary character of the Common Assembly in respecting opponents like himself: 'la première preuve que nous sommes un vrai Parlement, c'est l'indulgence que la majorité manifeste a` un représentant de la minorité'. He demanded that members explain what was meant by 'political authority', or the political system to which it refers: 'quelle serait cette autorité politique, quelles seraient ses attributions, en quoi consisterait le système politique de l'Europe.' (ibid)

Debré's argument was rejected by Nicolas Margue, who supported the 'mission' of the foreign ministers': 'que l'Assemblée est d'accord pour accepter la mission qui lui est confiée'. A motion put forward by French SFIO leader Guy Mollet (Soc), which only marginally differed from the motion of the Assembly presidency, passed by a vote of 51 to 4, with 4 abstentions (ibid.).

5.4 Constitution-writing by parliamentarians

US scholar Basil Karp notes a distinctive feature of the Ad Hoc Assembly in its having been 'drawn up not by scholars or government technicians, but by politicians...at the formal request of the governments' (1954, 181). This was perhaps not so unique as he claims, for at least the *Parlamentarischer Rat*, which wrote – under Allied supervision – the West German *Grundgesetz* in 1948/49, consisted of politicians named by the parties. Constitutional specialists played a major role among them, and only a few members had parliamentary experience from the time of the Weimar Reichstag, but members of the post-war Landtage were well represented.

The composition of the Ad Hoc Assembly goes back to the ECSC ministers, who agreed that the parliamentary dimension would play a key role in the new political community. A Constitution drafted by parliamentarians was the best way to obtain views and arguments *pro et contra* already in the preparatory phase. It was also a move to guarantee the supranational character of the European Political Community and to prevent it from being reduced to the form of other international organisations. Among the members, there were several constitutional lawyers, who understood that they were expected to create something new, and although using the experiences and practices of existing parliaments, the members regarded their task as political.

The pro-European orientation of a majority of members was obvious. Despite their parliamentary strength in France and Italy, Communists were excluded from the Ad Hoc Assembly, but Michel Debré and a two other Gaullists (Griffiths 2000, 92) were included and were fierce opponents of supranationalism. At the other end, were five members of the federalist Study Committee for the European Constitution, the Socialists Paul-Henri Spaak and Fernand Dehousse, the Christian Democrats Lodovico Benvenuti and Hermann Pünder, and the Liberal Max Becker (ibid. 72–73).

I would emphasise the political imagination of the parliamentarians. The drafting of the Constitution included familiar parliamentary procedures and practices, while recognising historical variations between parliaments when applying, *mutatis mutandis,* parliamentary principles to a supranational polity without precedent. Nobody was better suited to that than experienced parliamentarians, who could understand the politics of constitution-writing better than pure academics, and in debate present bold new ideas as well as reservations and objections against them. The party affiliations or nationalities of the members were of secondary importance: Schorkopf's division of parliamentarians into constitutionalists, governmentalists and pragmatists (2023, 16–17) hardly played any role in the Ad Hoc Assembly.

A key trait of the experienced parliamentarian is, in Max Weber's words, their ability to weigh 'the scope (*Tragweite*) of words' (Weber 1917b, 187), through the practice of debating *pro et contra* in plenum and in committees the broad lines as well as the details of the political alternatives. In parliaments, members had become accustomed to dealing with issues which they had never encountered before and to accept no justifications of governments and officials without a thorough questioning of their proposals. They could do that by calling attention to the possible, frequently unwanted, consequences of them, and by themselves drafting motions, initiatives, amendments, parliamentary questions and so on. Such competence was missing from most scholars, legal practitioners, utopian philosophers, futurologists or science fiction authors, to take some obvious examples of persons who also face an unknown future.

The European University Institute (EUI) website presents documentation about the Ad Hoc Assembly as a rule in five languages, in the four ECSC languages – French, German, Italian and Dutch – as well as in English. Although in conceptual matters, the translations are always problematic and, after 70 years, frequently look out of date, I have, for the sake of convenience, used the English versions if available, only checking the French or German if the English formulations sound odd or mistaken. In this book, I quote only the date and the type of sitting, and occasionally other documents given the same date. For the sittings of the Sub-committees, detailed records, including the speakers' own formulations, are available only in the French versions (*Compte-rendu*).

As opposed to verbatim reports made with the professional stenographic apparatus of modern parliaments, the Ad Hoc Assembly's documents are reports translated by the secretariat. How reliable the formulations are is an open question, but they are the only such documents we have available.

5.5 The members of the Ad Hoc Assembly

The first meeting of the Ad Hoc Assembly took place on 15 September 1952, two days after the termination of the Common Assembly sitting, with Paul-Henri Spaak (Soc), the President of that Assembly, as the Chair. In addition to the 78 members of the Common Assembly, the Ad Hoc Assembly co-opted three parliamentarians from France (Senghor, Silvandre, Plaisant), Italy (Bergmann, Bovetti, Santero) and West Germany (though not nominated at that particular sitting), thus having 87 ordinary members, as well as 13 'observers' from Council of Europe countries outside the ECSC (http://aei.pitt.edu/64508/ 1/A6595.pdfm%20101–102). The German SPD refused to send its members to the Ad Hoc Assembly, due to its late leader Kurt Schumacher's suspicions that the *Westbindung* would make the reunification of Germany more difficult. Younger SPD politicians, such as Willy Brandt, early supported the West European institutions, but for others it took longer to change their own and their party's position (on Brandt and Herbert Wehner, see Monnet 1978, 318, 412).

The members of the Common Assembly were, of course, not elected for the drafting of a Constitution for a European Political Community, nor were they elected as specialists for coal and steel. They included several front-bench parliamentarians of their parties. While they were not unwilling to accept the task of acting as a kind of constituent assembly for the proposed European Political Community, they probably did not realise all the problems they would face in its plenary and committee debates.

I have not found any full list of the members of the Ad Hoc Assembly. A list of original members of the Constitutional Committee and the Sub-committees are presented in the *Report of the Constitutional Committee* from January 1953. Obviously, there was rotation in the Assembly, some members left it and were replaced by new ones, and temporarily absent members had their deputies serve in some sittings. I have not found any document on the criteria for selecting the members or their deputies. I have made a list of those members whom I have identified to have intervened in the debates, mainly in the plenum or in the Constitutional Committee, whereas the Sub-committees had a more stable membership.

To give readers information about the political background of members (mainly on their parliamentary career and party affiliations), I have used internet search of member-states' corpora of parliamentarians as well as Wikipedia and related items in different languages. As the minutes use only the surname of members, there have been some problems of identifying them. Although there were no party groups yet in the Ad Hoc Assembly, I have situated them in the three parliamentary groups which were organised in the Common Assembly, namely, the Christian Democrats, the Socialists and the Liberals, the last being a heterogenous group from different parties, especially from France. Party affiliations were never mentioned in the records, although those in home countries were presented for the September 1952 list of Constitutional Committee members.

The Ad Hoc Assembly included observers with the right to speak and propose, but without voting rights, from the other nine Council of Europe member countries, namely Britain, Denmark, Greece, Ireland, Iceland, Norway, the Saar Protectorate, Sweden and Turkey. In practice, the British observers participated much more than others in the Assembly debates.

Table 1: List of the 64 members of the Ad Hoc Assembly

Paul-Henri Spaak (1899 – 1972), President of the Ad Hoc Assembly, leading Belgian Socialist politician, former Prime Minister, Chair of the Common Assembly of the ECSC, later foreign minister and the secretary-general of the NATO (https://en.wikipedia.org/wiki/Paul-Henri_Spaak)
Antonio Azara (1883 – 1967), Italian Christian Democratic politician and jurist, also minister in the 1950s (https://en.wikipedia.org/wiki/Antonio_Azara)
Max Becker (1888 – 1960), a West German Liberal (FDP) politician, member of the Bundestag 1949 – 1960 (https://de.wikipedia.org/wiki/Max_Becker_(Politiker))
Lodovico Benvenuti (1899 – 1976), an Italian Christian Democrat, who was later secretary general of the Council of Europe (https://de.wikipedia.org/wiki/Lodovico_Benvenuti)
Giulio Bergmann (1881 – 1956), Italian liberal (PRI) politician (https://it.wikipedia.org/wiki/Giulio_Bergmann)
Helmut Bertram (1910 – 1981), West German *Zentrum* politician (https://de.wikipedia.org/wiki/Helmut_Bertram)
Alfred Bertrand (1913 – 1986), Belgian Christian Social politician, minister, MEP (https://fr.wikipedia.org/wiki/Alfred_Bertrand_(homme_politique))
Pieter Alphons (P.A.) Blaisse (1911 – 1990) from the Dutch Catholic People's Party, later minister of economics in the Netherlands (https://nl.wikipedia.org/wiki/Pieter_Blaisse)

Martin Blank (1897 – 1972), West German politician (FDP, later DP) (https://de.wikipedia.org/wiki/Martin_Blank)
Giovanni Bovetti (1901 – 1965), Italian politician (DC) (https://it.wikipedia.org/wiki/Giovanni_Bovetti).
Heinz Braun (1888 – 1962) Social Democratic Landtag member and justice minister of the Saar until 1955 (http://www.saarland-biografien.de/frontend/php/ergebnis_detail.php?id=997)
Sieuwert Bruins Slot (1906 – 1972), Dutch parliamentarian from the Antirevolutionary Party, Vice-chair of the Assembly (https://nl.wikipedia.org/wiki/Sieuwert_Bruins_Slot)
Heinrich von Brentano (1904 – 1964), Chair of the Constitutional Committee, West German Christian Democrat, later foreign minister of the Federal Republic (https://de.wikipedia.org/wiki/Heinrich_von_Brentano)
Michel Debré (1912 – 1996) French Gaullist (RPF, UNR) politician, first Prime Minister of the Fifth Republic (1959 – 1962) (https://fr.wikipedia.org/wiki/Michel_Debré)
Fernand Dehousse (1906 – 1976) from Belgian Socialist Party, Professor of International Law, member of European Parliamentary Assembly (https://fr.wikipedia.org/wiki/Fernand_Dehousse)
Yves Delbos (1888 – 1956) French Liberal politician (Parti radical), foreign and education minister in the Third Republic (https://fr.wikipedia.org/wiki/Yvon_Delbos)
Francesco Maria Dominedò (1904 – 1964), Italian Christian Democratic parliamentarian (https://it.wikipedia.org/wiki/Francesco_Maria_Dominedò)
Maurice Faure (1922 – 2014), French Liberal Politician (*Parti radical*), MEP, Senator, (https://fr.wikipedia.org/wiki/Maurice_Faure)
Jean Fohrmann (1904 – 1973), Luxembourgian Social Democratic (LSAP) politician, MEP (https://fr.wikipedia.org/wiki/Jean_Fohrmann)
Eugen Gerstenmaier (1906 – 1986), West German politician and theologian (CDU), President of the Bundestag 1954 – 1969 (https://de.wikipedia.org/wiki/Eugen_Gerstenmaier)
Alberto Giovannini (1882 – 1969), Italian Liberal (PLI) politician and minister (https://it.wikipedia.org/wiki/Alberto_Giovannini_(politico))

Marinus van der Goes van Naters (1900 – 2005) politician from the Dutch Labour Party (https://de.wikipedia.org/wiki/Marinus_van_der_Goes_van_Naters)
Gerard Jaquet (1916 – 2013), French Socialist (SFIO) parliamentarian (https://fr.wikipedia.org/wiki/Gérard_Jaquet)
P.J. (Paul) Kapteyn (1895 – 1984) Dutch Labour Party politician (https://www.parlement.com/id/vg09ll25ddpx/p_j_paul_kapteijn)
Marga Klompé (1912 – 1986), Dutch Catholic (CVP) politician, minister, MEP (https://en.wikipedia.org/wiki/Marga_Klompé)
Hermann Kopf (1901 – 1991) West German Christian Democratic politician, (https://de.wikipedia.org/wiki/Hermann_Kopf)
Henk Korthals (1911 – 1976), Dutch Liberal (VVD) politician, minister and later MEP (https://en.wikipedia.org/wiki/Henk_Korthals)
Georges Jean Laffarque (1896 – 1969), French Liberal (Parti républicain) politician, senator, MEP (https://fr.wikipedia.org/wiki/Georges_Laffargue)
Theo Lefevre (1914 – 1973) Belgian Christian Social politician, prime minister 1961 – 1965 (https://fr.wikipedia.org/wiki/Théo_Lefèvre)
Maurice Lemaire (1895 – 1979), French Gaullist MP, Assemblée nationale, minister in the IV Republic (https://en.wikipedia.org/wiki/Maurice_Lemaire)
Nicolas Margue (1888 – 1976) from Luxembourg Christian Social People's Party, linguistic professor, former minister of agriculture (https://en.wikipedia.org/wiki/Nicholas_Margue#Publications)
Jean Maroger (1881 – 1956), French Liberal politician (CNI), senator (https://fr.wikipedia.org/wiki/Jean_Maroger)
François de Menthon (1900 – 1984), French parliamentarian and law professor (MRP) (https://fr.wikipedia.org/wiki/François_de_Menthon)
Hans-Joachim von Merkatz (1905 – 1982) Deutsche Partei (DP), later CDU, minister in Adenauer cabinets (https://de.wikipedia.org/wiki/Hans-Joachim_von_Merkatz)
Guy Mollet (1905 – 1975), French Socialist politician (SFIO), party leader 1946 – 1969, prime minister (1956 – 1957) (https://fr.wikipedia.org/wiki/Guy_Mollet)
Lodovico Montini (1896 – 1990), Italian Christian Democrat politician, senator (https://it.wikipedia.org/wiki/Lodovico_Montini)

Roger Motz (1904 – 1964), Belgian Liberal politician, MEP (https://fr.wikipedia.org/wiki/Roger_Motz)
André Mutter (1901 – 1973) from the French 'Peasant Union', later CNI, minister in the Fourth Republic (https://fr-academic.com/dic.nsf/frwiki/104026)
Gerard Nederhorst (1907 – 1979), Dutch Labour politician (PdA), MEP (https://nl.wikipedia.org/wiki/Gerard_Nederhorst)
Ferruccio Parri (1890 – 1981), Italian politician (PRI, later PSI), former Prime Minister (https://en.wikipedia.org/wiki/Ferruccio_Parri)
Georg Pelster (1897 – 1963), West-German Christian Democrat politician (https://de.wikipedia.org/wiki/Georg_Pelster)
Giovanni Persico (1878 – 1967), Italian parliamentarian, later senator, Socialist group in the Common Assembly (https://it.wikipedia.org/wiki/Giovanni_Persico_(politico_1878))
Marcel Plaisant (1887 – 1958), French senator (Gauche républicaine) (https://fr.wikipedia.org/wiki/Marcel_Plaisant)
Alain Poher (1909 – 1996), French politician (MRP, later UDF), senator, minister, presidential candidate 1969, as President of the Senate, acting French President in 1969 and 1974 (https://fr.wikipedia.org/wiki/Alain_Poher)
Victor-Emanuel Preusker (1916 – 1991), West German politician (FDP, later DP, CDU), minister (https://de.wikipedia.org/wiki/Victor-Emanuel_Preusker)
Hermann Pünder (1887 – 1976), Vice-President of the Ad Hoc Assembly, West German Christian Democratic Politician (Zentrum,1945 CDU), Mayor of Cologne (https://de.wikipedia.org/wiki/Hermann_Pünder_(Politiker))
Paul Reynaud (1878 – 1966), French Liberal politician (CNI), former Prime Minister (https://fr.wikipedia.org/wiki/Paul_Reynaud)
Armando Sabatini (1908 – 2003), Italian Christian Democratic politician (https://it.wikipedia.org/wiki/Armando_Sabatini)
Natale Santero (1893 – 1971), Italian Christian Democratic politician (https://it.wikipedia.org/wiki/Natale_Santero)
E.M.J.A. (Maan) Sassen (1911 – 1995), Dutch Catholic politician (KVP), minister, later European Commissioner (https://en.wikipedia.org/wiki/Maan_Sassen)
Eugène Schaus (1901 – 1978), Luxembourgeois Liberal politician (Parti démocratique), minister of justice (https://fr.wikipedia.org/wiki/Eugène_Schaus)

Johannes Semler (1898 – 1973), West-German politician (CSU) (https://de.wiki pedia.org/wiki/Johannes_Semler_(Politiker,_1898))
Léopold Sédar Senghor (1906 – 2001), French politician, later President of Sénégal (https://fr.wikipedia.org/wiki/Léopold_Sédar_Senghor)
Jean Silvandre (1896 – 1960), French Socialist politician (https://www2.assem blee-nationale.fr/sycomore/fiche/%28num_dept%29/6839)
Franz Singer (1898 – 1953), Saarland politician (CVP) (https://de.wikipedia.org/wiki/Franz_Singer_(Politiker))
Pierre de Smet (1892 – 1975), Belgian Christian Social Politician, minister, MEP (https://fr.wikipedia.org/wiki/Pierre_De_Smet)
Franz-Josef Strauß (1915 – 1988), West German politician, CSU party leader, minister, prime minister of Bavaria (https://de.wikipedia.org/wiki/Franz_Josef_Strauß)
Paul Struye (1898 – 1974), Belgian Christian-Social politician, President of the Senate, Minister of Justice (https://fr.wikipedia.org/wiki/Paul_Struye)
Pierre-Henri Teitgen (1908 – 1997), French politician, former minister and MRP party leader in the Fourth Republic, later law professor (https://fr.wikipedia.org/wiki/Pierre-Henri_Teitgen)
Piet Vermeylen (1904 – 1991), Belgian Socialist politician, minister of interior (https://en.wikipedia.org/wiki/Piet_Vermeylen)
Francesco de Vita (1913 – 1961), Italian liberal parliamentarian (PRI) (https://it.wikipedia.org/wiki/Francesco_De_Vita)
Gerrit Vixseboxse (1884 – 1963), Dutch politician (CHU) (http://www.biogra fischportaal.nl/en/persoon/96369911)
Pierre Wigny (1905 – 1986) from the Belgian Christian Social Party, law scholar, several times minister (https://fr.wikipedia.org/wiki/Pierre_Wigny)
Vinizio Ziino (1900 – 1986), Italian Christian Democratic politician (http://dati.acs.beniculturali.it/governi.owl/Bi1372)

5.6 The organisation of the Ad Hoc Assembly

The EUI website provides a summary history of the Ad Hoc Assembly (https://archives.eui.eu/en/isaar/52). The Assembly organised itself in an ordinary parliamentary manner. It was led by President Paul-Henri Spaak (Soc), and the vice-President was Hermann Pünder (CD). It held three plenary sessions (September 1952, January 1953 and March 1953). The main working instrument of the Assembly was the *Constitutional Committee* (26 members), led by Heinrich von Brentano (CD), with Lodovico Benvenuti (CD) and Sieuwert Bruins Slot (Lib) as the Vice-chairs.

The organisation and later the edition of the Draft was attributed to a *Working Party* (*Arbeitsgruppe, Groupe de travail temporaire*, 10 members), also chaired by Heinrich von Brentano. The Working Party served as a kind of presidium, drafted the timetable and itself took a stand in issues which were left controversial in the Committee or in Sub-committees, as well as an Editorial Committee taking care of the formulations in the Draft. These 'technical' working groups occasionally intervened in matters regarded by the members of the Committee and Sub-committees as 'strictly political'. Supranationality was manifested by the principle that the members of the Working Party 'would be appointed, not on the basis of allocation to countries but rather with reference to the tasks they had to perform' (Constitutional Committee, 22 September 1952).

At the installation of the Assembly, Sub-committees to the Constitutional Committees were elected to perform the detailed work of the Assembly. There were Sub-committees on the following: *Attributions*, Chair P-A Blaisse (CD) and rapporteur Lodovico Benvenuti (CD); *Political Institutions*, Chair Pierre-Henri Teitgen (CD), rapporteur Fernand Dehousse (Soc); *Juridical Instutions*, Chair Giovanni Persico (Soc), rapporteur Hans-Joachim von Merkatz (Lib); and *Liaisons*, Chair Marinus van der Goes van Naters (Soc), rapporteurs Johannes Semler (CD) and Pierre Wigny (CD). In the style of Francophone parliamentary institutions, the rapporteurs of the Sub-committees were perhaps the most important drafters of constitutional texts.

The objective of drafting a constitution differs from the objective of drafting ordinary parliamentary legislation, but work of the Ad Hoc Assembly largely followed parliamentary procedure, more precisely its Francophone variety with the rapporteurs acting as the key actors, It had a fixed schedule, namely, a parliamentary *guillotine* with 10 March 1953 as the cut-off point Within that timeline, the Assembly had plenaries with January and March dates decided in advance and the Constitutional Committee was to report to the plenary sittings, but the Sub-committees and the Working Party had flexible schedules.

In debates from October to December 1952, the Political Institutions Sub-committee served as a kind of political laboratory, debating in the best parliamentary committee style alternative solutions for new political questions by weighing their pros and cons. The members largely shared the idea that they their proposed Draft for the Political Community had to be visionary and could expect to receive enthusiastic support in public opinion, if explained properly. The debates in the Political Institutions Sub-committee provided a valuable source of justifications for parliamentarisation and supranationalisation, which were relevant also for later debates within the EU. I have looked at the other Sub-committees only sporadically. The Constitutional Committee represented a broader spectrum of views, and the first version of the Draft was agreed by it in December 1952.

To illustrate the intensive sitting programme of the Ad Hoc Assembly and its committees, I present the daily schedule of the sittings, as documented on the EUI website. In addition, the EUI website contains the reports of the committees as well as some statements of individual members, including Michel Debré's Counter-project (*Etablissement d'un pacte pour une union d'Etats européens*, 4 November 1952) and a motion of Lodovico Benvenuti, Giulio Bergmann and Fernand Dehousse to change the name of the Ad Hoc Assembly to 'Constituent Assembly' (24 February 1953).

Table 2: Sitting schedule of the Ad Hoc Assembly

Plenary sessions
15 September 1952, 7 January 1953, 8 January 1953, 9 January 1953, 10 January 1953, 6 March 1953,
7 March 1953, 8 March 1953, 9 March 1953, 10 March 1953,
11 March 1953 (extraordinary session), 12 May 1953 (extraordinary session)
Constitutional Committee
22 September 1952, 23 October 1952, 24 October 1952, 25 October 1952, 27 October 1952,
15 December 1952, 16 December 1952, 17 December 1952, 18 December 1952, 19 December 1952,
20 December 1952, 6 January 1953, 14 January 1953, 5 February 1953, 21 February 1953, 23 February 1953,
24 February 1953, 25 February 1953, 26 February 1953, 23 June 1953 (extraordinary session)
Working Party I (Groupe de travail temporaire)
22 September 1952, 6 October 1952, 7 October 1952, 8 October 1952, 23 October 1952

Committee for the Working plan (Comité de plan du travail)
25 October 1952, 27 October 1952
Working Party of the Constitutional Committee
28 October 1952, 19 November 1952, 6 December 1952, 16 December 1952, 7 January 1953,
8 January 1953, 9 January 1953, 29 January 1953, 30 January 1953, 31 January 1953, 2 February 1953,
11 February 1953, 12 February 1953, 13 February 1953, 14 February 1953, 16 February 1953,
17 February 1953 (Comité de redaction special), 26 February 1953, 5 March 1953, 6 March 1953,
7 March 1953, 9 March 1953, 11 March 1953, [continuing with numerous sittings until January 1954]
Committee of redaction
16 December 1952, 18 December 1952, 12 February 1953
Attributions Sub-committee
28 October 1952, 12 November 1952, 13 November 1952, 14 November 1952, 15 November 1952,
20 November 1952, 21 November 1952, 1 December 1952, 2 December 1952, 3 December 1952,
4 December 1952, 5 December 1952, 6 December 1952, 6 February 1953,
7 February 1953 (jointly with the Political Institutions Sub-committee), 7 February 1953, 9 February 1953
Political Institutions Sub-committee
28 October 1952, 14 November 1952, 15 November 1952, 17 November 1952, 18 November 1952,

20 November 1952, 21 November 1952, 3 December 1952, 4 December 1952, 5 December 1952,
6 December 1952, 6 February 1953, 7 February 1953, 10 February 1953, 11 February 1953,
14 February 1953, 18 February 1953

Juridical Institutions Sub-committee
28 October 1952, 24 November 1952, 25 November 1952, 15 December 1952, 2 February 1953,
17 February 1953

Liaisons Sub-committee
28 October 1952, 19 November 1952, 24 November 1952, 25 November 1952, 1 December 1952
2 December 1952, 9 February 1953, 10 February 1953

For my purposes, the plenum and the meetings of the Constitutional Committee, Political Institutions Sub-committee and the Working Parties have been the most important. Of the other Sub-committees, I have been content to notice mainly their rapporteurs' comments in the plenum and in the Constitutional Committee. The Working Party's interventions on 6 and 18 February 1953 altered the name of the planned polity from 'European Political Community' to 'European Community'. (See the discussion in Chapter 6.)

The final product of the deliberations was called the *Draft Treaty embodying the Statute of the European Community,* in French *Projet de Traité portant Statut de la Communauté Européenne.* It was passed in the plenum on 10 March 1953. Besides dropping of 'Political' from the title (see Chapter 6), the term 'Constitution' was replaced by the more modest term Statute. Primarily when analysing the debates, I shall use the original name and not the overcautious final version.

The Draft Treaty was passed with 50 votes for and with 5 abstentions. According to Griffiths the result was 'flattering', because 28 members 'did not register their vote'. The abstentions came, of course, from Michel Debré and two other Gaullists and from the Antonio Giovannini (Lib), who was also against the strong 'federalist or supranational elements'. The seven West German Social Democrats never participated in the work of the Ad Hoc Assembly, the non-voters included Paul Struye (CD), who opposed making the Community indissoluble (Griffiths 2000, 92–93). Griffiths' reporting of these results is in line with his style of treating the 'losers' in history by focusing only on the numbers and discarding the debates.

5.7 The Ad Hoc Assembly as a parliamentary institution

The Ad Hoc Assembly was a proto-parliament, following the style of Weber's 'working parliament' (see Weber 1918) in that it served only a specific purpose. Although the Assembly had a strict time limit, its work was by no means a linear move forward. There was no government proposal prepared with the help of an extensive staff of officials and advisers, but it was the parliamentarians themselves who had to initiate motions and conduct the preliminary debates on them in Sub-committees. By the end of December 1952, the Constitutional Committee had agreed upon a preliminary Draft Resolution, roughly comparable to a government proposal in ordinary parliaments, which was submitted to the plenum in January.

The members were tasked with inventing what the new European institutions could and should do, while knowing approximately what was realisable in the member states. Committee rapporteurs presented a report to the Constitutional Committee and to the plenum, and in the general debates the members could in parliamentary manner move amendments, which were then debated in the Sub-committee or in the Working Party. The amendments were by no means ineffective: several of them led to revisions of the December Draft, precisely because there was no government involvement or backing. The Assembly's rank-and-file members utilised their parliamentary imagination and experience when confronting committee chairs and rapporteurs. Through careful argumentation, plenum members were willing to reconsider their own positions or reformulate the committee positions, not uncommonly resulting in agreeing with the amendments or parts of them.

In the politics of the member states, there was tendency in the post-war years towards a clearer government-vs.-opposition divide and stronger party discipline, but this did not hold for the Ad Hoc Assembly. This proto-parliamentary Assembly was in many respects closer to the idea of parliament not only in debating *pro et contra,* but also in that debates or even single speeches could contribute to a revision or modification of the stands originally taken.

6 The Politics of Naming

The creation of new institutions entails for the participating actors the task of naming them, which is different from naming something that already exists but does not yet have an official name. The actors well understand that this naming was also a part of creating something new. Entitling new entities is a thoroughly contingent act and, as such, a political act: the names could always be different. Naming something that does not yet exist conceptualises the item as a future-oriented *Vorgriff,* a topic related to the 'horizon of expectation', as Reinhart Koselleck (1972, 1979) put it.

Before a detailed analysis of debates in the Ad Hoc Assembly, I will discuss the politics of naming around a few central topics that distinguish some major political stands taken within the Assembly. The topics offer a rhetorical framework that shades light on the politics of the Assembly and serve to guide the more empirical analysis of debate in the subsequent chapters.

6.1 Naming rhetoric

The naming of political institutions cannot, of course, begin out of nothing. There are historical repertoires for possible and acceptable names, which help the actors and the targeted audiences to identify the type of the institution. An entirely new type of title for a political institution very difficult to create if it is to receive approval and credibility among its intended audience. Rhetorically, those who create the names of new institutions must judge the relationships between change and continuity, or between innovation and legitimation in their politics of naming.

Following classical and Renaissance rhetoric, Quentin Skinner emphasises key alternatives for rhetorical redescription with the scheme of *paradiastole* (see esp. Skinner 1996, chapter 4 and 2007). When applying the scheme to naming a new institution, we can identifying in terms of Skinners description the following possibilities: inventing an entirely new name, extending the legitimate range for an existing name, increasing a name's political weight as well as revaluing a name in disrepute.

For example, 'supranational' was in the early 1950s a rather new concept, and it was understood above all as a counter-concept to intergovernmental (see Chapter 7.1). It could be interpreted as a new version of international, but one which marks a devaluation of the 'national' that had been such a key concept in the 'Westphalian' world and European order. Such paradiastolic revaluation (*Umwertung der Werte* for Nietzsche) was, of course, highly contested in the Ad

Hoc Assembly: not all who supported supranationality were willing to devaluate nationality, as was the case with, for example, Antonio Boggiano-Pico's opening speech in the Common Assembly (quoted in 4.3.1).

More generally, the names for the political institutions used in the debates of Ad Hoc Assembly were seldom direct counter-concepts to other proposed alternatives; instead, attempts were made to make the proposed names compatible with the alternatives by means of modification and specification. Another rhetorical strategy was to discard older conceptual pairs, such as the distinction between 'federation' and 'confederation' by insisting that the supranationalism proposed by the Ad Hoc Assembly could not be covered by this nineteenth-century opposition (see esp. Chair Paul-Henri Spaak's opening speech in the final plenum on 9 March 1953, to be discussed in 7.1.2).

The combination of innovation and legitimation in the politics of naming for the European Political Community required the members to adopt the attitude of an 'innovative ideologist', as sketched by Skinner (1974). If one wants to realise conceptual revisions, they must be legitimised to the audience as being compatible with some of the already existing denomination practices.

6.2 Naming disputes

The naming disputes were not merely a symbolic prelude to be followed by the study of 'politics proper'. The naming disputes illustrate rather the gravity of the conceptual and rhetorical issues at play that guide the detailed analysis in the later chapters.

Political controversies in the Ad Hoc Assembly are marked by naming items that did not exist before. The Assembly debates and decisions mark a unique stage in the politics of post-war European integration. That there were hardly any precedents for the naming process will be illustrated in this chapter by the debates over the key names 'European Political Community', 'Ad Hoc Assembly' and 'European Parliament'. The naming disputes on additional topics, such as supranationalism, European government and the titles of the Parliament chambers will be discussed in later chapters.

6.2.1 European Political Community

The task of the Ad Hoc Assembly, assigned by Konrad Adenauer on the behalf of ECSC foreign ministers on 11 September 1952, was to create a 'European Political Community'. What was the background of that name, how was it related to the preceding debates, and why was just 'European Political Community' chosen as the only alternative to be debated? None of the words –

'European', 'Political' or 'Community' – was self-evident but required deliberation.

How could the six member countries of the ECSC, at the occasion of extending their cooperation from coal and steel issues to foreign and defence policy with the European Defence Community, declare themselves as 'European'. This was never discussed in the Ad Hoc Assembly. Their forerunners, the Council of Europe and the ECSC, had already used 'Europe(an)' in their names in the sense of being within Europe, knowing that the borders of Europe went well beyond their own borders. Their 'European-we' was not an exclusive but an inclusive we: in other words, as stated on French–German unity at the founding of the ECSC, an extension of what was to be striven for. The EPC was a political community 'in Europe' with the expectation of one day becoming 'of Europe'.

Of course, there was a famous precedent which the European Political Community followed, in part, explicitly (see Paul-Henri Spaak's speech in the final plenum, 9 March 1953). The 'United States of America' was, at the time of the Declaration of Independence in 1776, an ensemble of thirteen former colonies, now called states, but with the clear intention that additional states could and would be encouraged to join them, under the name given for the new country. In the horizon of expectation of the European Political Community, there was the similar idea of making the Community sound so attractive that other European states would sooner or later join it. This remains the idea of the European Union in extending an invitation towards new member states.

Such use of 'European' entails a rhetorical revaluation of 'Europe', from denoting a mere geographical or historical entity to suggesting a political one with a normative value. The counter-concept that was tacitly devalued was, of course, nation or national, which had been compromised not only by 'national socialism', but also by the experience of the two world wars.

'Community' was not either an obvious choice. The Consultative Assembly's Resolution from 10 December 1951, quoted above, called the new entity the 'European Political Authority'. This term had already been used by Georges Bidault in the first sitting of the Consultative Assembly, as well as by the Council of Europe's General Affairs Committee on 7 August 1950 (see Chapter 3). The Consultative Assembly referred to 'a supranational Political Authority' on 30 May 1952 in the context of setting up the EDC, although its statement had already mentioned drafting a statute for a 'supranational European political community' (see above 5.1), the term that Adenauer adopted in launching the Ad Hoc Assembly.

'Authority' is, of course, an ambiguous concept, derived from the Latin *auctoritas* (see, for example, Arendt 1968), and it does not necessarily have anything to do with authoritarianism. The term seems to have been again borrowed from the United States, from the 'Tennessee Valley Authority', a centrepiece of Franklin Delano Roosevelt's New Deal, referring to an extraordinary 'technocratic' office that could transcend the ordinary political and administrative borders for the sake of a regional cooperation (see Schorkopf 2023, 40). When Michel Debré spoke of 'Political Authority' in the Common Assembly on 12 September (see 5.3), he accepted that something extraordinary was needed to enable cooperation on European level. As he advocated for confederation, it might be the case that 'European Political Authority' was meant to avoid connoting a regular supranational institution.

On 20 November 1952, Pierre-Henri Teitgen (CD), speaking in the Political Institutions Sub-committee, commented that 'numerous delegates also in the Council of Europe have wanted a rapid creation of a Political Authority in order to avoid a technocracy without responsibility'. He seems to have shared the terminology of the Council of Europe members but, without opposing a 'European Political Community'. When Fernand Dehousse (Soc, 20 December 1952) and Heinrich von Brentano (CD, 7 January 1953) used the expression 'Political Authority' in the Constitutional Committee, they pointed out its executive aspect which, for Brentano 'would be assisted by genuine Political Parliamentary Control'. Brentano's point was to contrast 'Political Authority' with the 'High Authority' of the ECSC, which was associated with technocratic rule.

But was 'community' anything better? The German term *Gemeinschaft*, in particular, had romantic roots with its extreme expression in the Nazi ideal of a *Volksgemeinschaft*, a both exclusive and repressive form of 'togetherness'. Ferdinand Tönnies's famous opposition between *Gemeinschaft* and *Gesellschaft* also interprets the former as connoting a tight-knit and closed order, which was criticised by, for example, Helmuth Plessner in *Grenzen der Gemeinschaft* (1924). The French *communauté* was hardly different, and Schorkopf emphasises its links with the inter-war corporatist idea of a 'third way' between capitalism and socialism (2023, 50–51).

Nonetheless, when 'community' was established in both the ECSC and the EDC, it was not debated in the Ad Hoc Assembly. The alternative 'European Union', as proposed by the Political Report of the Hague Congress (see Chapter 2) and by Robert Schuman for the Council of Europe (see Chapter 3), was never proposed in the Ad Hoc Assembly, probably due to the fixed guidelines given to the Assembly. We might speculate that 'Community' with its all-inclusiveness served as an alternative to the hierarchical 'authority'. It could be acceptable for both those who wanted to convey something of the romantic or corporative ideals to the European level – with the advisory Economic and Social Council including representatives of labour as well as commercial and consumer corporations – and for those who wanted it as a neutral term for supranational cooperation or joint projects compatible with a parliamentary government.

'Political' was also only marginally problematised. 'European Political Community' was used throughout almost all of the debates of the Ad Hoc

Assembly, and the term also appears in later scholarship concerning the project (see, for example, Schorkopf 2023). The Draft of the Working Party on 18 February 1953 changed, however, the proposed name to the 'European Community', which was accepted by the Constitutional Committee on 26 February 1953 and in the final Draft Statute of 10 March 1953.

From a conceptual and rhetorical point of view, one could imagine opposed reasons for dropping 'Political'. It might have been realised that, as the ECSC and EDC are political institutions through and through, use of the term would be redundant. On the other hand, 'political' might have been avoided since in most European languages it was commonly seen as something suspicious, such as referring to the intrigues of cunning politicians.

The debates of the Working Party on 11 February 1953 merely hinted at the dropping of 'Political' from the name. A debate arose on the motions of Pierre-Henri Teitgen and Pierre Wigny (CD) to abandon the word 'supranational'. Wigny defended it with the idea of minimising the words in the Constitution, that is, 'qu'une Constitution doit être as courte as possible'. Fernand Dehousse is 'd'accord' with this principle but regards 'supranational' as an essential defining feature of the Community, and the term was retained in the Draft Treaty from 10 March (Article 1, spelling 'supra-national'). Dehousse disputed the power of the Committee of Redaction and the Working Party to do such omissions. He also noted the omission of 'politique' and here his polemics against that seems aimed at the Working Party. The British observer Noel remarked that *politique* was 'supprimé à la demande de M. Benvenuti qui le jugeait trop restreignant'. What might it mean that 'political' was considered too restrictive? (11 February 1953)

Dehousse makes the point that by dropping 'supranational' from the name, the singular political profile of the parliamentary project with its unique constitutional programme would be lost. Did Lodovico Benvenuti (CD) and Pierre Wigny think that leaving out 'political' would lower the profile and avoid provocative catchwords, thereby making the project easier to accept for citizens, parliaments and governments? Or did they believe that it was only an issue of reducing the number of words in the Draft Treaty?

In an amendment dated 6 March 1953, François de Menthon (CD) wanted to return to the original title. 'The title already adopted by the Assembly in January, viz: "Draft Treaty setting up a European Political Community" to be retained in the place of the new title proposed by the Committee, viz: "Draft Treaty embodying the Statute of the European Community"' (Amendment 18). He moved to replace 'a European Community' in paragraph 8 by 'a European Political Community' (Amendment 19), and in the title of Part I (Amendment 20) and Article 1 (Amendment 20).

In the plenum on the same day (6 March 1953), Benvenuti briefly explained the change. 'The adjective "political" has been deleted in order to avoid the construction that the Community was instituted, as if it were, in opposition to the two other communities – whereas in reality it formed an organic unit'. This is a confusing statement. The explanation alludes to playing down the political aspect in all three communities, with a view to making the project look less 'dangerous'. My thesis is that the 'political' of the specialised communities ECSC and EDC concerned policy, but that of the EPC concerned the polity as a type of regime (see Palonen 2003 and 2022b), which could have justified the original title.

In the debate on the article, still on 6 March, de Menthon moved that his amendment to retain the original title be 'reserved'. This resulted in something close to the classical indirect rejection, *adjournment sine die* in Westminster. Only in the last sitting on 10 March did the amendment reappear on the agenda. De Menthon would have preferred not to alter the original title but being 'anxious to avoid any last-minute dispute which might split the Treaty, he withdrew his amendments.'

For me as a conceptual historian of politics, this is a sad story in which over-caution and certain constitutional conventions prevented a conceptual debate. There was no debate justifying the naming of the new supranational institution the 'European Political Community', as opposed to all other European projects that carefully avoided a reference to 'political' in their names. The project for constituting a parliamentary polity on a democratic basis would have justified calling it political. Whether the members understood the parliamentary and supranational moments as politicising moves, but did not want to say that publicly, remains an open question.

Despite the late change in the title of the proposed Community, I shall use throughout this volume the original title. This is also the practice in the scholarly literature, and for me the title marks a double momentum of politicisation: intergovernmentalism was replaced by supranationalism, and parliamentary government was extended to encompass a supranational polity.

6.2.2 Self-naming of the Ad Hoc Assembly

Another topic that raised debates both in the early and late stages of the Ad Hoc Assembly was the naming of the Assembly itself and its Constitutional Committee. These debates give an indication of the profile and the ambitions of the Assembly.

In the opening plenum on 15 September 1952, de Menthon noted that, in the documents for the sitting, several different titles had been used. Chair Spaak called it 'Ad Hoc Assembly, formed out of the ECSC Assembly', but was willing to discuss other titles. De Menthon proposed 'Constituent Assembly', while an unnamed French member suggested 'Preconstituent Assembly'. Spaak opted for Ad Hoc Assembly as a title not used previously, and this was accepted by the plenum.

The debate in the Constitutional Committee was opened in the Working Party on 6 October. The Chair Brentano, referred to the informal discussions held in the Working Party and in the Presidency. For him, 'Ad Hoc Assembly' was an unfortunate (no *heureuse*) title, but the Working Party had no power to modify it. Fernand Dehousse admitted that he was responsible for the 'l'expression "Assemblée ad hoc"', but he regarded the term as poor (*mauvaise*) from the viewpoint of finding words 'qui frappent son imagination'. In other words, the title did not call to mind a European identification.

As for the Committee, Brentano moved for the title 'Commission preconstituante de l'Assemblee Ad hoc' and but hoped that the Assembly would change it later. P.-A. Blaisse (CD) supported the title 'Constitutional Committee'. Giovanni Persico (Soc) suggested 'Committee for the study of Constituante', which André Mutter (Lib) supported. Wigny proposed 'Committee for constitutional problems', supported by Dehousse and Blaisse. Finally, Chair Brentano proposed to use 'Constitutional Committee of the Ad Hoc Assembly' at least until the January 1953 plenum (ibid.).

In the Constitutional Committee's 23 October sitting, proposals on the naming (*appellation*) were again debated. Brentano accepted the Working Party's proposal to replace the initial proposal of 'Pre-constituant Committee' (*Commission préconstituente*) with 'Constitutional Committee' (*Commission constitutionnelle)* as more appropriate and more readily understandable. Nobody returned to the initial title.

References to an overarching European state was by no means common in the Ad Hoc Assembly. Michel Debré opposed such a state and proposed to the committee the heading 'Commission d'études constitutionnelles', which was supported by Guy Mollet (Soc), who thought the Committee should not raise in the public too high expectations that might turn out to be illusory in the end. Brentano responded to Debré by referring to the Luxembourg resolution defining the objective of the Ad Hoc Assembly as a 'mandat d'élaborer une reorganisation européenne' and not merely to study it. Dehousse referred to the use of 'Constitution' in the statutes of organisations such as the ILO, and Hermann Kopf (CD) remarked that the German *Verfassung* had a broader content than the French *constitution*. Yves Delbos (Lib) moved for a compromise, 'Commission de preparation de Communauté politique'. Persico approved of speaking of a constitution and understood the Working Party's motion as 'un travail constitutionnel à l'usage d'une future Assemblée constituante'. 'Constitutional Committee' was in the end approved with 2 votes against and 1 abstention.

'Constitutional Committee' expressed the ambition of the Assembly. It signalled that the members were responsible for writing a new type of Constitution, one that was supranational and would later be the groundwork for the parliamentary Constitution for the European Political Community.

Guy Mollet proposed changing the article of the Community from 'la' to 'une' and the French title was accepted accordingly as 'Assemblée pour une Communauté Politique Européenne', the English title retaining the definite article in 'Assembly for the European Political Community'.

In the January 1953 plenum, the name of the Assembly was not brought to a debate. However, on 24 February, members Lodovico Benvenuti, Guilio Bergmann (Lib) and Fernand Dehousse in a cross-party initiative moved 'that the Ad Hoc Assembly, when its March session opens, should change its name to that of *Constituent Assembly*', returning to what de Menthon had proposed in the September 1952 plenum. Historically, the preparation of a Draft Treaty closely resembled other contemporary examples of constituent assemblies, such as the *Parlamentarischer Rat* in the Western Zones of Germany in 1948/49.

The movers indicated that the Assembly accomplished its mission and considered the comments received but were aware of the difficulties that still lie ahead: 'If the Governments and Parliaments so desire, the basic preparatory work of the Community whose birth we are now witnessing will eternally remain.' (ibid.) They concluded: 'Surely, after such achievements, the Assembly cannot go down in the history of free Europe under the mysterious name "Ad Hoc Assembly"' charged with preparing a draft Treaty to set up a European Political Community.'

The motion was never taken up in the March plenary. The ambitious aim of the motion to justify the Draft by a well-considered title was not followed up on. The 'Ad Hoc Assembly' is still the term of choice in scholarly use, although Schorkopf (2023) entitles his chapter *Verfassungsversuch.*

Could changing the name to 'Constituent Assembly' have improved the chances to get the Draft Treaty ratified by the member states? This is, of course, impossible to say, but it is not very plausible.

6.2.3 European Parliament

A third noteworthy issue in the Ad Hoc Assembly's politics of naming concerns what, when and how the 'European Parliament' was named. As discussed above, this term was occasionally used by authors of the post-war European movement, at the Hague Congress on Europe and among the federalist wing within the Consultative Assembly of the Council of Europe. Here, I merely consider the discussion in the September 1952 sitting of the Common Assembly of the ECSC and the subsequent debates of the Ad Hoc Assembly.

In his address to the Common Assembly on 11 September 1952, Jean Monnet used the formulation: 'C'est la première Assemblée européenne qui soit investie d'un pouvoir de decision' (Journal official 1952/53). Although he qualifies the Common Assembly as parliamentary, he does not speak of a

European Parliament. Next day Konrad Adenauer made the same point but spoke on the first supranational parliament in Europe: 'Vous êtes en Europe le premier Parlement souverain établi sur une base supranationale.' (Journal official, 12 September 1952) Indeed, Monnet's and Adenauer's common point was to speak of a 'parliament in Europe': as to speak of a 'European Parliament' for the six countries of the ECSC or EPC could raise immediate objections. If we, however, compare with the naming of United States of America, we could also make a point for speaking of a 'European Parliament' within the 'Europe of the Six'.

A day after Adenauer's address, Theo Lefevre (CD) explicitly uttered in the Common Assembly: 'notre Assemblée qui est la première à mériter le nom de "Parlement européen"'. Lefevre's point is to downplay the lacking parliamentary qualities of the Consultative Assembly, and to claim for the Common Assembly was to be 'a European Parliament', although of course not 'the European Parliament' (Journal official, 13 September 1952).

The parliamentary qualities that the Ad Hoc Assembly proposed for the European Political Community were not unanimously supported by its members. The notorious adversary of supranationalism, Michel Debré, maintained in the Constitutional Committee: 'il faut qu'un parlement européen ne soit que l'émanation des parlements nationaux et que l'exécutif européen soit fondé sur la légitimité des gouvernements nationaux' (24 October 1952). He saw 'a European Parliament' only as an interparliamentary institution of the national parliaments.

The following day (25 October 1952), Antonio Azara (CD) raised in the Committee the expectation that the Ad Hoc Assembly would be able to create *une assemblée politique européenne,* which would be elected as soon as possible. Chair Brentano welcomed the idea but thought the timetable was unrealistic. In the debate, Marius van der Goes told of having heard Brentano speak of *Le parlement general européen,* which van der Goes opposed, saying that no document had been submitted to the Constitutional Committee referring to such a parliament, only to chambers with limited powers and competence. Brentano responded that in his comment to Azara he merely stated that the Committee could not deviate from its mandate in order to 'faire immédiatement élire un parlement général européen'.

In the further debate, however, Azara argued that if he would have said that to the German audience, the objection would have been: 'Do we not already have several 'Parlements européens', of the Council of Europe, the Common Assembly and the Ad Hoc Assembly? We are now proposing *un nouveau Parlement.*' Hermann Kopf (CD) found Azara's proposal interesting and thought that *un Parlement Européen démocratique élu* might lead the peoples of Europe better to assimilate (25 October 1952).

Several dimensions are involved in the debate: the contrast between van der Goes and Azara was at the moment between the minimalists and the maximalists of European unification, which related to whether the Ad Hoc Assembly should stick to its given objective or serve as an occasion for a wider European project. In the Political Institutions Sub-committee on 14 November 1952, van der Goes again demanded limiting the powers of the Ad Hoc Assembly to a 'strict minimum', and polemised against those who wanted to create 'un vrai "Parlement" de six'. Van der Goes wanted to have 'the existing parliaments serve as electoral colleges', as he opposed direct elections. He would follow the practice of the Council of Europe, which for him still served as an umbrella organisation for Europe (see his view in the Sub-committee on 16 November 1952).

On 25 October 1952, Brentano still opposed immediate elections, but was using the expression 'general European Parliament', in contrast to the thematically limited Common Assembly: 'general European Parliament' marked the difference of a parliament to mere assemblies. This was more clearly the case with Azara's and Kopf's exchange on how a directly elected 'European Parliament' would improve the legitimacy of Europe. However, they also did not specify criteria for distinguishing a proper parliament from other assemblies.

Following the Political Institutions Sub-committee debate on 20 November, however, *le Parlement européen* became a widely used French expression for the Parliament of the European Political Community. Eugène Schaus (Lib) asked whether the President of the High Authority planned to be *ex officio* a member of the European Executive Council, 'est renversée par le Parlement européen'. Fernand Dehousse spoke generally of the Executive as 'responsible devant le Parlement européen'. Brentano judged that it would be a negation of the European idea if the European Parliament could not elect the chair of the executive, 'de ne pas donner le Parlement européen le pouvoir de designer le Président de l'Executif'. Chair Teitgen in responding to a question by Schaus, replied affirmatively: 'il puit être reverse par le Parlement européen'.

The Sub-committee members affirmed the parliamentary responsibility of the Executive Council and its ministers. At this stage, the parliamentary system of government for the European Political Community was widely supported, and at least in French, *le Parlement européen* was commonly used for the two chambers together. What did not yet directly appear in the task given to the Ad Hoc Assembly, namely the application of the parliamentary system of government to the Political Community, was widely supported by the Sub-committee, and through it the expression 'the European Parliament' has gained a new and more precise meaning.

In the Sub-committee of 3 December 1952, Fernand Dehousse proposed to replace *organes législatifs* by *pouvoir législatif*. To that Pierre-Henri Tietgen responded with the name '*le parlement de la Communauté*). For van der Goes, Parliament was linked to a state, even a supranational one, which he accused of being 'État en sense unique'. Teitgen regarded Parliament as a 'maximalist expression'. Dehousse also saw that the word had until then been used for an organ of the state, but in the France under *l'ancien regime parlement* it was a juridical institution. Van der Goes said that he did not oppose the term 'Parliament'. Lodovico Montini (CD) remarked that the term depended on how the executive was named. After the debate, the Sub-committee agreed on the term 'Parliament of the Community' as the official title, and in German as 'das gemeinsame Parlament', which avoids the term 'Gemeinschaft'.

The Sub-committee's decision on 6 December 1952 also applied the English expression, 'the European Parliament'. The Sub-committee 'adjourned the question of the duration of the term of office in the European Parliament' and took a stand in favour of the term being 'independent of the terms of office in the national Parliaments', again strengthening the supranational aspect. Teitgen spoke of *Parlement européen* in a specific sense, contrasting it to the assemblies of the ECSC and EDC. This was an obvious way to facilitate its usage, which is also linked to the adoption of the parliamentary government. In the final plenum of the Ad Hoc Assembly, on 7 March 1953, Pierre Wigny opposed the term 'Peoples' Chamber' for the lower house with the interesting argument that 'the resort to universal direct suffrage would imply not a Parliament for the peoples but a European Parliament'. In his view, the supranational concept of Europe clearly enjoys priority over the popular sovereignty.

The point of difference with earlier uses was that the European Parliament no longer was a parliament in Europe or a European parliament among the others, but *the* Parliament of the European Political Community, that is, of a general, although thematically limited supranational polity. The European Parliament was a representative example of applying the principle of parliamentary government to the European polity.

There were also some debates on the naming of the two chambers of the European Parliament. This concerned less the first, or Peoples' Chamber, but to a considerable extent, the Senate. The debate concerned whether such a highly parliamentary title would be appropriate to a chamber elected by the member states' parliaments. As will be discussed in Chapter 8, the Ad Hoc Assembly came to regard the Second Chamber as a fully parliamentary institution equal in powers to the Peoples' Chamber. Having the power to appoint the President of the European Executive Council (see Chapter 9) might even have given the Senate a certain superiority over the Peoples' Chamber, although such questions were decided only through the actual practice.

The naming of the European Parliament might, furthermore, be seen as analogous to the naming of the government of the EPC as 'European Executive Council'. The 'baptism', as Fernand Dehousse said, of this institution took place in the Political Institution Sub-committee on 4 December 1952. His original proposal was *Collège exécutif européen*, which would have put the emphasis on the collegial cabinet of the ministers. After some further remarks, Dehousse arrived at the expression *le Conseil des Ministres européens*, European Executive Council, with the emphasis that it, unlike the Parliament, was meant to sit permanently. For Dehousse, the best name would have been Government (*Gouvernement*), but this alternative was regarded by Chair Teitgen as 'un peu prétentieux' (ibid.).

Already in the Political Institutions Sub-committee on 21 November 1952, Dehousse spoke of the 'Government of the Community', and on the previous day in the Sub-committee, Wigny had preferred to speak of the 'government' rather than of the 'executive' also at the European level, referring to the government's parliamentary responsibility. Even Nicolas Margue (CD), a rather sceptical member, 'saw in the Executive Council the origin of a European government, whose political idea should be represented by a President' (Constitutional Committee, 20 December 1952).

The cautious view was upheld and article 17 of the Draft version alludes to the European Executive Council. Nonetheless, the members seem to be speaking of European government in the similar colloquial, unofficial sense as they spoke of European parliament. In this book I follow this terminology in chapter and section headings, regarding them as analytic scholarly concepts.

When the Sub-committee did include 'European' with 'Executive Council', it was referring to the European Political Community, which was held up as a model of the proposed political institution that would be open to new members.

In Dehousse's report to the Constitutional Committee on 15 December 1952 there was, however, no mention of 'European Parliament'; instead, the two chambers were dealt with separately and were referred to together as simply 'Parliament'. In this sense, the 'European Parliament' had turned into a colloquialism for the 'Parliament of the Community', in parallel with the 'European Executive Council'. This was the practice of, for example, the rapporteur of the Sub-committee of Attributions, Benvenuti, as well as Mollet and Max Becker (Lib) in the Constitutional Committee debate on 17 December 1952. On 18 December 1952, Dehousse spoke on the responsibility of the executive before the two parliamentary chambers and, in the next paragraph, on the question of how to establish that responsibility before *le parlement Européen*. Teitgen also described the relation of the executives of the ECSC and EDC to the Parliament in this way.

The practice of speaking of the Parliament as a counterpart to the European Executive Council continued in the plenary debates from January to March 1953. However, the versions of the Drafts for the Constitution were asymmetric insofar as they used the term 'Parliament' but not 'Government'. The Ad Hoc Assembly's majority did not regard the Parliament as less 'European' than the government, despite restricting their explicit use of the term to 'European Executive Council'.

We could speculate on the reasons for this asymmetry. One reason could be the bicameral character of the Parliament, comprising the lower house (Peoples' Chamber), which was elected directly, and the upper house (Senate), elected by member-state parliaments. It would perhaps have been easier to call the directly elected chamber a European Parliament, whereas in the Senate, the justification for using 'Parliament' was more problematic, since a link to the member states persisted (despite the Senate's exclusion of the imperative mandate and its freedom to disregard instructions from the voting chamber). Another point is that the real novelty of the European Political Community was the plan for it to have a permanently sitting European Executive Council, whereas the Parliament had only two sitting periods per year. To provide the permanent executive with the adjective 'European' can be seen as strengthening both the supranational and the parliamentary aspects of the government.

In the later sections, I shall deal more closely with the parliament and the government in discussing the plans for the European Political Community. They also have much to do with the politics of naming – why is the chair of the Executive Council called 'President' and not 'Prime Minister', for example. The contexts of the debates on naming are directly connected to the institutions and procedures and the debates on them. The absence of such debates can also be significant. Therefore I am postponing the detailed discussion on the parliamentary and governmental politics of naming to the context of the 'substantial' debates.

6.3 Naming the polity

The politics of naming is built into the practice of drafting a constitution. Any name, title, designation or expression used in the items dealt with on the agenda is contingent and potentially controversial. A Constitution for a new, supranational entity with a parliamentary government as the guiding principle of the polity faces major challenges.

For political regimes, institutions and their practices, a limited repertoire of names were available and surely known to the parliamentarians of the Ad Hoc Assembly. For writing the Draft Treaty for the European Political Community, the problem was not merely continuity or discontinuity with practices at the national level or with the practices of international institutions, but also a choice between a cautious versus an audacious naming policy. Another choice was between adapting to the conventions used by the national governments, parliaments and citizens, versus provocative proposals to alter the conventions by raising the expectations for the European project.

The watering down of the name 'European Political Community' to 'European Community' was perhaps an adaptation to the expectation that 'Political' would increase opposition towards the project as a whole. The debates in the Assembly were full of speculations about the potential responses of the audiences, which were still difficult to predict, despite the refined techniques for conducting opinion polls. Michel Debré used the extremely pessimistic forecasts of the public opinion to justify his opposition to any supranational Europeanising project, including of inciting increased 'nationalism', of which the majority of members saw Debré himself to be a typical representative. Strongly pro-European members, such as Fernand Dehousse, on the contrary, expected that intentionally bold moves by the Assembly would raise interest for Europeanisation in the public opinion.

Applying familiar designations at the new, supranational level could also be bold moves. Although for the reasons discussed, 'European Parliament' remained a widely shared but still unofficial title for the Parliament of the EPC, the very idea of speaking of a Parliament – perhaps more specifically of a parliamentary government (see below) – remained provocative not only for British observers, but also more generally as an innovation signalling the novelty of the polity to be constructed. In other words, the Assembly did not compromise parliamentarism when deciding to use 'Parliament' in the name.

The normative superiority of the term 'Parliament' over 'Assembly' was not problematic in the debates. Despite remnants of the interwar polemics against parliamentarism, persisting for example in the early Federal Republic (see Ullrich 2009), Parliament was a title to be merited by meeting certain criteria, which other European assemblies did not meet. However, the Ad Hoc Assembly members did not have a chance to alter British observers' views on the supposed impossibility of applying parliamentary government to a supranational polity.

Pierre-Henri Teitgen's view that 'government' would be a too pretentious name for what the Assembly proposed to call instead with the neologism 'European Executive Council' illustrates that to obtain changes, indirect moves were sometimes necessary: calling the members of the European Executive Council 'ministers' did not provoke opposition within the Assembly. The members had also understood that parliament and government were analytic concepts which were seldom used in the names of specific institutions.

The politics of naming within the Ad Hoc Assembly illustrates well what Quentin Skinner (1974) calls the situation of innovative ideologists. To appear as innovators, they must propose something new, but simultaneously appeal to something that has already been accepted. It was easier to accept speaking about the European Parliament, as the title had already been used in the 'less parliamentary' context of the Consultative Assembly and in the Common Assembly. For the Ad Hoc Assembly, no better alternative was found, and I think the members were content to neutralise that title.

Whereas the Ad Hoc Assembly managed quite well to transfer the parliamentary vocabulary to the supranational level, we can hardly speak of an innovative naming strategy around supranationalism. Although there are no direct comparisons of accepting a supranational vocabulary during the months of Ad Hoc Assembly sittings, we may nonetheless speculate that the term underwent a change: the highly divisive and partisan concept of supranationalism was neutralised by referring to institutions and practices independent of nation-states.

7 A supranational polity

There is, of course, no canonised definition for what is supranational (or supranationalism / supranationality). Consequently, the meaning of a concept lies in its uses, as Ludwig Wittgenstein famously put it (1953, § 43). Although the parliamentarians of the Ad Hoc Assembly might have not known the dictum, they followed it by never defining the concept but using it in different contexts and for different purposes. The anonymous 'Chronique' in *Politique étrangère*, indeed, formulates the same point: 'En réalité, il n'existe d'abord que des projets et des statuts concrets auxquels l'on avait donné le nom de "supranational"' (Initiation 1955, 638).

7.1 A colourful conceptual history

Recent studies have alluded to a complex and politically diverse conceptual history of supranationalism. Hugo Canihac has identified multiple usages of the concept from nineteenth century to World War II, by which he wants to discredit the teleological views of many European Union studies. In contrast to them he is 'interested in describing a process of conceptual transformation, underlining the uncertainties and contingencies of the current meaning of the concept' (2020, 709).

According to Canihac, 'Supranationality thus began to be used in French debates as a polemic concept against liberal nationalism' in the second half of the nineteenth century (ibid. 714). The first transformation took place before First World War, which he describes as 'an integration of the traditionalist, conservative vocabulary of supranationality within liberal language: the term was redefined to justify a limitation of the powers of sovereign states' (ibid, 716).

This transformation took place above all in legal language, first in German private law, as *überstaatliches internationales Privatrecht* of Ernst Zitelmann (ibid. 718–719). After the second Hague Peace conference in 1907 the terminology taken over by a pacifist tendency among international law scholars such as Hans Wehberg, who in *Das Problem eines internationalen Staatengerichtshofs* (1912) already spoke on 'supranational law and court', and the US scholar Alpheus H. Snow used the same year 'supranational' or 'supernational' for a law governing the nations (see Canihac 2020, 721–722, more generally Koskenniemi 2001, 215–225).

Another critique of state sovereignty was represented by French jurists indebted to Durkheimian sociology with different political views, such as Léon

105

Duguit, Georges Scelle and the Catholic traditionalist Louis le Fur. They came to defend a decentralised and vaguely federalist, syndicalist or corporatist view against the state sovereignty (see Koskenniemi 2001, chapter 4.). Canihac insists that their common point was to insist on the stability of law against the instability and arbitrariness of parliamentary politics (2020, 726–736). Canihac also mentions the criticism of state sovereignty and parliamentary politics from a free-market perspective by the famous Austrian economist Friedrich A. von Hayek (ibid. 734–735).

This does not exclude the possibility that some politicians after World War I had federalist ideas. French Foreign Minister Aristide Briand's plan for an 'Organisation of a System of European Federal Union' (1930) within the framework of the League of Nations was probably the most ambitious project from the interwar era. It focused on security policy as opposed to the plans for a customs union, and his 'federalism' was not opposed to national sovereignty but planned to establish 'a representative and responsible body in the shape of a regular institution known as the "European Conference" composed of the representatives of all the European Governments Members of the League of Nation' (Briand plan 1930, 11).

The ambiguity of supranationality (see 'Initiation à l'idée du "supranational"', 1955) is illustrated in how some ideologists of Nazi Germany, fascist Italy and Vichy France had sketched a Europe beyond the national states. The most famous publication was Carl Schmitt's *Völkerrechtliche Großraumordnung* (1941, see Soutou 2021, 102–104). In France, a continuity in the legal doctrine persists, for example, in the work of Paul Reuter from 1930 s through the Vichy regime to his co-operation with Jean Monnet in the High Authority of the Coal and Steel Community (ECSC) (see Cohen 1998).

European unification was, however, equally promoted among Resistance movements. Altiero Spinelli wrote the well-known Manifest of Ventotene in 1941 (http://www.federalunion.org.uk/archives/ventotene.shtml). The German *Kreisauer Kreis* also had pro-European ideas (see, for example, Soutou, 2021, 494–500).

Historically many versions of supranationalism had an aversion against politics, the parliamentary system and professional politicians. A universalist, frequently impersonal conception of religion, law or economics was likely to support expert power by using the epideictic rhetoric of acclamation, delegitimising dissensus and debate. Such power could also be supported by decentralised federalist types of politics based on the representation of interests instead of electoral and parliamentary types of politics based on the representation of citizens as individuals. From this historical perspective, both the limited interest of the post-war European movements in parliamentary politics and suspicion of British parliamentarians concerning supranationalism become understandable. The challenge of combining supranationalism with parliamentarism in the context of the Ad Hoc Assembly thus had high obstacles to overcome.

7.2 Supranationalism in early European integration

Authoritarian groups wanted to expand nationalism to the European level, whereas Spinelli and Monnet were consciously anti-nationalists (on the contrast between Gaulle's and Monnet's views on Europe, see Duroselle 1966; on Monnet's links to the French solidarist tradition, see Koskenniemi 2001, 345–346). Jean Monnet formulated his Europe plan in Algiers in August 1943:

> The countries of Europe are too small to give their peoples the prosperity that is now attainable and therefore necessary. They need a wider market…To enjoy the prosperity and social progress that are essential, the States of Europe must form a federation or a 'European entity' which will make them a single economic unit (Monnet 1978, 222; see also Gehler 2002/2014, 104).

The extent to which the use of supranationalism in the post-war debates on European integration was informed by the longer conceptual history of the term remains an open question (see Initiation, 1955). A discussion of supranationality, its history and later practices in the EU has been presented by Kimmo Kiljunen 2004 (see esp. his interpretation of the supranational union between federation and confederation, 21–23).

The supranational principle was first institutionalised in the ECSC (see Chapter 4.1) with the establishment of the High Authority, initially perhaps aiming at 'autonomes Verhandlungshandeln durch Experten', as Schorkopf points out (2023, 57). In Monnet's early plans for a supranational Europe, the High Authority of the ECSC seems to have been an administrative office of 'specialists for Europeanisation'. To Paul Reuter, the High Authority consisted of independent men, related to the fashion that techniques could replace politics and experts be set against parliamentarians (see Cohen 1998).

The French expression *haute autorité* is a common title for an administrative organ of specialists from different interested partners. There still exist such expert boards on health (*Haute autorité de santé*), for example, or the organisation that oversees the conduct of the French Football Federation (see chttps://www.fff.fr/7-la-gouvernance/129-la-haute-autorite-du-football.html). Franz Schorkopf points out that the Schuman plan used the term 'international authority' but, to mark a difference to intergovernmentalism, the term 'haute autorité' was chosen, which the German term *Hohe Behörde* does not correspond to exactly (2023, 40–43, on the Tennessee Vallee Authority as a potential model for the High Authority, see section 6.2.1).

In the planning stage of the ECSC, the participating politicians from the member countries convinced Monnet to accept both a Council of Ministers and a Common Assembly composed of parliamentarians, an arrangement which he later praised (see Chapter 4.1 and below). An innovative feature of the Common Assembly consists precisely in its combining of the supranational with the parliamentary momentum of Europeanisation. This was then expanded by the Ad Hoc Assembly and its constitutional draft to form a proper parliamentary government.

7.3 Supranationalism in the Ad Hoc Assembly

In this section, I analyse the Assembly's debates and look for different rhetorical usages of supranational[ism], frequently related to counter-concepts or to quasi-synonymous concepts. I have gone through the debates of the Ad Hoc Assembly in its different fora and tried to identify, select and classify a limited number of *topoi*, forming a conceptual cluster of supranationalism. I shall discuss the policy issues which were controversial within the Ad Hoc Assembly in section 7.4. It was not clear for the Ad Hoc Assembly whether the policy issues should be dealt on a supranational level and, if so, how the Political Community could, within the existing treaties, extend the range of supranational Europeanisation.

7.3.1 Against nationalism

The first *topos* we will discuss is the obvious counter-concept of nationalism, specifically, the understanding of the nation-state as the only legitimate basis for organising a polity. In the debates preceding the Ad Hoc Assembly, I have quoted Dutch Federalist Hendrik Brugmans's polemic against nationalism at the Hague Europe Conference (2.2.1) and Robert Schuman's statement from May 1949 (4.1). Within the debates of the Ad Hoc Assembly, the condemnation of nationalism was less common, partly because it was an obvious a part of the peace project of reconciling historical enmities (see the final paragraph of the Preamble of the Draft Treaty, 10 March 1953).

However, the national point of view had not vanished from the Ad Hoc Assembly. An obstinate defender was the Gaullist Michel Debré, who repeatedly opposed supranationalism (see especially his 'Counter-project', dated 4 November 1952, in the Proposition de resolutions 10, 1 January 1953). In the Constitutional Committee on 24 October, Debré raised the question 'Peut-on envisager ou non une construction politique abstraite des réalités nationales?' He maintained that European parliaments and governments should be founded on a national basis: 'Il faut qu'un parlement européen ne soit que l'émanation des parlements nationaux et que l'exécutif européen soit fondé sur la légitimité des gouvernements nationaux' (24 October 1952). His claim was to regard 'nations' as indispensable 'realities', without which no legitimate government was possible.

In the Assembly plenum of 7 January 1953, Debré repeated his view that 'sovereign competence and powers could not be divided between separate authorities' and that doing so attempt to do so would in fact 'accentuate [the] nationalism' of the national authorities. He turned the common accusation of nationalism around, arguing that opposing nationalism in the name of supra-nationalism would have the opposite effect. Supranational projects assumed 'that there was a European nation already in existence', whereas he recommended 'an association of nations' and opposed the severing of links to the overseas parts of the European states. In other words, Debré assumed a unified nation as a condition for polity formation and excluded *a priori* other possibilities to realise such a formation.

Some other members came close to Debré's view. For Nicolas Margue (CD), 'Europe was not an end in itself…it must ensure the existence of the nations', though they had to sacrifice a part of their national sovereignty for the European project. He defended a minimalist version of supranationalism as means that would be acceptable on behalf of the small nations, with his native Luxembourg as the most extreme example (Plenum, 7 January 1953). Alfred Bertrand (CD) insisted that 'the man in the street still thought in a nationalistic way and not as a European', implying that he himself did not think in that way. For him, nonetheless, 'national States…had fundamental rights which could not be infringed by Federal or Confederal authorities' (Plenum, 8 January 1953).

In the final plenary debate on the Draft Treaty, Jean Maroger (Lib) stated that the Draft 'did not satisfy him'. He opposed both concepts, 'nation' as well as 'Europe', and remarked that the parliamentary majority in the Community would include Germany, which would become the dominant political and military power, besides being the dominant economic power. Maroger then launched into a diatribe, reciting his disappointments with the Draft (10 March 1953). Despite similarities with Debré's stand, Maroger remained pro-European though retaining his doubts on the form of supranationality as it was contained in the Draft Treaty.

To respond to accusations, the rapporteur of the Attributions Sub-committee Lodovico Benvenuti (CD), in his report to the Constitutional Committee on 20 December, made it clear that the European Political Community was no 'super-state', as did P.A. Blaisse (CD), who replied to Debré that nobody wanted a super-state (Constitutional Committee, 17 December 1952). Benvenuti alluded to the formulations that the Common Assembly's oldest Member, Antonio Boggiano-Pico, used in his opening address in September 1952 on the 'fundamental and inalienable rights' of national states. Benvenuti added: 'We all are attached to the traditions, the culture and the special characteristics of our different countries', but the task of the supranational institutions 'is to afford them protection'. He then proposed to include in the Preface of the Constitution 'an enumeration of the general tasks which fall to the Community founded on a union of peoples' (20 December 1952).

Contrary to Debré's view on the unity of a nation, Benvenuti's point was that the diversity of the countries provides a precondition for a supranational polity; it affords a medium for uniting 'powers and competence'. Benvenuti speaks of the proposed institution's 'restrictive character' – but that was understood as expandable, as he mentions the procedures for constitutional amendments. The 'Community has been constituted with the agreement and encouragement of *all* the other free states of Europe' (ibid.).

Hans-Joachim von Merkatz (Lib) spoke on 24 October of 'fusions' of national realities: 'La future Communauté doit-elle être l'expression des gouvernements nationaux or une fusion des réalités nationales?' A different angle was thematised by Sieuwert Bruins Slot (Lib) on 17 November 1952, who declared himself a federalist, but warned against a too rapid discarding of national sovereignty in his justification for a transition period towards the establishment of the supranational community. Such views were shared by several Dutch members of the Ad Hoc Assembly.

An example of relativising the importance of nationality was, for Alberto Giovannini (Lib), the supranationality of the Assembly itself, in the sense that party divisions were already considered more important than nationalities: 'dans cette Assemblée, ses membres se sont comptés dans les scrutins, non pas selon leur nationalité, mais selon leur opinion politique' (15 September 1952). In the final plenary debate on 10 March 1953, Franz-Josef Strauß (CD) spoke more militantly than anyone against 'the devil called nationalism', but reaffirmed that the Community did not mean that 'the European States would be liquidated'.

In a sense, 'nationalism' was commonly criticised in the Ad Hoc Assembly, while nations, nationalities and nation states as units of political organisation were accepted. Except Debré, the members did not see these units as hurdles that preventing the formation of a supranational European Political Community. Realising the supranational project required, however, special procedures, for which the members proposed different formulations and rhetorical figures or set distinct conditions to be filled for.

7.3.2 Supranationalism vs. intergovernmentalism

If nationalism was the counter-concept *par excellence* for supranationalism, the project for Political Community was frequently presented in the language of federalism. The objective given to the Ad Hoc Assembly by the ECSC foreign ministers was the alternative of a 'federal or confederal structure' as the 'ultimate' goal of the European Political Community. The members of the Working Party agreed, however, already on 6 October 1952 not to stick to this nineteenth-century legal classification, because precise interpretations of the concepts differed between countries and languages. The claim that they would draft their own views instead of sticking to the older classification was a mainstream view in the Ad Hoc Assembly.

For the Assembly, a more important divide was between supranational and intergovernmental institutions. A confederal system could allow a minimal degree of supranationalism, whereas a higher degree of it would not necessarily be federal, nor would it necessarily mean a unitary state. Supranationality was manifested by the principle that members of the Working Party 'would be appointed, not on the basis of allocation to countries but rather with reference to the tasks they had to perform'. (Constitutional Committee, 22 September 1952)

At the opening of the plenum of the Ad Hoc Assembly on 9 March 1953, Chair Paul-Henri Spaak (Soc) presented to the ECSC foreign ministers the Draft Treaty, resulting from the debates of the Assembly. His speech contained remarkable conceptual commitments regarding the supranational and parliamentary politics of the planned European Political Community. Spaak began by contrasting independent sovereignty versus the interests and security of all, referring to a speech George Washington made as President of the Federal Convention when presenting the project of a Federal Constitution on 17 September 1787. Using Washington's words, Spaak justified a partial sacrifice of national sovereignty in favour of higher values, and in the context of his judgement of the post-war political situation in Europe early in the Cold War. '[W]e alone have the responsibility of giving back to the old Europe her strength, her greatness and her glory'. The 'we' of Spaak could consist of the Ad Hoc Assembly, the political leaders of the ECSC countries and of 'Europe' as such.

Spaak emphasised that the Draft Treaty transcended the 'federal or confederal' divide as well as one between maximalists and minimalists of Europeanisation and spoke of a 'middle path' when specifying the novelty of the Draft as its 'setting up [of] a Political Community of a supranational character'. He contrasted this work with the 'piecemeal affair' of the preceding efforts at Europeanisation.

Hans-Joachim v. Merkatz was among those who used the language of federalism. He regarded the changes as an evolution rather than a revolution (Constitutional Committee, 17 December 1952). Sieuwert Bruins Slot pointed out in the January plenum that 'although various nationalities might be important players [for organising Europe politically], the Federal authority ought to be the principal actor and should have as strongly a federal character as possible'. He gave his judgement that 'in the modern world, the national states alone could not save the day', and therefore 'the "Balkanisation" of Europe in economic terms must come to an end' (8 January 1953).

Federalism was understood as a state system in the declaration of the ECSC ministers, giving to the Ad Hoc Assembly the task of constituting either a federal or a confederal state. The concept of the state was only occasionally used for the Political Community in the Ad Hoc Assembly. In the opening plenum on 15 September 1952, Giovanni Persico supported creating a State of the European Community, 'l'Etat de la Communauté européenne', as soon as possible, but among the members, he was an exception. In contrast, Marinus van der Goes (Soc) did not see the task of the Ad Hoc Assembly as being to create a Constitution for a European State (Constitutional Committee, 23 October 1952).

On 18 November 1952, the Political Institutions Sub-committee debates raised the problem of the 'Head of State' (*Chef d'État*). Chair Pierre-Henri Teitgen took a stand for a rotating head between the member states. Eugène Schaus (Lib) enquired whether it would be possible to consider a state without a head of state. Merkatz responded that the Community is not a new state, but a construction *sui generis*, using a term that would later be proverbial to characterise the EU. Perhaps this also illustrates the difference between federalism and supranationalism.

For the Ad Hoc Assembly members, supranationalism was, however, less a synonym for federalism than a counter-concept to intergovernmentalism. The Draft Treaty of the Ad Hoc Assembly from March 1953 emphasised this in the possibility that the Political Community could sign treaties and intervene against any member-state governments that broke with such treaties (see Article 4 on the Community's juridical personality and Articles 67 to 74 on the treaties).

The Constitutional Committee's first debate on supranationality arose on 23 October 1952 when debating whether the ECSC's High Authority's representative could attend the Committee's meetings. Michel Debré wanted to keep the new Political Community at a distance from an openly supranational ECSC High Authority. Nicolas Margue was concerned that the ECSC representatives would 'mix their experience with their political wishes' (*désirs politiques*), that is, the High Authority's supranationality would be extended to the EPC. Johannes Semler (CD) also rejected attendance by the High Authority, but on the grounds that it would 'constitute un organisme supranational seulement sur le plan technique et non sur le plan politique', thus on opposite grounds to Margue. For Semler, the Political Community represented a higher level of Europeanisation (23 October 1952).

Attendance by the High Authority was defended by Fernand Dehousse, who had invited its members to the Constitutional Committee. He regarded the High Authority as providing a political and psychological basis conducive to European integration, as it was up until then the only existing supranational organisation. The Committee had 'liens de parenté' with the ECSC's Common Assembly and Council of Ministers, although they were juridically separate entities. Dehousse's main point was that the task of the Constitutional Committee would be better served with the presence of the explicitly supranational institution's representatives, as they could then share their experiences of how a supranational institution functioned in practice (ibid.).

Dehousse was supported by several members of the Committee. Max Becker (Lib) argued that the European Political Community would have an internationally recognised juridical personality, Giovanni Persico regarded the High Authority as the only supranational institution already existing at the state level (*le seule organisme étatique supranational*), and Lodovico Montini (CD) supported the inclusion of the High Authority for its experience and due to its character as a living example (seed [*germe*]) of Europeanisation. Chair Heinrich von Brentano let a vote be conducted separately on representation of the High Authority in the Committee, and it was accepted unanimously; their attendance in the sub-committee was passed by against three votes (23 October 1952). These decisions marked a clear majority in favour of a supranational Europe, although Debré and two other members expressed their reservations. In the debate, the degree of supranationality was at stake.

In the Constitutional Committee debate on 23 February 1953, the relationship to the Council of Europe was on the agenda. It marked a confrontation of principles: How could a supranational institution be represented in an intergovernmental one? The discussion presupposed the Council of Europe as still 'the general framework of Europe', whereas the Political Community was considered a supranational avant-garde within it.

A dispute arose about whether the representative of the Political Community should be offered a 'deliberative' vote within the Council of Europe's Committee of Ministers, as Johannes Semler moved and was supported by Max Becker, or merely a 'consultative' vote, as Michel Debré proposed, to maintain the Committee's unanimity before an intergovernmental organisation. Fernand Dehousse indicated the possibility to revise the statute of the Council of Europe in order to enable indirect supranationalisation and eventually the parlia-mentarisation of the Council. He was fiercely opposed by Debre's insistence on preserving the power of national governments. Finally, the Constitutional Committee agreed to Pierre Wigny's amendment, including the statement that, until the eventual modification of the Statutes of the Council of Europe, the members would have a merely consultative vote in the Committee of Ministers (Constitutional Committee, 23 February 1953).

The Council of Europe was seen among several Ad Hoc Assembly members as an umbrella for all Europeanising institutions, but the demand for a representative of the European Political Community to have a deliberative vote in the Committee of Ministers was an attempt to introduce a supranational element in an intergovernmental institution. Conversely, the Danish observer

Frode Jacobsen argued that the European Political Community should be obliged to consult with the Council of Europe, which would, as Dehousse pointed out, have paralysed this supranational institution with a possible veto by an intergovernmental organisation (ibid.).

When the Ad Hoc Assembly debated its relationship to the existing European institutions, the degree of supranationalism turned out to be a dividing line. A few members remained suspicious towards the ECSC and especially its supranational High Authority, while others wanted precisely the opposite: to make use of the supranational experience of the High Authority by allowing its representatives to attend the Constitutional Committee's meetings. The hopes to broaden European cooperation was shown in the ambiguous relationships of the Assembly members to the Council of Europe, including the proposal that Senate members could be members of the Consultative Assembly (see below) while simultaneously having a voice in the Council's Committee of Ministers. These Ad Hoc Assembly members were, rather unrealistically, hoping that the Council of Europe would allow indirect representation of the supranational European Political Community. The debates illustrate that members still preferred to avoid the hard choice between the intergovernmental and supranational polities, and that they were not fully ready to regard themselves as an avant-garde of Europeanisation, providing a model that others could follow later.

In the Ad Hoc Assembly, the contrast between supranationalism and intergovernmentalism was thus manifested in different situations. A shift from federalist-type intra-polity problematics to inter-polity issues, exemplified by the competition between the intergovernmental and supranational paradigms of European co-operation, is clearly visible. An important part of this shift lay in disputing the governments' monopoly in foreign policy, as the ECSC and the EPC were regarded as able to sign international treaties and to oversee member state governments.

The Ad Hoc Assembly members faced a largely unwanted situation of regarding the Council of Europe and the European Political Community as alternative polity paradigms. Many of the members who had also participated in the Consultative Assembly wanted to mediate rather than openly compete with the Council of Europe, including a support for the Council's minority which wanted to change it to a supranational direction. Some members, such as Guy Mollet, were unwilling to make a final break with Britain and other Council countries outside the ECSC (see below).

7.3.3 The delegation paradigm

How could a supranational polity be realisable in a world in which nation-states and intergovernmental institutions remained dominant practices? This question was hardly debated in the Ad Hoc Assembly in terms of principles, but we still can identify typical models for enabling and justifying supranationality. The dominant paradigm was a partial 'delegation of sovereignty' from nation-states to supranational institutions.

A good illustration of this model was the speech of Guy Mollet on 17 December 1952 in the Constitutional Committee. He points out that 'supranationality should be a delegation and not abandoning of sovereignty'. This is an ambiguous formula. In a sense, it could be easily agreed that supranationality in this context would consist of member states' delegation of their sovereignty, thus, not questioning the legal and political doctrine of state sovereignty. Mollet's formula tends to give the impression that member states might at any movement take back 'their' sovereignty, however, he does not seem to consider the possibility that the delegated sovereignty might not be so easily reversible.

Later in the debate on 17 December, Mollet used the formulation that the range of competence of the Community should be limited but real: 'strictement limitées mais, en ce domaine, un reel pouvoir supranational'. This formula was frequently repeated, for example, already on the same day by Francisco María Dominedò, CD), who contrasted expanding versus deepening the supranational aspects of the polity, which then became a major topic of debate. The priority of expanding EPC's competence to include supranational economic integration was demanded, still in the 17 December sitting, by Marius van der Goes, and P.A. Blaisse moved on 21 December 1952 for an amendment to expand these economic competence. Nicolas Margue, on the contrary, opposed a 'toute forme de auto-extension' of the powers and competence of the Political Community.

In the plenum of the Ad Hoc Assembly on 9 January 1953, an interesting controversy between minimalists and maximalists took place. The Attributions Sub-committee had proposed inserting the following a sub-paragraph: 'The Competence and powers conferred to the Community by its Statute shall be restrictively interpreted'. Three Italian members, Lodovico Montini, Francesco Maria Dominedò and Francesco De Vita (Lib), proposed an amendment to delete this sub-paragraph. The rapporteur Benvenuti explained the motives for retaining the formula but stated that De Vita's amendment had now been adopted.

In the debate, Nicolas Margue wanted to 'see the original text restored' and Pierre Wigny justified the use of 'restrictively' so that 'in doubtful cases, the Member States and not the Community should be given the benefit of the doubt'. Piet Vermeylen (Soc), on the contrary, thought that it was 'the duty of those responsible for applying the texts to interpret them', and President Paul-Henri Spaak believed it would be 'merely redundant to talk on a restrictive interpretation'. The motion of de Vita et al. was, however, eventually defeated and the phrase 'restrictively interpreted' remained in Article 7 of the Draft Treaty. This controversy was another judgement of the balance of forces between the cautious and the audacious approaches to understanding supranational power, showing at this point a preference for the former. This victory of the minimalists followed the paradigm of delegating sovereignty.

The powers to decide on the economic integration were a central topic of the Working Party's debates. On 29 January 1953. Pierre-Henri Teitgen interpreted the situation such that the member state governments had not yet delegated sovereignty over economic issues to the Political Community, and that decisions by the Working Party must accept this fact. In matters going beyond the ECSC and EDC Treaties, the Community should have the ability (*faculté*) to issue recommendations to the government, express opinions (*avis*) and prepare treaties as an extension of its activities. This argument also conformed to the 'restrictive interpretation' of the Ad Hoc Assembly's mandate, but it also indicated ways through which the Political Community could expand its powers over matters of economic integration.

In the Report to the January 1953 plenum of the Ad Hoc Assembly, dated 20 December 1952, Benvenuti spoke on behalf of supranationalism, wishing to counter conventional prejudices against it. He saw supranational institutions as necessary for the paradigm of delegating sovereignty. He broke with the zero-sum logic of sovereignty, insisting that supranational powers could be better protectors of diversity than nation-states (see 7.3.1).

The delegation paradigm was not the only justification for supranational Europe. In the plenum on 8 January, Gerard Nederhorst (Soc) distinguished national sovereignty from 'European sovereignty, which was not yet full grown...and was not in any state properly to accomplish its mission'. He saw in 'transferring [of] national sovereignty in economic matters to the European plane' a consequence of the ECSC Treaty. The next initiative, he felt, should come from the Ad Hoc Assembly. In other words, he regarded European sovereignty as parallel to national sovereignty and as a concept that should be elaborated by the Ad Hoc Assembly and in the European Political Community.

Ferruccio Parri (Lib) contested the delegation model in the plenum on 8 January 1953: 'The Community should spring from original autonomous law and not from derived jurisdiction', and this applied also, he thought, to defence and foreign policy. The European Political Community, as an independent legal entity, was also his ground for regarding European sovereignty as parallel to national sovereignty.

The creation of the European Political Community with parliamentary, governmental and juridical institutions of its own marked a break from the exclusive model of delegation of national sovereignty, by which it was frequently justified. Thus, not all Ad Hoc Assembly members regarded the supranational Political Community as dependent on the delegation paradigm. The paradigm was used to legitimise the proposals for a supranational Political Community, although cautioning that such delegation was not possible *ad infinitum* and required popular support to be realised. European sovereignty provided an alternative vision, which, however, demanded a detailed elaboration and formulation in a both juridically and politically acceptable form.

7.3.4 The parliamentary condition

Analytically, it is important to separate the supranational and parliamentary aspects of European politicisation. Some key members of the Ad Hoc Assembly appealed to parliamentary control as a necessary condition for getting into acceptable form the supranational Political Community.

The Constitutional Committee debated the report of the Working Party on 25 October 1952. Antonio Azara (CD) was insistent regarding which issues should be debated in the Committee. For him, the primary question concerned the European political assembly, which he wanted created as soon as possible and which could be on no other basis than universal and direct suffrage. Only its members had the authority in the public opinion to achieve the necessary abandonment of national sovereignty. In Azara's view, a directly elected Parliament provided the necessary condition for the acceptance of this abandonment.

Sieuwert Bruins-Slot, speaking on 17 December 1952 in the Constitutional Committee, was willing to give up national sovereignty in economic matters. For him, the creation of a federal authority was the main aim, the methods were secondary as long as the Parliament of the Community would obtain sufficient powers. Speaking in the plenum on 7 January 1953, Marinus van der Goes claimed that 'a common economic system should…occupy the foremost place' in the Draft Statute, and this was achievable 'only by a constitution of a supranational power'. A 'European outlook in the public' was necessary before elaborating a European electoral system. For both, as for further Dutch members, the supranational parliamentary government was first and foremost an instrument to render legitimate the economic integration into the free market.

P.-A Blaisse prefaced in his amendment (plenum, 9 January 1953) with the formula 'Recognising the essential importance of economic powers and competence for the European Political Community'. Henk Korthals (Lib) supported the motion with a radically anti-national argument: 'If the European unity was to be realised, economic struggles between the nations should be abolished'. Blaisse's motion was agreed to (plenum, 9 January 1953).

In his Report dated 20 December 1952 and presented to the plenum in January 1953, Benvenuti used a parliamentary argument as a justification for supranationalism. He emphasised a difference in this from the ECSC and EDC treaties: 'It would be inadmissible for the future rules of the Community to be established without the participation of the Community's Parliament'. Parliamentarisation, combined with a separation of powers, was for him a major justification for the supranational Political Community: 'The initiative in matters of legislation thus remains with the executive institutions, the "veto" of the governments is maintained but the Parliament is associated with the exercise of those normative powers of the Community which are most important for the development of a future European legislation'. He saw the extension of parliamentary control to the supranational level as a guarantee against centralisation and arbitrary rule. Benvenuti's motion was seconded by Brentano, who emphasised that '[t]he Political Authority to be created would be assisted by genuine Political Parliamentary Control' (7 January 1953).

In a Working Party sitting on 29 January 1953, Teitgen thought that it was impossible to define the Political Community's competence in foreign policy. Brentano remarked that the Community had already received the *élan necessaire* an extension of competence, as it had already been given real powers containing the delegation of sovereignty.

In foreign policy, Teitgen thought that all recommendations voted on by the European Parliament could also be submitted to the member state parliaments. Brentano agreed and noted that in this way the Community could obtain the required publicity. Benvenuti argued that the European Executive Council, in agreement with the Committee of Ministers and under the control of the European Parliament, could set down the broad outlines of a common European foreign policy. Teitgen thought that the member states would prefer recommendations rather than decisions, or a discussion by their parliaments rather than one in the Committee of Ministers. Brentano judged that asking for the opinion of national parliaments would be a flexible (*élastique*) and efficient solution.

Teitgen's point was to break with the traditional governmental priority in foreign policy at the national level in favour of its parliamentarisation at the European level while, however, requiring the standpoint from the member state parliaments to be heard. In contrast, Benvenuti wanted to guarantee the priority of supranational foreign policy by making the Executive Council the primary actor, leaving the European Parliament and the Council of Ministers with veto powers. No share was left in this scheme for the member state parliaments. A part of the issue was whether the debaters held the member state governments or their parliaments to be the main danger and brake on Europeanisation. The priorities of supranationalism versus those of parliamentarism seemed to clash. For Teitgen, the point was to parliamentarise foreign policy on both the European and the national level, while Benvenuti wanted to secure for Europe the priority for supranational foreign policy by making the Executive Council the main actor and leaving the national parliaments outside.

The parliamentary argument in favour of supranationality is the political core in Fernand Dehousse's Report of the Political Institutions Sub-committee, presented to the plenum in January 1953:

The impelling idea of the proposals of the Committee resides in the election by universal suffrage of a popular Assembly...in the participation of the peoples themselves, by the direct selection of their representatives, in the construction and direction of a united Europe, the scale of whose development has hitherto been mostly determined by the Governments. (7 January 1953)

Dehousse's specific argument was directed against intergovernmentalism and its strict separation of foreign and domestic politics. He intended overcoming of the governmental monopoly by making parliamentary representatives not only controllers but also participants in the 'construction and direction' of the Europeanisation in the EPC.

The dividing line regarding the primacy of the supranational or the parliamentary aspect of politicising Europe roughly corresponds to the contrast between *policy-* and *polity-*focused views. Dutch members from the Catholic Blaisse to the Social Democrat van der Goes tended to regard the Political Community as a means for demanding economic unification, including policies for a free market and a customs union. In contrast, constitutionalist polity politicians, such as Dehousse, Teitgen or Benvenuti, were mainly interested in creating new supranational political institutions. The policy strategy highlights Europe's common interests in having open borders and free markets; the polity strategy contested the idea of nation-states as being the only 'natural' polity units but recognised the existing nation-states as initial ways of organising polities, and as such, more difficult to overcome than in interest struggles between them.

7.3.5 Europeanisation as freedom from dependence

In the Constitutional Committee debate on 19 December 1952, Max Becker presented an amendment calling for the same rights for citizens in all member states, in other words, European citizenship, a term which Benvenuti explicitly used in a remark to him. Becker justified his motion by insisting that the armed forces of the EDC could not remain national. He also proposed that the Community had a right to intervene against the member states in order protect democratic liberties. Such liberty also safeguards national sovereignty, he added, referring to the communist *coup* in Prague in 1948. Yves Delbos (Lib) drew the further conclusion that Becker's amendment would allow a citizen of one country to vote in another. Pierre Wigny regarded Becker's amendment as juridically 'une innovation technique dangerouse', but politically 'séduisante'. Fernand Dehousse moved for its 'maintenance for a further study', which was supported by Brentano and passed (19 December 1952).

Becker's amendment added to the debate on supranationalism a new, individual dimension that was taken up in the UN Charter, in the European Convention of Human Rights (1950), in the West German *Grundgesetz* and in

Council of Europe. Supranationalism was not merely a matter between the states, but its point was the freedom and rights of individuals within the Political Community, independently of the powers and borders of member states. The supranational institutions of the Political Community should gain the right to intervene against violations of political liberties in member states. Both aspects became important parts of the Draft Treaty and were not opposed in the Ad Hoc Assembly. Voting rights and European citizenship were introduced much later, and the idea of border-crossing electoral districts has still not been realised.

At stake here is a dimension of the politicisation of European supranationality in terms of recognising individuals as political actors. It does not concern only extending their freedom of movement from interference by their 'own' state within the Political Community, but also enlarging their freedom from dependence on the arbitrary rule of their 'own' states and other dependence-producing units, including the weakening or relativising of their 'national identity' in favour of a European one. In terms of Quentin Skinner's neo-Roman concept of liberty, this included, as Becker put it, action at the European level against regime changes that threaten to reduce or extinguish liberty in the political institutions of member states.

Something of the neo-Roman vision on Europe as a perspective on expanding individual freedom is also included in Chair Paul-Henri Spaak's final speech on 9 March 1953 in the plenum:

The Statute applies to the limited sphere of the European Community the accepted constitutional principles of our countries. It is the first attempt to associate the peoples themselves in the building of that Europe on which the whole future depends, by introducing universal direct suffrage in the election of the Peoples' Chamber of the European Parliament.

With a move typical of an 'innovative ideologist' à la Skinner (1974), Spaak justified the novel and unprecedented character of the Draft Treaty by calling for the existing principles of member states to be extended, applying their principle of popular sovereignty through direct election to the European level. Was the latter principle also a rhetorical move to justify what is not explicitly said by Spaak, that is, the application and extension of parliamentary government to a supranational polity? Or was parliamentary government seen by Spaak and the members of the Ad Hoc Assembly as a move that legitimised the acceptance of supranationalism, as Benvenuti's view quoted above?

Europeanisation as an extension of freedom of individuals and a guarantee of free political institutions was a vision shared by the openly Europe-minded members of the Ad Hoc Assembly. In continental European thinking, agreeing upon a constitution has been understood as an extension of political freedom. Extending this constitutional freedom beyond the borders of the nation-states, partly freeing the individuals from their quasi-natural dependence on their 'own' state can, in retrospective terms, be seen as a major political contribution of the Draft Treaty for the European Political Community and its combining of supranational and parliamentary institutions.

7.4 Supranational policies

The policy controversies in the Ad Hoc Assembly were related to the activities of the two supranational polities, the ECSC and the EDC. Whether the Political Community could exercise its own economic and financial policy, the establishment of a common market was a regularly disputed topic. The same holds for a common foreign and defence policies beyond the EDC. I also discuss the membership and association policy, showing their relationships to the Council of Europe.

A point of controversy was whether the Ad Hoc Assembly could take stand on policy issues. Such questions were regarded by many members as national, best left to the ECSC and EDC or to the future Political Community, whereas the Constitution would deal only with polity issues. However, it proved impossible to separate the two, as policy issues had consequences for the legitimacy and practices of the polity. Dutch members in particular regarded extending economic competence for entering a common market as a condition for accepting the Political Community as such. Consequently, the sections on foreign and economic policy were included late in the Draft Treaty and debated extensively at different occasions from January to March 1953, but the range of issues regarded as 'constitutional' were kept restricted, in order not to bind the Community in advance by the Constitution.

7.4.1 Economic policies

World wars and the world-wide recession had contributed to protectionism and other national restrictions, limitations and rationings in business and commerce. For individuals, they severely curtailed both freedom from interference and freedom from dependence on the state and on employers as well. The main motives of the post-war European 'freedom movement' concerned freedom from both interference and dependence, but faced vested interests of different kinds, some of them experienced as protection of the citizens, many of whom, it was assumed, would be more willing to accept dependence rather than freedom. For the possible extension of the Political Community to have a decision-making power in economic and financial policies, the common market and the Community's right to raise taxes from the member states were debated.

In the Constitutional Committee on 17 December 1952, P.-A. Blaisse supported a modest auto-extension of the competence of the Community towards a common market. Pierre Wigny praised the Committee for having avoided making too little or too much in the way of rules and conditions in the Constitution, leaving space for extending to, above all, a common market, but making this area dependent on member states (18 December 1952).

On 20 December 1952, Blaisse proposed to include in the statute of the Political Community an amendment extending the economic goals of the Community to include the creation of common market. Gérard Jaquet (Soc) wanted to abolish the articles on economic goals and, for the moment, not to extend the economic EPC's competence beyond coal and steel. Giulio Bergmann judged the extension as important in the common struggle against privileges and economic monopolies as well as in the removal of customs barriers. For him, the Political Community should also serve as an instrument for economic and social progress. Pierre Wigny wanted to base the Community on hope, not fear, but did not support including economic goals in the Statute, because a constitution must be short. Nicolas Margue opposed a *carte blanche* for expanding the Community's competence (Constitutional Committee, 20 December 1952).

Blaisse's amendment was not passed. Nonetheless, in the General Resolution of the Constitutional Committee, the Community's 'mission' included 'to contribute...in particular to a progressive establishment of a common market' (ibid.). The Resolution also affirmed: 'Without transfer of sovereignty by Member States to the Community, the latter's institutions, particularly its Parliament, will never be able to take any effective action or cause the Member States to take essential measures.' This point of view was directed against 'consultative bodies' (ibid.)

In the plenum of 7 January 1953, the rapporteur Benvenuti called for new areas of competence of the Community, such as 'the right of taxation, which should be voted by the Parliament'. In economic matters, he distinguished between the Community's opinion (*avis*) and binding approval. New 'sovereign powers' of the Community would require ratification by the member states' parliaments. Van der Goes urged for 'a common economic system [that] should...occupy the foremost place' in the Draft Statute, and this was achievable 'only by a constitution of a supranational power'. Victor Emmanuel Preusker (Lib) supported 'a common market, a customs union and a common European currency' but thought that they were not possible without the issuing of clear principles by the Community (7 January 1953).

In the continued debate, Gerard Nederhorst saw a contradiction between the EPC's boldness in the political field versus a 'conservative attitude as regards economic powers'. Blaisse thought that 'a unity based on common interests' was the objective and spoke again for the customs union and common market (8 January 1953).

In the Working Party on 29 January 1953, Brentano saw that, in economic matters, it would be possible to set down general principles for a limited topic, such as for the common market. Blaisse proposed annexing to the Statute the principle that the member states be committed (*s'engagent*) to complete a convention for dealing with customs (30 January 1953).

Wigny regarded the Constitution's main aim (*but principal*) to be the establishment of a common market for the Community. Benvenuti would have preferred to leave the economic integration to have adopted by the member states together. Dehousse supported Blaisse's proposal as a practical move for disciplining economic forces and proposed that a two-thirds majority be sufficient for approving a succession of treaties in economic matters. André Mutter (Lib) admitted that the economic integration was progressing slowly, but it would be better not to include in the political Statute anything on economics. Blaisse again insisted on the priority of the common market. Teitgen agreed but thought that it should not give to the governments the impression of a leap into the dark (*saut dans l'inconnu*). On 30 January, Wigny asserted that once the common market and free trade was approved, the member states would realise them without undue delay. After a thorough debate, Chair Brentano declared that the final aim to be the economic union, with a common market being one step in that direction (31 January 1953).

In the final plenary session, Benvenuti (7 March 1953) adopted the view of the Dutch members that the common market as decisive for determining the political character of the Community. The debates illustrated political aspects of the common market and the co-ordination of economic policy, which had been doubted by some French members. Benvenuti clearly formulated the idea and was applying for the political advantages of the economic integration, independently of the policy details (7 March 1953).

Debates on the community taxation arose more prominently in the final plenary session, when François de Menthon moved for deleting from the financial resources 'the contributions paid by Member States' (Article 77:2). He opposed 'the surrender of one of the main competences of national Parliaments' and thought that taxes could be included in a 'separate protocol submitted to the States concerned for ratification'. (7 March 1953)

Several members responded. Alfred Bertrand (CD) and Wigny referred to powers of the ECSC member states, and Wigny mentioned that 'only the Executive had the right to propose taxes with the unanimous agreement of National Ministers'. Vinizio Ziino (CD) pointed out that 'if the national Parliaments approved the present Treaty, they would implicitly be authorising the Community to levy taxes'. De Menthon said that he 'was not averse to introduction of European taxation' but supported a similar procedure as in the ECSC. Benvenuti pointed out that in previous debates, 'there had been no opposition to the Committee's view'. De Menthon's amendment was rejected (ibid.).

To sum up, the common market, including the customs union and the indication of a move towards a currency union, were accepted in principle by the Political Community, but national reservations remained. The same was the case with the European tax system when there were contributions from member states, which, as a concrete manifestation of the will to organise supranational institutions, was opposed only in a formal sense due to concerns that its inclusion in the Statute would frighten public opinion in the member states. There was a clear willingness to expand the common market and other 'economic freedoms' after the Political Community was established, avoiding too rapid reforms.

7.4.2 Foreign policy

In the preliminary treaty on the European Defence Community by the Europe of the Six, a foreign and security policy pillar was added to the supranational competence of the European Political Community. Here the contrast between intergovernmental and supranational aspects dissolved the classical divide between foreign and domestic politics.

National interests in maintaining control of foreign policy still persisted among the member states. Another controversy in the Ad Hoc Assembly concerned the degree and the form of a common supranational policy, as compared to the traditional foreign policy and diplomacy of the member states. Certain foreign policy topics, such as the continuous possession of colonies by France, Belgium and the Netherlands, were never properly debated in the Ad Hoc Assembly.

The Constitutional Committee's resolution on 20 December 1952 supported extending the powers of the Community it to have parliamentary control on joint foreign policy matters. The aim was: 'To clarify and systematise these possibilities, which are already implicit in the E. D. C. Treaty, and to make room for the intervention, in this process, of the European Executive Council, a political institution responsible to a democratically elected Parliament'. It further affirmed the legal personality of the Community as a safeguard for its ability to exercise independent politics: 'In international relations the Community possesses the legal personality to enable it to discard its duties and to achieve its objects'. This legal status would be comparable to the 'corporate bodies' in member states. For their part, the states were to 'undertake to take the necessary…measures to ensure the performance of the obligations resulting from the decisions or recommendations of the Community's institutions and to assist the Community to accomplish its mission'. Furthermore: 'Member States undertake to refrain from any measure which would be incompatible with the present Statute'. (20 December 1952)

This vision left much to interpretation, but contained in legal and political terms a strong statement that the Political Community would not allow member states to discard the policies of the Community. In this sense, supranationalism enjoyed within the Community a political and legal priority over the national interests. This was hardly disputed but did not prevent struggles over the interpretation.

In his plenary speech, Francisco Maria Dominedò stated that 'it would be inadequate to speak of the co-ordination of foreign policy, although there should be a minimum of European foreign policy', if supranational means more than a 'co-ordination' between member states (8 January 1953). Ferruccio Parri insisted on the autonomy of European law and the priority of the European Community (ibid.). Dominedò's amendment, that the European Political Community 'shall further lay down general objectives in foreign policy of the Member States within framework...of said [the ECSC and EDC] treaties', was agreed by the plenum on 9 January 1953.

In the Working Party on 29 January, Pierre-Henri Teitgen abstained from affirming the standpoint that the Community's right to take stand on certain foreign policy issues. Brentano thought that, in foreign policy, a preliminary consultation with the member states was a condition for extending the EPC's powers. Benvenuti preferred the European Executive Council to be the body that would set the broad outlines of a common foreign policy, in agreement with the Committee of Ministers and under the control of the European Parliament. For him, supranational foreign policy was the main point, whereas Teitgen and Brentano supported a parliament-controlled foreign policy.

On 6 March 1953, the plenum debated de Menthon's amendment to restrict the co-ordination of foreign policy (Article 2, point 4) 'in spheres of common interest'. After several members, including Brentano, Teitgen and Dehousse, spoke against it, it was rejected by 26 votes to 22, with 3 abstentions. In the 7 March sitting, Teitgen, Dehousse and Merkatz presented an amendment to include de Menthon's point: 'To ensure the co-ordination in foreign policy of Member States in questions likely to involve the existence, the security and the prosperity of the Community', thus with an emphasis on the co-ordination instead of the implicit veto power of member states, as de Menthon's amendment had indicated. This amendment was agreed to.

In the final wording of the Draft Treaty, the co-ordination of foreign policy contained: a procedure for building 'a common attitude...at any international conferences'; 'a pact for the peaceful settlement' of disputes between the member states; and statements on the information and control of member states' treaties and agreements as well as on the formation of the Community's own diplomatic representation (Article 67). This affirmed the supranationality of the Community, including its recognition as a partner in international contexts. However, the Parliament's foreign policy was limited to initiatives and motions.

Indeed, there was hardly any dissent among the members on a supranational common foreign policy, except de Menthon's last minute intervention. Several members would have gone further in the supranational direction (see van der Goes on 30 January 1953 in the Working Party).

7.4.3 Full and associated members

Numerous members of the Ad Hoc Assembly had experienced the Consultative Assembly of the Council of Europe. As discussed in section 7.3.2, avoiding a break with it, even regarding the Council as a broader framework of European unification, was a mindset shared by many members. The French Socialists Guy Mollet and Gerard Jaquet were reluctant to give up a close relationship with Britain. Mollet opposed the deepening of the continental Community, which for him was economically too narrow and excluded the countries with socialists in power, at that time Britain and the Scandinavian countries. He also saw a risk of separating Catholic from Protestant Europe. Mollet supported the creation of the Europe of the Six, which was limited to defence, coal and steel, but including real control by the Assembly over the High Authority (17 December 1952). Benvenuti shared Mollet's criticism that the parliamentary control over the Executive was too vague. The Political Community looked for him, in contrast to Mollet, like a small Council of Europe, except that the EPC included a European Executive. In this respect the shift to electing the Executive Council by the Senate marked a major move towards parliamentarisation (see chapter 9.3).

The Assembly discussed the partial rights of the European Political Community members to participate in the debates of the Consultative Assembly as well as their joint membership in the Senate and in the Consultative Assembly (see 7.3.2). The Draft of the Constitutional Committee from 20 December 1952 insisted that the 'Senate would also make it possible to establish a liaison between the European Parliament, the national parliaments, and the Consultative Assembly of the Council of Europe'. The two Councils of the Political Community were to 'meet periodically with the representatives of the Associated States', meaning, above all, Council of Europe member states. The conference was not regarded as an organ of the Community. Treaties of Association would be negotiated by the European Executive Council and ratified by the Community's Parliament.

In a special resolution attached to the Constitutional Committee's statement, the proposed relationships between the Political Community and the Council of Europe were presented in detail. The document is another expression of the Committee's persistent hopes to change the Council of Europe by allowing the supranational Community to be integrated within the Council's intergovernmental order. The statement is also included in the final version of the Draft Treaty from 10 March 1953.

The Preamble of the Draft Treaty declared on behalf of the member states that they were 'determined to invite other European peoples, which share the same ideal, to join with us in our endeavour'. That is all that was said on about new states' possibilities to join the Political Community. The chapter on association did not contain anything about the conditions and procedures for applying for full membership in the Community.

In the Working Party on 7 October 1952, Fernand Dehousse proposed the membership issues as a central topic on the agenda of the Ad Hoc Assembly. For him, the issues included the procedures for gaining membership as well as the terms for exclusion and withdrawing from membership. This topic seems never to have been submitted to a thorough debate in the meetings of the Assembly. If the supranational and parliamentary European polity was to be attractive to other states, they should at least know how to apply for membership and how such applications would be decided.

The plenum on its final day (10 March 1953) debated de Menthon's amendment to restrict eligibility for membership to countries outside the Council of Europe that fulfilled the requirement of protecting human rights and fundamental freedoms. Marga Klompé (CD) and Hermann Kopf (CD) pointed out that with the amendment the membership in the European Community would become dependent on the Council of Europe. In the vote, the amendment did not gain a majority.

7.5 Supranational politicisation

Analysing supranationalism conceptually with the rhetoric of *topoi* (see Palonen 2006 and 2021b), I view the concept through different thematic profiles and political agendas. The task of the Ad Hoc Assembly was to prepare a Constitutional Draft for the European Political Community, to be submitted to the governments and parliaments of the six member states. Supranationalism was discussed cautiously, carefully and dispassionately, aiming at justifying something new, as opposed appealing to rooted beliefs and fixed categories of thinking. No eloquent declarations or provocations to nation-states or their national traditions were made.

The sovereignty of the nation-states was not militantly denied, but most members regarded a transfer of a lesser and greater degree to the Political Community as justified by common interests or common principles, such as human rights and democracy. The concept of European sovereignty was brought to the agenda as an alternative to the delegation model.

The most powerful arguments for supranationalism as a politicising move were connected to seeing in it an alternative to the intergovernmental paradigm of international politics. Experiences from the post-war European movement and the Council of Europe, in which the federalist wing was discontent with the status of a mere Consultative Assembly, were a major reason for opting in favour of a supranational European Political Community. Instrumental policy goals and parliamentary principles were used to support supranationalism. Even the minimal provision of a vote of no confidence for the ECSC's Common Assembly, and the ill-defined status of the High Authority as something between a political and bureaucratic institution, were important legitimisations for the Ad Hoc Assembly to propose a full parliamentary system of government and justify supranationalism before the member states. The Ad Hoc Assembly members seem not to have any doubt about the compatibility of supranationalism with parliamentary government: they were convinced that, on the European level, a parliament that selects and controls the supranational government would facilitate both the legitimacy and the efficiency of the government.

The supranationalism of the Political Community contained a specific interpretation of the concept of Europe. Knowing that the six member states together formed a rather small, although important, part of Europe, the debates in the Ad Hoc Assembly on the Draft Treaty strove to retain explicit links to the Council of Europe, despite its lack of supranational and parliamentary styles of doing politics. Still, there was in the Assembly an *élan* of avant-garde with the insight that nobody else was willing or capable of initiating Europeanisation in supranational terms. In such a situation, the Ad Hoc Assembly, as the *de facto* Constituent Assembly for the European Political Community, felt that they should not shrink from supranational powers, even if the Ad Hoc Assembly presently had a limited range of them. Their willingness to take the initiative was combined with the tacit expectation that other countries would follow – as was the case with the ECSC, which had begun as a Franco-German peace project. Similarly, although not in the same pace, it was expected that the items on the agenda of the European Political Community would be enlarged in the course of time and through their experiences with the policies they first dealt with.

Supranationalism refers to an 'ism' concept, or what Reinhart Koselleck (1972) calls a *Vorgriff* oriented towards the future, as opposed to a concept describing an existing or past state of affairs. In the context of the early 1950s, the *Vorgriff* character of supranationalism was marked by its disjunction from nationalism and intergovernmentalism. These had turned into defences of the status quo, nationalism even into a reactionary utopia, which even the Gaullist Michel Debré used to conjure up the ghost of popular reaction in order to oppose the supranational plans. Intergovernmentalism, for its part, was characteristic of the limits of international organisations from the League of Nations to the Council of Europe.

More precisely, with a reference to the parliamentary practices of the Ad Hoc Assembly, supranationalism marked a *Vorgriff* also in the sense of an agenda-setting concept. When considering the rhetoric of *topoi* discussed in this chapter, supranationalism included a comprehensive programme (policy) to promote a new type of polity or political order in different respects. The programme included transcending a mere delegation of sovereignty to joining the parallel project of parliamentarism and using these two together with Europeanisation as an opportune moment to obtain freedom from dependence. It further included a regulative idea for controlling or sanctioning member states, if they limited individual rights and freedoms or threatened the activities of free political institutions and practices.

Because of its strong links to Europeanisation, the supranationalism of the Ad Hoc Assembly was limited and therefore of a singular kind. It was practically impossible to include the 'overseas territories', especially those forming part of the French Union. Their existence was used by Debré as an argument against the European supranationalism, as noted by Assembly members Leopold Sedar Senghor and Jean Silvandre in the January 1953 plenary debates, who for their part proposed the territories as a reason for adding seven seats to France in the Peoples' Chamber as compared to those of West Germany and Italy. The emphasis on European identity was even more explicit in the attempts to include the Council of Europe and its member countries outside the ECSC in the form of partial memberships and associations with the assemblies.

The degree of supranationality as well as its thematic scope were the main problems for the policy aspects of supranationalism. In both economic policy and foreign policy, the Draft Treaty and the debates moved between the original task of providing a political backup for the ECSC and EDC and the broader ambition to efficiently realise supranational politics so that it would serve as a further impetus for extending and deepening supranational powers in matters of policy.

The European limits to supranationalism, however, kept the project of the European Political Community on a feasible footing. With Europeanisation as a vision on the horizon of the currently living persons, it offered a chance to break with the experiences of the war and totalitarianism and to provide a range of freedoms worth being set on the agenda of debates beyond the actual Draft Treaty. In the debates, numerous ideas were 'reserved for a future use', such as a common currency (*la monnaie unique*), which Dehousse mentioned in the Constitutional Committee on 17 December 1952, and European citizenship, with possible voting rights in member countries other than that of one's nationality or in electoral districts that crossed the borders (as brought to debate by van der Goes for the 'Third Stage of the European Community', Political Institutions Sub-committee, 14 November 1952).

Finally, as an agenda-setting concept, supranationalism did not as such contain any definite policy proposals. On the contrary, its debates illustrated well how different alternatives to the issues were thrown in debates and spelled out rather explicitly and weighed against each other, occasionally allowing members to change their view during the debates. Even if supranational Europe was a commonly accepted principle, this left ample space and time to debate how it could be best realised at the policy and polity levels. This was even more the case when the issue on the agenda concerned what the full significance might be of a supranational parliamentarism.

Today, supranationalism has become a rare concept even among EU scholars, the academic jargon preferring to speak of it as a trans- or cross-national phenomena. Richard Griffiths (2000) analysed the Ad Hoc Assembly in the traditional language of the advocates and adversaries of federalism. Despite that, I think that the concept of supranationalism would be worth rehabilitating, not only for a proper understanding of the Ad Hoc Assembly's work for the European Political Community; it would equally be of value for today's EU politics, especially from the parliamentary perspective.

8 The European Parliament

The Declaration of the ECSC ministers' guidelines assigned to the Ad Hoc Assembly the task of working on 'a bicameral representative system'. This criterion was vague enough to allow considering a broad range of possible types for a political regime besides parliamentary government, including the US type of presidential government and the Swiss type of semi-plebiscitarian system. There was, however, no precedent for applying parliamentary principles to a supranational polity, and the Assembly debated in multiple rounds how to apply and transfer parliamentary principles to this new level.

8.1 Histories of parliamentarisation

Parliamentarism has not been a *Vorgriff* devised by some theorists, but it has been formed through concrete political practices. As an ism-concept, it was launched by Victor Hugo in 1852 to describe a regime ironically described by Louis Bonaparte. In the British debate, the term was long used mainly about France, although elsewhere Britain was the exemplary parliamentary system of government (see Palonen 2020, 74–76). In Britain, the formation of parliamentary government was a result of slowly established practices, such as: the selection of cabinet ministers among the Houses of Parliament in the eighteenth century Britain (Selinger 2019); or the result of specific moves, such as Sandys' motion in 1741 for a vote of confidence against the Walpole government (Turkka 2007); or interpretation of a changed situation, such as the acceptance that, after the 1832 Reform Act, a government which has lost the confidence of parliament must resign (see Andrén 1847). In other countries, such as Norway and Sweden, parliamentarism came about also as a result of practical considerations.

However, after the First World War, the principle of parliamentary democracy was written into the constitutions of Germany and Austria as well as the newly founded states. Within a few years, however, a trend towards strengthening the executive government was visible across Europe. During the inter-war era, the parliaments lost power, and coups d'états or other transitions to authoritarian or totalitarian regimes abolished the parliaments (see e.g. Gusy ed. 2008). Even in countries which retained the parliamentary system, governmental powers were strengthened, or corporative elements were introduced (for France, see Roussellier 1997, 2015; for Belgium and the Netherlands, see Beyen and te Velde 2016). Parliamentarism had lost much of its reputation.

After the defeat of Nazism and fascism in the Second World War, the parliamentary system was rehabilitated without significant controversy. It prevailed in four ECSC member countries and was re-established in Italy and West Germany. Despite the common acceptance of parliamentary government in the *Parlamentarischer Rat,* which drafted the West German *Grundgesetz*, the Weimar experiences left it unpopular in public and academic opinion and in the early Federal Republic (Ullrich 2009). West German members in the Ad Hoc Assembly, however, did support parliamentarism.

The support for parliamentary government in the Ad Hoc Assembly was also justified by referring to the experiences of the powerless, merely Consultative Assembly of the Council of Europe, which it did not want to repeat in the European Political Community. The Common Assembly of the ECSC lacked the elementary parliamentary powers of legislation and finances, but it did possess the vote of censure, and members also otherwise immediately began to empower parliamentary practices from within (see Chapter 4), which provided a model for the Ad Hoc Assembly. The Ad Hoc Assembly regarded parliamentary government as compatible with the stable government they sought for the supranational Community, wishing to avoid the practices that led to frequent instability in France and Italy. How this might be possible on the supranational European level within a bicameral parliament became a topic of intense debate in the Assembly.

8.2 The Parliament of the Community

In the Draft Treaty from 10 March 1953, the powers and competence of the Parliament of the Community are briefly presented in Article 10:

Parliament shall enact legislation and make recommendations and proposals. It shall also approve the budget and pass a bill approving the accounts of the Community. It shall exercise such powers of supervision as are conferred upon it in the present statute.

These principles were hardly discussed at all by the Ad Hoc Assembly. For its members, as experienced parliamentarians, the powers and competence were a self-evident and indispensable part of the well-known practices of parliamentary politics. They did not have any doubts about their applicability to a supranational parliament. The tacit subtext of this paragraph was that the European Political Community would be the first to apply parliamentary principles to supranational politics.

Still, this paragraph does not yet suffice to justify speaking of a supranational parliamentary system of government. For that question it is equally important to take note of what was said in the Draft Treaty and in the debates about the Chambers of European Parliament, their elections, the status of the members. Above all, within the horizon of parliamentary politics such as presented by Walter Bagehot (1867/72) and by Max Weber (1918), the government is a part of the parliamentary system, including its election, dismissal and different forms of control and supervision. How to realise such a parliamentary system of government was perhaps the most interesting topic of debate in the different stages and fora of the Ad Hoc Assembly.

Many of the general principles of parliamentary politics (as discussed in section 1.5) were never debated in the Ad Hoc Assembly. However, the details of the questions of parliamentary procedure, of the free mandate of members and of the politics of time were involved in the debates about realising parliamentary government in a supranational polity.

When discussing parliamentary government, the parliament and the government aspects should be discussed together. However, in the Draft Treaty, the section on Parliament precedes that of the Executive Council, saying that the latter is elected by, responsible to and dismissible by the Parliament. I have decided to deal first with the Parliament, as did the Ad Hoc Assembly.

8.2.1 The organisation of Parliament

The driving force of both drafting and debating was the Political Institutions Sub-committee, with Chair Pierre-Henri Teitgen (CD) and rapporteur Fernand Dehousse (Soc). In its first sitting on 28 October 1952, the Sub-committee agreed on an internal division of tasks as follows:

Chair Pierre-Henri Teitgen for the First Chamber
Rapporteur Fernand Dehousse for the Second Chamber
Pierre Wigny (CD) for the Executive, including the possible Council of Ministers
Antonio Azara (CD, absent from the meeting, for the European elections)
Hans-Joachim von Merkatz (Lib, absent from the meeting) on the Economic and Social Council
P.-A. Blaisse (CD) from the Sub-committee on Attributions on the ECSC and EDC.

The discussion in section 6.1.3 refers to what a representative political assembly requires in order to be called a parliament. The possibility to overturn the government by a vote of no confidence has become the decisive criterion for speaking of a parliamentary system, as discussed by Bagehot, Weber and later scholars (see section 1.5). This presupposes, in addition, several other criteria, including: the long-term aspects of parliamentary politics, such as the presence of the distinctive parliamentary procedure; the members a status based on the 'neo-Roman' concept of freedom from dependence (in the sense of Skinner 1998, 2002); a rhetorical culture of debating *pro et contra;* and the parliamentary way of dealing with time politically (see Palonen 2018).

The main question in the agenda-setting of the Ad Hoc Assembly was how to apply well-known parliamentary practices to the supranational Parliament of

European Political Community. The Assembly did not have time to thoroughly reflect upon all the formal aspects of the parliamentary quality of politics, yet they did regard many of them as key issues to be resolved already in the Draft Treaty stage.

Today, it is obvious that the rhetoric of debate was not part of the *Zeitgeist* of post-war Europe. On the contrary, a rather naïve view of letting 'the matters themselves' decide the items on the agenda was the dominant mood. This held at least for the debates in the early West German Bundestag (see Palonen 2021b, also Loewenberg 1969). Parliamentary rhetoric surely played a role in the lively debates of the Ad Hoc Assembly. Indeed, several members admitted being persuaded by the arguments of previous speakers and having altered their own standpoints due to the debates. I regard rhetorical studies on Ad Hoc Assembly's debates as challenging but will not pursue them here, beyond discussing the rhetoric of *topoi*.

The special difficulties for rhetorical studies of the debates of the Assembly also involve their multilingualism, for which only a portion have been translated and without always indicating the original language of the speaker. Another problem lies in recognising that the documentation was not based on verbatim records with a professional stenographic apparatus, as used in member state parliaments. Both problems also limit the conclusions one may draw from the type of conceptual analysis which I conduct in this volume.

The Ad Hoc Assembly decided to adopt the Rules of Procedure of the ECSC Common Assembly (see Working Party 8 October 1952), the main lines of it being determined in the opening session in September 1952. As analysed in section 4.3.2, they deviate from the Westminster model in the Francophone direction in three respects: the motion was sent into committee without a preceding plenary debate; the list of speakers was made in order of request instead of relying on the President's judgement to enable a rotation of speeches *pro* and *contra* on the motion on the agenda; and the President was not a neutral arbiter, but could intervene in the debate by leaving the chair to the Vice-President. These deviations tended to render the Ad Hoc Assembly less dissensual, and therefore less able to present opposing points of view as a medium for improving the understanding of the question on the agenda.

However, the Ad Hoc Assembly had been given the task to obtain a result of reaching agreement on the Draft Treaty for the European Political Community within a half-year. Not obtaining a Draft after thorough deliberations would have been a huge disappointment for the European project. Excluding the Communists and the extreme right from the Assembly supported the result-oriented debates. Michel Debré served as *advocatus diaboli* and urged the pro-European majority to sharpen their arguments and specify their proposals. The Francophone model of rapporteurs also contributed to the result-oriented debate by not letting marginal minorities delay the deliberations.

The absence of explicit party groups as well as the dissent among the national delegations brought occasions for genuine debate, in which members were obliged to consider what had been said previously and to be willing to alter their own stands. The model of deliberating in the Constitutional Committee, in the Sub-committees and in the plenum (supplemented as well with deliberations in the Working Party and Committee of Redaction) also supported the completion of the Draft on schedule.

A central aspect of the parliamentary character of an assembly concerns the status of its members. The classical criterion of forbidding the imperative mandate and its surrogate of imposing binding instructions from the electors or from the party can be seen as a special case of freedom from dependence on arbitrary powers (as discussed in section 1.5), or in Skinner's term, as the 'neo-Roman' concept of liberty. In intergovernmental assemblies, such freedom hardly exists, and the same holds for the West German Bundesrat, which are bound to take the stand of their *Länder*, which then can be negotiated with the Bundestag in the *Vermittlungsausschuss*.

In line with the ECSC Treaty and the speeches of Jean Monnet and Konrad Adenauer (see 4.2.1), the Common Assembly members understood well that a supranational institution demands exclusion of the imperative mandate. The free mandate was, of course, also a basic liberty of the Members of the Parliament of the European Community. However, a discussion on it, regarding Senate elections by member state parliaments, arose in the Ad Hoc Assembly. In the Working Party, Pierre Wigny regarded it necessary to find 'un équilibre entre la volonté européenne et les susceptibilités nationales'. He presented a kind of agenda-setting for the Assembly, asking the Parliament to elaborate on the 'status of the parliamentarians: eligibility and incompatibility of members, their immunities and privileges, representing constituency or Europe; imperative or free mandate; duration of the mandate' (7 October 1952).

In Political Institutions Sub-committee on 14 November 1952, Chair Pierre-Henri Teitgen prepared a Note on the First Chamber, dated 12 November. It concluded on the status of the members: 'The deputy, once elected, will be a deputy of the Community, not of his country'. The Treaty should absolutely exclude an imperative mandate.

For the Second Chamber, the situation was slightly more complicated. In his Note presented to the Political Institutions Sub-committee on 17 November 1952, Fernand Dehousse left a range of possibilities open. Whether vote in the Chamber would take part *par tête* or (as governments might require) by national delegation was another question, in other words, whether the Senate or the Bundesrat model was to be applied. In his Note, Dehousse analytically distinguished a vote by delegation from an imperative mandate: although in a vote by delegation, the practice where a dissenting minority view would have to follow the majority in the Chamber, was close to an imperative mandate. Dehousse strongly supported individual voting in the Second Chamber, which, of course, excluded the imperative mandate.

In the debate, Hans-Joachim v. Merkatz (Lib) supported a vote per delegation for the ratification of treaties, which did not mean an imperative mandate, but followed the Bundesrat practice. Eugène Schaus (Lib) argued that the senators could receive instructions from their governments. In contrast, Sieuwert Bruins Slot (Lib), Marinus van der Goes (Soc) and Lodovico Montini (CD) opposed the imperative mandate. The observer Lord Walter Layton argued that, if the UK were to join the EPC, the British government would determine the members for the Second Chamber and prefer voting by delegation. Pierre-Henri Teitgen regarded the absence of instructions to members as a necessary condition for forming an independent Second Chamber: ambassadors of countries could not give binding instructions. Schaus abstained from supporting the resolution excluding the imperative mandate (Political Institutions Sub-committee on 17 November 1952).

On 20 December 1952 in the Constitutional Committee, Dehousse responded to the Danish observer Frode Jacobsen that no imperative mandate was allowed for senators, and that they represent states only in the sense of being indirectly elected. In his Report to the Plenum, Dehousse further pointed out regarding the Second Chamber the importance of distinguishing between 'Governments, which are transitory phenomena, and States, which are lasting'. It is the states which should be represented in the Senate. Its members should be 'national representatives' with a free mandate and not 'docile diplomats under governmental instructions', which would also guarantee that the opposition would be represented (7 January 1953).

The commitment to the free mandate – also for the Council of National Ministers (see section 9.1) – contributed to a double, supranational and parliamentary momentum in the Draft Treaty. In this respect, the Ad Hoc Assembly remained consistent and made no compromises with the member state governments.

William Selinger (2019) emphasises how, in contrast to a narrow interpretation of the separation of powers doctrine, the British parliamentary practice since the eighteenth century was to elect cabinet ministers among the Members of Parliament while allowing them to retain their parliamentary seat while serving as ministers. This practice was in line with Walter Bagehot's view (1867/72, 125–129) and opposed to the practice in the German Empire, against which Max Weber vehemently argued (1918, 222–227). The main point was for ministers to consider themselves as politicians and not just as officials of their ministries, thereby also retaining their parliamentary status of freedom from dependence.

The Ad Hoc Assembly debated the practical consequences of having a free mandate at the supranational level. The ECSC emphasised the independence it would give to the High Authority members from paid or unpaid interests. In the

Ad Hoc Assembly, rapporteur Dehousse interpreted that permanent officials and administrators of the Community would be barred from being members of its Parliament. Merkatz added that Community officials could be candidates, but if elected they should be suspended from their positions (Constitutional Committee 24 February 1953).

Regarding the classical problem of the compatibility of seats for parliamentarians, Teitgen, in his Note to the Political Institutions Sub-committee on 14 November 1952, regarded that, in the First Chamber, incompatibility between the two would, for national parliamentarians, 'isolate the European Chamber from concrete realities, and would diminish the authority of its members', even 'lead some personalities of high standing to refrain from seeking election to the European Chamber'. Restricting the membership to national parliamentarians alone, however, 'might deprive the European Assembly from other personalities'. Therefore for him it would be best 'to allow a plurality of offices without making them obligatory'. For a directly elected First Chamber, restricting the membership to national parliamentarians would not make sense, although nothing should prevent them from being elected directly to the First Chamber.

For Teitgen, 'a parliamentary mandate would not be incompatible with the "ministerial", or assimilated [equivalent], functions in the "executive" organ of the Community'. He also asserted: 'The European parliamentary mandate would, in any case, be compatible with the functions of a minister in a national government' (ibid). When the European Executive Council was to become a permanent institution, it would, of course, have been difficult to combine a ministerial position in a member-state, but there should not be any juridical obstacles to that in the Treaty. Van der Goes also argued against applying national incompatibilities on the European level (Sub-committee Political Institutions, 6 December 1952). In a debate in 1960, he opposed, however, the European Commissioners' retaining a seat in Parliament (see Palonen 2022a). In the Assembly plenum on 7 March, Victor-Emanuel Preusker (Lib) asked whether membership in Parliament was incompatible with ministerial membership on the European Executive Council, and Dehousse responded 'certainly not'.

In the plenum on 7 January 1953, Nicolas Margue argued that 'there should be incompatibilities between European and national Parliaments'. These incompatibilities had more to do, however, with his reservations about supranationality than they were about excluding a 'cumulation of mandates'. At the European level, the Political Institutions Sub-committee agreed that there need not be an exclusion, that is, that membership in the European Parliament was compatible with being a minister on the European Executive Council or in a member state government (11 February 1953).

The free mandate of members in all elected institutions of the European Political Community and the compatibility between parliamentary mandates as well as between European and national ministerial membership in the European Parliament were strong stands for adopting a full-scale parliamentary government on the European level. The full-term professionalisation of not only ministers but also of parliamentarians at the national and European level would later alter the problematic, but parliamentarians' freedom from dependence was no longer in question.

The power of parliaments tends to roughly correspond to the length and intensity of their sitting time. The English Parliament after the Glorious Revolution of 1688/89 began convening every year in order to prevent the monarch and the government from making decisions against the Parliament while the Parliament was on leave. Western parliaments in the twentieth century tended to sit regularly throughout the year and were, of course, willing to convene if needed also during their 'vacation' (see the juridical study of Ridard 2018). In contrast, the Supreme Soviet convened twice a year for a couple of days, and Soviet bloc parliaments followed it with certain variations (see Ilie and Ornatowski 2016 on differences between the Polish and the Romanian pseudo-parliaments).

The parliamentary assemblies of international organisations tend to practice short sitting times in order not to disturb the ordinary parliamentary rhythm of the member countries. Neither the Consultative Assembly nor the Common Assembly radically deviated from the advisory assemblies of inter-governmental organisations, although the Common Assembly understood that it could empower itself by extending its sitting period (see Wigny 1958).

For the European Political Community, a limited annual sitting period was planned. In the Political Institutions Sub-committee on 6 February 1953, Teitgen supported two annual periods, of which one dealt with the budget. Dehousse pointed out that it was difficult to find periods outside the sessions of national parliaments and the UN General Assembly. He was particularly insistent that the length of the sessions should not, as in the case of the ECSC and Council of Europe assemblies, have a time limit. His proposal of convening the second Tuesday of May, in accordance with the date of the Common Assembly, was agreed.

In the Constitutional Committee on 24 February 1953, the schedule (two sessions annually and extra sessions by invitation of the President, of members or of the Executive Council) was not as such questioned, but it does seem that coordination had been made with the schedules of the national parliaments, the Council of Europe and the ECSC. Van der Goes hinted at the possibility of combining the equal powers of the two Chambers, however, with priority for the Peoples' Chamber as examiner of the items on the agenda.

In the plenum 7 March 1953, however, a debate arose regarding Article 21. Whereas the Committee proposed two regular annual sessions, Franz-Josef Strauß (CD) moved for three sessions, one in February besides those in May and October. In the debate, Preusker defended the amendment: 'The practice of holding two sessions annually could not be applied in view of the task which a European Political Parliament would have; rather it would be necessary for work to go on continuously'. Such a view that not only extended, as the amendment did, but made permanent the Parliament's political presence would have been a major affirmation of the weight of the supranational European Parliament. Against this, Dehousse referred to the Committee's Working Party, which had 'considered it inadvisable for the European Parliament to become in any way permanent'. Dehousse stuck to the compromise position, which did not allow the supranational parliament to sit as regularly as member state parliaments (7 March 1953).

Even more than the compatibilities between the national and European levels, the stand against a 'permanent' European Parliament looks anachronistic in not considering the possibility that, for full parliamentary powers, the professionalisation of its members was indispensable (see the discussions regarding the Bundestag, Palonen 2021b). In general, the Ad Hoc Assembly seems to have underrated the importance of the politics of time for the range of parliamentary powers needed within the European Political Community, not to mention as a necessary dimension for conducting parliamentary-style politics as such.

There would have been a discrepancy in sitting times between that of the Parliament, with only two annual sitting periods, and that of the permanently sitting European Executive Council. Could this have allowed the executive to govern by decree outside the sitting times of the Parliament? If we, however, consider the striving for greater stability in the European government, the discrepancy might be intentional to protect the government against the otherwise nearly continual threat of its dismissal. On the other hand, as discussed in Chapter 9, the Draft Treaty had other measures for guaranteeing stability, and arranging a permanent sitting of the Senate would have been difficult to realise as mainly parliamentarians were to be elected from the member states.

We must, of course, distinguish between the Ad Hoc Assembly's own organising practices and those aimed at the Parliament of the European Political Community. Regarding the Rules of Procedure, the Ad Hoc Assembly did not want to bind the future Parliament's hands. Forbidding the imperative mandate and instructions as well as allowing compatibilities, the Assembly wanted to guarantee the well-known necessary conditions for giving the European Parliament a genuinely parliamentary character. These provisions marked, more importantly, a break with the practices in intergovernmental organisations, and can therefore be also regarded as a well-founded application of common parliamentary principles to the supranational level.

The European Parliament and the EU member states have more recently limited or forbidden the accumulation of parliamentary mandates. Professionalisation of parliamentarians has also been recognised in the annual sitting times of the European Parliament, which today do not differ from that in member states.

However, for the members of the European Commission, retaining Parliament membership was narrowly rejected by the European Parliamentary Assembly in 1960, due to de Gaulle's rise to power and the exclusion of the parliamentary mandate for ministers in the French Fifth Republic (on the debate see Palonen 2022a). The Commission was not then recognised as a government responsible to the European Parliament, as the European Executive Council was intended to be. Allowing concurrent membership in the Commision and the Parliament could have steered the Commission in a parliamentary direction.

8.2.2 The bicameral system

The task given to the Ad Hoc Assembly mentioned a bicameral system of representation. In the debates of the Assembly, this principle was never properly questioned, even if occasionally doubts were raised. For example, Giovanni Persico (Soc) spoke of 'one or two chambers' (Constitutional Committee, 17 December 1952). The political point and the context of expressing bicameralism deserve a short discussion, as does the defence of bicameralism that was given in response as well as defences of bicameralism more generally.

In a debate of the Political Institutions Sub-committee on 20 November 1952, Heinrich v. Brentano saw bicameralism as complicating the relationship to the ECSC and to the EDC. One of the issues provoking disagreement concerned whether the installation of the European Political Community would require a transition period before its implementation. In a debate in the Sub-committee on 6 December 1952, Chair Teitgen remarked that if member state parliaments were made to elect both chambers of the European Parliament in the transition period, they were tending to produce similar results. Although he for the moment gave up bicameralism, he was soon willing to admit with Dehousse, Schaus and Lodovico Montini that it was instead the transitory period that should be abandoned.

In the Constitutional Committee on 20 December 1952, the British observer Lord Walter Layton was unsure of the value of bicameralism if the chambers did not significantly differ from each other, for example, if both had a system of representation based on weighted voting. In the debate, Hermann Kopf (CD) found the bicameral system too complicated and impractical for the legislative tasks of the Parliament. Instead of that, the Committee of Ministers could have some legislative powers or a conference of the heads of government, as proposed by Michel Debré in his counter-project (dated 4 November 1952), could be used. P.A. Blaisse also supported a single chamber for the transition period (20 December 1952).

Taking the other side, Schaus thought that unicameralism would be incompatible with the principle of separation of powers. Others saw a second chamber as legitimate under certain conditions. Johannes Semler (CD) was ready to abandon the Committee of Ministers and make a Second Chamber of the representatives of governments and oppositions. Dehousse judged that a bicameral system would exclude government representatives (ibid.).

In his Report to the Assembly plenum on 8 January 1953, Dehousse defended the bicameral system: 'The establishment of a second Chamber would guarantee to the Community a fuller degree of parliamentary control. It would also make possible to establish a liaison between the European Parliament, the national parliaments, and the Consultative Assembly of the Council of Europe'. Unlike the common justification of chambers balancing each other, he saw in the Second Chamber an additional force to strengthen the parliamentary control over the executive. When the chambers are elected differently and vary in their political composition, it would be easy to regard them as potential obstacles to each other, but Dehousse saw in them a way to exercise controlling powers from different perspectives. This would hold true under the condition that the Second Chamber was also 'of parliamentary character' and not a 'mere Council of National Ministers', as in the ECSC (ibid.).

In retrospect, it is striking to note that the bicameral system, combining the direct elections with appointment by the parliaments, has hardly ever been put on the agenda of the European Communities for serious discussion since the Treaty of Rome in 1957. What debates there were on bicameralism followed a line explicitly rejected by the Ad Hoc Assembly, namely, understanding the Council of Ministers as the second chamber, together with, as understood later, the summits of the European Council. Considering Dehousse's arguments for bicameralism as a double control over government: What important political chances for European integration may have been lost due to not discussing the possibility of a bicameralism based on a directly elected Peoples' Chamber and a parliament-elected Senate, as proposed in the Draft Treaty?

In the Ad Hoc Assembly it was, however, the powers of the two chambers which provoked interesting debates. In his Note to the Political Institutions Subcommittee, dated 16 November 1952 and discussed on the following day, Dehousse developed some general considerations without yet taking a definite stand:

> These relations may be envisaged on the basis of a strict equality; or, on the contrary, on the basis of the primacy of one of the two Chambers.
> Equality may lead to a deadlock.
> As regards the primacy, in the world of today it could only be vested in the popular Chamber, that is, in the First Chamber.

In the debate on 17 November 1952, opposed views on the topic arose. Schaus spoke for equal powers between the two Chambers, whereas Brentano argued that the competence of the Second Chamber should be limited and should not appropiate (*empiéter*) that which the member states wanted to retain. In the 6 December sitting of the Sub-committee, which debated the possible dissent between the two Chambers of Parliament, Dehousse referred to a conciliation committee, or that one Chamber would be accepted as having priority. He opted himself for the priority of the Peoples' Chamber: a second reading was possible in the case of dissent, but for avoiding delay, the First Chamber's vote should, under certain conditions, be decisive. Teitgen proposed to leave the entire decision to the Ad Hoc Assembly. The Constitutional Committee decided on 14 December that the Senate 'has the same powers and the same rights as the Peoples' Chamber' with 16 votes for to 2 against.

In the later debates, different opinions on the equality of the chambers were expressed, however, in a way concerning what kinds of powers would be given to them, for example, in electing the Executive Council's President, and in the determining what kind majorities were required. For this reason, I postpone further discussion of to this to Chapter 9.

8.2.3 Legislation and initiative

The Constitutional Committee's December 1952 version of the Draft did not have a section on legislation. Since the 18 February Working Party's Draft, such a section has been added, although not under the Parliament chapter. When no major distinctions were made here between the chambers, I think it is appropriate to discuss legislation before discussing the composition and powers of the two chambers.

In his proposal for rapid organisation of direct elections for the Political Community, Antonio Azara had spoken already in October on parliamentary initiative as one of the Community's powers (see below 8.3.1) The theme was introduced by the Attributions Sub-committee rapporteur Lodovico Benvenuti in his Report to the Constitutional Committee, dated 20 December 1952 and presented to the January plenum of the Ad Hoc Assembly. Admitting that the ECSC and EDC Treaties conferred only weak powers to parliamentary assemblies, and that this could not be altered without changing the Treaties, Benvenuti concluded: 'It would be inadmissible for the future rules of the Community to be established without the participation of the Community's Parliament'. In other words, the major advantage of the European Political Community lay for Benvenuti in the parliamentarisation of the legislation and the control over the executive powers. He concluded his argument with a separation of powers doctrine: 'The initiative in matters of legislation thus remains with the executive institutions, the "veto" of the governments is maintained but the Parliament is associated with the exercise of those normative powers of the Community which are most important for the development of a future European legislation'.

The European Parliament has only lately gained such normative powers, and it still has no power in certain matters of legislation. The Draft Treaty of the Ad Hoc Assembly remains in this respect more parliamentary than any subsequent project for empowering the European Parliament.

In the Draft of the Constitutional Committee, dated 26 February 1953, the Article 51 began by stating: 'Both the European Executive Council and the Members of Parliament shall be entitled to initiate legislation. The passing of legislation shall require the assent of both Chambers'. Here a formal equality of the government and the parliamentarians was mentioned, thus recognising parliamentary initiative on the supranational level of the European Parliament on equal terms with the member state parliaments. The right to initiate legislation was given to individual members, not to party groups, as in the West German *Parteienstaat* theory (Leibholz 1951), or it required a certain number of signatures, as in the current European Parliament. In the final version of the Draft, no such paragraphs existed, apparently due to a word-saving redaction of the text.

The Westminster model was not followed in the next paragraph. Instead of three readings, even the second reading in the Senate was optional:

After the adoption of the bill by the two Chambers, a second deliberation shall be held automatically in the Peoples' Chamber and in the Senate, if requested by one quarter of the Senate within three clear days. The second deliberation shall begin ten days after the request has been made. A second deliberation in accordance with this procedure may not be requested more than once for the same bill. (Article 52 in the 10 March version)

The formulation indicates that in ordinary cases the Peoples' Chamber would have the first word in debating legislation, but one quarter of Senators might request a second round of deliberation in both Chambers. In the debate on 9 March 1953, Piet Vermeylen (Soc) proposed the same right also for the Peoples' Chamber members. Dehousse referred to the revised formulation of the Working Party: 'Legislation shall require the assent of each of the two Chambers in succession, voting by a simple majority of its Members'. Here no order of ranking of the Chambers was mentioned, but legislation could be initiated in either of the two Chambers, which would correspond to the agreed principle of equal powers between them. Vermeylen's amendment would have strengthened their equal powers, but Dehousse insisted that it 'unduly delayed the second reading, the main purpose of which must still be to afford a guarantee to small states'. Such a view seems to give a partial veto right to the Senate, not for guaranteeing a more thorough parliamentary debate, but related to its membership giving greater weight to smaller states.

According to Article 52:4, within the period of 'eight clear days', 'the President of the European Executive Council may request the Parliament to hold a new debate'. A suspicion arises, whether here a weak suspensive veto for the Council President was implied. A distrust towards the unpredictable conduct of directly elected parliamentarians was not unknown in the Ad Hoc Assembly, instead of trusting in the creative powers of parliamentary debate or in the political imagination of individual members.

The article on proposals is interesting when compared with the corresponding articles in the ECSC's Common Assembly. In the Draft Treaty, the proposals concern the relationships between the Community and the member states. Article 55 declares:

> The Community may make proposals to the Member States with the object of attaining the general aims defined in the Article 2.
> Such proposals shall be made by the European Executive Council, either on its own initiative or as a result of a motion of the Parliament or by one of the Chambers.
> The European Executive Council may request Member States for information on the action which they have taken in regard to the proposals of the Community.

The Draft claims that proposals are a supranational right over the member states, exercised through the European Executive Council, either as such or by mediating the proposals of the parliamentary chambers. A decision by the Executive Council was required regarding which proposals if any, would be addressed to member states. To what extent the Council had to forward the motions passed by the parliamentary chambers to member states, is not mentioned. The 'request' to member states on measures taken also remains at the level of 'information', without indicating the sanctions the Community could impose on them for neglecting or misinterpreting its initiatives in specific cases.

Article 54 adds recommendations to the Parliament's competence. 'Under the conditions and within the limits in which it is entitled to legislate, Parliament may also make recommendations which shall be binding as regards the aims specified therein, but shall leave the means of implementation to the Authorities to whom the recommendation is addressed.' This corresponds to the distinction between decisions and recommendations but adds to the powers of the parliament a less formal and more rapidly applicable instrument of guidance and regulation of the polity, subject to the interpretation of the government.

As minimalistic as these considerations of the Draft Statute on legislation and initiative appear, they must be regarded as the results of a thorough parliamentary debate. In the Ad Hoc Assembly, the members wanted to establish the ordinary parliamentary powers of members' initiatives in legislation, leaving, however, to the President of the European Executive Council a weak suspensive veto. In its implications, the recommendations are then an instrument of a more open power struggle between the 'will' of the parliament and the 'force' of the government.

8.3 The Peoples' Chamber

In the initial meetings of the Assembly, the term 'First Chamber' was used for the popularly elected chamber, a practice opposite to the names used in the Netherlands or in the Swedish Chambers from 1868 to 1970. Pierre-Henri Teitgen consistently used the term 'First Chamber' in his Note dated 12 November 1952.

The term 'Peoples' Chamber' appears on the agenda of the Political Institutions Sub-committee on 3 December 1952, when rapporteur Fernand Dehousse proposed, referring to article 38 of the EDC Treaty, 'States Chamber' for the second and 'Peoples' Chamber' for the first chamber. The latter proposal was agreed, although Lodovico Montini did not regard it as *très concluant*. Later, there were no major disputes on the name of the first chamber, except a remark of Pierre Wigny (quoted in 6.1.3).

8.3.1 Direct elections

A major part of the Ad Hoc Assembly's debates dealt with the election of the Peoples' Chamber. The main controversy was whether the direct general election by universal suffrage should be practised already with the first election of the Chamber or whether a transition period was necessary before the general elections. A second dispute concerned the electoral system, the choice between proportional representation and a majoritarian system. A further topic was whether the communists should be allowed to enter Parliament and if not, how their membership could eventually be prevented. In section 8.3.3, I shall deal with the distribution of seats both between and within the member states as well as two special cases, which were difficult to apply to the electoral systems, namely the French overseas departments and the Saar question.

Neither the Luxembourg resolution of the ECSC foreign ministers nor their Questionnaire sent to the Ad Hoc Assembly in October 1952 contained any guidelines for electing the parliamentary chambers of the European Political Community. The Ad Hoc Assembly could debate on the electoral system freely.

The first to argue for direct and rapid election of the first Chamber was Antonio Azara in the Constitutional Committee of 25 October 1952. For him the creation of a European political assembly could not have any other basis than universal and direct suffrage. Only directly elected members would possess the authority to obtain the consent of public opinion for the necessary relinquishment of sovereignty. In Azara's view, the Assembly should be constituted as soon as possible, and the elaboration of the electoral law should have priority in the Committee. The Assembly should replace the assemblies of the ECSC and the EDC and have a right to constitutional initiative. The motion was to be debated in the Ad Hoc Assembly's plenum in January 1953.

Committee Chair Heinrich v. Brentano, however, saw it as necessary to connect Azara's proposal to the debates on the Questionnaire of the ECSC ministers. Fernand Dehousse welcomed Azara's proposal in its direct appeal to the European peoples, seeing, however, constitutional problems around it. Hermann Kopf seconded Azara's proposal as a good means for obtaining the support of the European peoples.

Pierre-Henri Teitgen began his Note on the First Chamber to Political Institutions Sub-committee (dated 12 November 1952) with the question of whether the First Chamber should be elected directly or chosen by the parliaments of the member states. For him, only the former alternative would win over the public opinion and be able 'to invest the First Chamber with the necessary authority, and to endow the Community with the dynamism it needs'. In other words, he regarded the mode of election as a highly political question and decisive for the legitimacy of the Political Community among the citizens of member states. With it, the Political Community would be in a strong position to support the Europeanisation of politics.

Teitgen in his Note seems to have been the first to mention the possibility that a supranational Political Community could dispense with drawing the electoral districts to coincide with the member states. He judged, however, that it would 'obviously be quite premature to contemplate electoral districts across the frontiers'. The idea and the debate on it indicated that, when obtaining an occasion to use their own political imagination, pro-European members such as Teitgen could freely develop supranational and parliamentary visions beyond the formal objective for writing a Draft for Constitution.

Indeed, the Sub-committee agreed on 14 November that 'the Treaty might provide for the adoption of a definite regime, in which the deputies would no longer be elected on the basis of a single national electoral area'. This resolution did not, however, play any further part in the debates in the Ad Hoc Assembly and has in this form hardly ever been debated later, either. The idea and the resolution of the Sub-committee deserve therefore to be recovered from oblivion.

Direct elections were opposed by Marinus van der Goes, who still was hoping to avoid a break with the Council of Europe (see above 6.1.3). Hans-Joachim v. Merkatz agreed with Teitgen's view on the 'dynamism' with direct elections. Pierre Wigny did not see a difference in the democratic quality between the different modes of elections. He insisted, however, that a directly elected chamber would have the advantage of having a direct link to public opinion, but he was willing to accept a transition period of 5–6 years during which time the national parliaments would elect the European First Chamber. Teitgen agreed to adopt Wigny's view to let the member state parliaments elect the first 'legislature' and recommended leaving the decision on direct elections to the Assembly plenum. Sieuwert Bruins Slot did not see the failure of the Council of Europe to be its election by national parliaments, but rather its lacking competence. He referred to the Dutch First Chamber as a parliament whose lack of direct elections did not lead to a lack of authority. Teitgen's proposal to make a distinction between transitory and definitive electoral systems for the First Chamber was unanimously accepted (14 November 1952).

Van der Goes justified his motion for giving time 'to set up an electoral system which was both watertight and democratic'. Theo Lefevre (CD) saw a danger that, if unprepared, the first elections could lead to a scenario where 'Fascist and Communist elements would fling themselves upon Europe'. (ibid.)

Council of Europe Secretary Jacques Camille Paris reminded that article 38 of the European Defence Community had presupposed an Assembly on a 'democratic basis', which would require direct elections as the definitive system of voting. He was supported by Merkatz, whereas Bruins Slot evoked the election of the President of the United States as a counterexample, to which Teitgen remarked that the US grand electors had an imperative mandate (ibid.).

Against direct elections van der Goes argued that there were no European parties. Wigny emphasised the expectations for a positive construction, where a European Assembly would be assembled along grand ideological lines and not grouped according to nation. Teitgen further pointed out that without European elections there would be no European parties and he emphasised his joy at contributing to something genuinely novels in the Sub-committee (ibid.).

The Dutch government presented a letter to the Political Institutions Sub-committee's sitting on 5 December. It held the direct elections to be, at least for the moment, contra-productive, as it would weaken the spirit of solidarity, allow destructive forces to enter the parliament, and take place at a time when both common parties and common programmes were missing. The Dutch members of the Ad Hoc Assembly had been the most critical of immediate direct elections. However, in the sitting, van der Goes did not regard the Dutch government's stand as beyond dispute.

Dehousse presented to the Sub-committee a dramatic alternative: direct elections or no Political Community. Teitgen responded that the Sub-committee could not abandon its goals in face of the first difficulty it encountered; the Sub-committee should be prepared to encounter controversy. Dehousse remarked that European parties and programmes would not arise until the elections are declared. Van der Goes allied with Teitgen in opting for a single Chamber for a transition period (5 December 1952).

The next day in the Sub-committee, Fernand Dehousse made a personal declaration against an eventual transition period, which he considered as only delaying the establishment of the European Political Community. The postponement of direct elections to the Parliament also deprived from the Political Community of its substance and its powerful idea (*idée-force*) as well as containing a risk for non-ratification of the Treaty on the European Defence Community by losing the Political Community in its oversight over it. Teitgen proposed a resolution of the Sub-committee: 'The Sub-committee has carefully considered, at the second reading, the question of the desirability of a transitional regime.' By 5 votes against 1, the Sub-committee declared its opposition to any sort of transitional regime (6 December 1952).

To the Constitutional Committee, Dehousse presented his Report from the Political Institutions Sub-committee. He again appealed to the new and dynamic *idée-force* of electing an assembly by universal suffrage, by which 'the peoples themselves' could elect their representations for the construction and realisation (*gestion*) of a united Europe. This would replace the government-led rhythms of development and modalities of realisation (Report from 15 December 1952).

Dehousse relied in his argument on the force of popular sovereignty which, through the parliamentary representation, could counter both the inter-war trend of reducing parliaments to ratifying instruments of government policy and the weakening of the European-level powers by the opposing national governments. For Dehousse, the independence of parliaments towards government was in principle worth defending. His reliance on the critical force of citizens voting in elections, without explicit procedural and institutional provisions to strengthen the parliamentary powers of debate and control, are less convincing. Governments traditionally gained additional powers outside parliamentary control and weakened the parliamentary forms of controlling government and administration in context where electoral results, and not parliamentary debates, determined the election and longevity of the government (Bagehot 1872, revised edition; see Palonen 2014a and 2018).

Launching direct elections for a European Parliament in the six member countries of the Political Community could provoke unpredictable results. Dehousse argued that they would be teaching citizens to think of themselves as Europeans instead of focusing on their nationalities (Report from 15 November 1952). How far this goal would have been realistic in the 1950s, we cannot know. Still, we can speculate that if the Europeanisation within the six countries had received a boost from below through direct elections, the subsequent European history might have been quite different.

In the Constitutional Committee debate on 17 December, Blaisse supported, contrary to the Dutch government, the election of the Peoples' Chamber partly by universal suffrage, partly by national parliaments. He thought that, at the beginning, a one-chamber parliament and Council of National Ministers would suffice, while the Senate could be created in due time along with the growing powers of the Community. Van der Goes still regarded a direct election of the first chamber without European parties as premature. Becker noted, however, that real political parties had in fact been formed in the Council of Europe and thus in Parliament they would presumably be similarly formed in ideological terms. Wigny had some doubts about the representativity of the First Chamber, due to the absence of obligatory voting, a topic which others were not interested in discussing at all (Constitutional Committee, 17 November 1952).

In the Committee on 20 December, Merkatz remarked that the parliamentary responsibility of the Executive Council required further discussion. Dehousse emphasised that this responsibility of the Executive Council before the Parliament, applied to foreign policy and such other powers as amendments of the statute could give to it. Margue saw in the Executive Council the origins of a European Government, the political orientation of which should be represented by a President.

In the Assembly plenum on 7 January 1953, Dehousse presented the work of the Political Institutions Sub-committee and defended again the idea of direct elections to the Peoples' Chamber:

The impelling idea of the proposals of the Committee resides in the election by universal suffrage of a popular Assembly…in the participation of the peoples themselves, by the direct selection of their representatives, in the construction and direction of a united Europe, the scale of whose development has hitherto been mostly determined by the Governments.

Dehousse's main point was to combine Europeanisation of the polity with a breaking up of the governmental monopoly on international politics by making parliamentary representatives not only controllers, but also participants in the 'construction and direction' of Europeanisation. He pleaded for politicisation of Europe from below, although not in the sense of a ruling parliament, *régime d'Assemblée*, as the French slogan goes. Dehousse illustrated 'the system… based on principles of internal logic – of political logic in the best sense of the term'. In the history of European integration, such a vision is exceptional, as opposed to making adjustments, adaptations and agreements according to the smallest common denominator, and therefore the report of this Sub-committee is of special interest from a politicisation perspective.

In the plenum of 9 January 1953, again, a controversy arose on the election of the Peoples' Chamber by direct and universal suffrage. Wigny had moved that for the first legislature 'the members shall be nominated by the national Parliaments'. Van der Goes and other Dutch members had moved for 'an active transition towards a genuine European direct suffrage, and measures shall be taken to ensure that the parliamentary system operates during this period' (9 January 1953).

Wigny repeated the argument about lacking European parties, which led to a situation in which 'most of the populations were not yet ready to express their views on questions of European nature', but he could support direct elections 'immediately, provided the vote was compulsory and failure to vote was punishable'. The point raises the question of whether it is better to compel political illiterates to vote or to prevent them from voting in a politically hazardous manner, a topic that nobody but Wigny took up. Van der Goes justified his motion for giving time 'to set up an electoral system which was both watertight and democratic'. Lefevre saw a danger, as mentioned above, that if the first elections were unprepared, 'Fascist and Communist elements would fling themselves upon Europe'. (ibid.)

Against these amendments, Paul Reynaud (Lib) referred to the failure of the Council of Europe and maintained that 'the peoples…could not be left outside the door for another four years. Nothing would be achieved without popular support'. For Armando Sabatini (CD), only with direct elections 'would [it] be possible to achieve clear-cut alignment of parties'. Teitgen argued that direct elections would never be realised if waiting 'until European political parties had been formed', but they would be formed 'as a result of such elections', which 'represented the sole means of establishing European institutions on a firm basis'. Natale Santero (CD) supported direct elections on the additional grounds that 'indirect elections would subject the Assembly of the Community to all the vicissitudes entailed by the decline of ordinary and extraordinary powers of the Assemblies of different countries'. (ibid.)

On 6 February, the Political Institutions Sub-committee agreed on the principles for electing the Peoples' Chamber: 'The deputies shall be elected by universal, equal and direct suffrage, open to both men and women', and this formula was adopted in Article 13 of the final Draft Treaty. It must be remembered that women's suffrage was introduced in France, Italy and Belgium only in the aftermath of the Second World War. The second paragraph of the Article adds: 'The Community shall enact legislation defining the principles of the electoral system'.

For parliamentarisation of the European Political Community, the acceptance of direct elections into the Peoples' Chamber was a necessary condition, without which other moves in favour of a supranational parliamentary government would have been difficult to accept. With Dehousse, we can also emphasise the value of parliamentarising foreign policy: the European Political Community could then follow a more parliamentary line in foreign policy than do member state governments. Although a minority remained unconvinced of the 'maturity' of the electorate for participating in European elections, the remark of Teitgen, that this was the eternal argument used against earlier movements to expand suffrage and that, as John Stuart Mill (1861) pointed out, there were 'educative' powers to enfranchisement, seem to have supported the acceptance of direct elections.

From the hindsight of 70 years, it is, of course, possible to question the validity of that educative interest, given the low turnout in EP elections as well as the still fragmentary quality of the European party system. The counterargument, inspired by the work of the Ad Hoc Assembly, is that the elections never have been connected to such a powerful supranational parliamentarism as was proposed in the Draft Treaty for the European Political Community.

8.3.2 Proportional or majority representation

Another issue that provoked heated disputes in the Ad Hoc Assembly was the seemingly technical question of opposing proportional representation to its majoritarian alternative. At the time, almost all member states had a proportional system, a partial exception being West Germany, which had a majoritarian element in the first vote (*Erststimme*) for the constituency, while the second vote determining the composition of the Bundestag was in proportion to party support. The French Third Republic for most of the period followed a two-stage majoritarian system, while the British simple-majority system had adherents also in the continental Europe (for more on West Germany, see Ullrich 2009).

In a Note from 12 November 1952, Pierre-Henri Teitgen moved for proportional representation with a combined list, including only those who 'admit the fundamental principles in the statute of the Council of Europe'. By 'combined list', he meant that electoral alliances between parties were allowed, both nationally and locally. For the practical organisation, including whether the vote should be obligatory, the decisions should be left to the member states.

A main purpose with the 'combined list' was to weaken the Communist parties' representation, under the assumption that pro-European parties could agree on common lists, whereas communists would not be accepted to any alliance. Eugène Schaus supported direct elections and raised the question of whether the communists, a major part of the electorate in certain countries, should continue to be excluded. Merkatz saw that integrated lists had prevented their election in West Germany (in 1952 the KPD was still represented in the Bundestag and several of the Landtage). Later in the debate, van der Goes, Merkatz and Teitgen all wanted at least to minimise the presence of Communist parties. Merkatz regarded them as reporting directly to Moscow, and Teitgen saw their presence as reducing the number of French representatives. Van der Goes regarded the possibility of their winning seats as grounds for looking for some alternative to the list system (12 November 1952).

Today, the fear of communists sounds overrated. If we look at the parliamentary election results of around 1950 in the ECSC countries, we get the following numbers (years and percentages):

Italy	1948, 30.8 (S+ PCI)
	[Popular front with Nenni Socialists]
	1953, 20.2 (S+PCI)
France	1951, 26.4 (PDF)
West Germany	1949, 5.7 (KPD)
	1953, 2.2 (KPD)
Belgium	1950, 4.9 (PCB)
The Netherlands.	1952, 6.2 (PCN)

Luxembourg 1951, 3.4 (PCL)
(Source: Wikipedia).

In France and Italy, the Communist parties were in the early 1950s major parliamentary parties, but they played only a marginal role in the other four countries. Their membership in the Peoples' Chamber was again debated in the Political Institutions Sub-committee on 3 December 1952. Dehousse declared himself to be a partisan of a *fidéle* representation, even with the communists, to which Teitgen remarked that two states would withdraw from the Community if communists were represented. Lodovico Montini referred to the Italian experience of fighting against communists by creating large electoral districts. Dehousse preferred to fight against communists who had been elected and were represented in Parliament. Van der Goes was afraid that the admission of communists, as a foreign and illegal party, would be the death of the Community. Teitgen judged that, in France, all non-communist parties could be presented in a common list, but in that case few people would vote because the victory of the united list would be too obvious. The Sub-committee decided to leave the decision on the electoral laws to the Statute of the Community (3 December 1952).

Both a parliamentary and an exclusive strategy were applied to 'fighting against' communists. Teitgen's and van der Goes's view on the lethal effects of communists in the Parliament of the Community looks harsh, but at least Teitgen recognised that it is difficult to exclude them by means of the electoral system.

In the plenum of 7 January 1953, van der Goes linked excluding communists to a majoritarian system. He considered a 'European outlook in the public' was necessary before elaborating a European electoral system, and for eliminating the communists a 'majority system with a double ballot' would be preferable. In the Political Institutions Sub-committee on 6 February 1953, Yves Delbos (Lib) supported the majoritarian system (see below) with the argument that it would allow elimination of the communists without irritations. Natale Santero agreed with Delbos's proposal and thought that 'the low number of Communists elected by the majority system would not disturb anyone'. Teitgen referred to the constituency of Lot in France and pointed out that majoritarian elections did not necessarily prevent electing communists (6 February 1953). In the plenary debates the 'communist argument' did not play any role, and it seems that the majority agreed with Montini and Dehousse to struggle against them in the Parliament rather against electing them to Parliament in the first place.

Majoritarian systems were also supported in principle. Giovanni Persico opted for dividing the states into as many electoral districts as the state has votes in the First Chamber, because the proportional system is difficult to understand among the voters (Constitutional Committee 20 December 1952). This would require a majoritarian system.

Yves Delbos was the main proponent of majoritarianism. He defended it in the Political Institutions Sub-committee with the interesting argument that the proportional system favoured parties with national, but not European, programmes. Regarding Europe, most parties were internally divided, and the majority system 'allows [one] to judge the personal opinions of the candidates on Europe, independently of their parties' (6 February 1953). Delbos had in view a European divide different from that between Liberals vs. Socialists in the Peoples' Chamber.

In the same sitting, Eugène Schaus declared himself to be a partisan of the majority system, but said that for the moment it could not be adopted because it did not permit the representation of minorities. Teitgen asserted that the Political Community would surely be constituted, and after that the divide on Europe would lose its significance and be replaced by the 'lines of different political doctrines'. Europe required independent persons, and for that parties were better than the representatives of special interests. He referred to French experience with two-stage majoritarian elections, which had never functioned well. He further pointed out that the small parties, which frequently had a majority in national parliaments, would be weakly represented in the Peoples' Chamber, which discrepancy would lead the national parliaments to oppose that of the Community (ibid.).

Dehousse was struck by Delbos' exclusively French view and said that the majoritarian system was entirely alien to Benelux Countries. Dehousse thought that ideological battles between Christian, Liberal and Socialist parties would take place also on the European level. As the Peoples' Chamber should be the 'motor' of Europeanisation and, as such, enjoy great authority. This would be impossible without representation of the parties of the main currents of thought (ibid.).

Delbos replied that he did not oppose parties, but he did not want to set them above Europe. He saw the representation as being split between the 'European movement' and anti-European national parties, and he did not think that the majority system would exclude small parties. He was referring to the British example where, however, the simple majority system was practised. He did not say whether he would prefer that for the European elections (ibid.).

Heinz Braun (Saar SPD) noted that, though his party got 35% of the votes, it would not be represented in a majority system. Teitgen reminded the plenum that non-partisan movements had not succeeded in post-war France, and the same would hold for the European movement after the establishment of the Community, and although crypto-communists could hide behind such lists. Delbos asked what common ground could there be between for example Paul-Henri Spaak and the German Social Democrats? Delbos's amendment was rejected with by a vote of 8 to 0. The proposal of the Committee for proportional representation allowing electoral alliances, in lines of each member state's own system, was agreed with 7–0 votes (ibid.).

In the Constitutional Committee on 25 February, Yves Delbos returned to his proposal for two-stage majority elections (*un scrutin uninominal majoritaire à deux tours*) and argued that this system would consider the European dimension better than parties focusing on domestic issues. Teitgen predicted that a majoritarian system in the first elections would have grave consequences. It would give the impression of excluding a minority, whereas the proportional system would work inside the majority alliance. Delbos's amendment was rejected with 5 to 2 votes against, and 5 abstentions (ibid.).

In the final plenum on 10 March 1953, Delbos again took up his motion to elect the Peoples' Chamber by a majority vote. He thought that 'conflicting views about Europe existed within certain parties' and advocated voting for a single candidate, 'a system which made it possible for men of high integrity to be elected on a specific programme, after an electoral campaign fought solely on a European ticket…The deputies elected would be first and foremost Europeans.' This view, based strongly on the French experience, was supported by Maurice Faure (Lib) with the argument that without a majoritarian system the pro-European candidates in France would be easily defeated. Against these views, Henk Korthals (Lib) considered 'that the European elections would centre…on principles; for instance, what direction should be taken by Europe. For that reason, they should build up European parties'. Lodovico Montini was willing to postpone the decision on the electoral system, but 'was convinced that parties were a genuine instrument of democracy'. Delbos's amendment was rejected (ibid.).

What would have become of the European Parliament if the Peoples' Chamber, had been elected by a majoritarian system, is impossible to know. Delbos had a point in claiming that acceptance of European integration marked a dividing line that crosses conventional party lines. This does not mean to divide voters into pro- vs. anti-Europeans, but for example between the extension versus the deepening of Europeanisation. The nightmare scenario of Teitgen was surely an oversimplification. Still, there were not any guarantees that a majoritarian system would have supported pro-European forces, and it is likely that it would have prevented the representation of new party groups and national and other minorities in the EP.

The majoritarian system would presumably have strengthened a European-level divide between governmental and opposition parties in the Parliament. The mood in the Ad Hoc Assembly, as manifested in the demand that the opposition be represented in the Senate (see below), would not have regarded such a dualistic parliament as a desirable outcome, preferring instead that minority representatives in the European Parliament would play a constructive part in politics.

Europeanisation still plays a role as a political dividing line in EP elections with a proportional system – as indicated in the higher support for the pro-European Green parties in EP elections in countries such Germany, France and Finland. Maybe, with the cautiously pro-European stand of Conservative, Socialist and Liberal factions in the EP, it would still be better to keep their divergences mitigated within the same electoral alliance. As for Eurosceptics, the oxymoronic possibility of 'an international of nationalists' has never been realised as seen, for example, in the fundamental disagreement between the Italian Lega and the Austrian FPÖ on the South Tyrol/Alto Adige issue.

8.3.3 The distribution of seats

The distribution of seats in Peoples' Chamber of the European Parliament was another major subject of controversy in which the interests of member countries were directly involved. The Constitutional Committee's proposal deviated from arithmetical proportionality in favour of minor states, so that two of the three major countries could not together form a majority in the Chamber. From the supranational perspective, distributing parliamentary seats by considering the member states as electoral districts (eventually including the divisions within them) is questionable, and how to transcend such districting in the long term was, as mentioned, debated in the Sub-committee.

The seat distribution in the Peoples' Chamber was first debated in the Political Institutions Sub-committee on 14 November 1952. Montini recommended taking the practice of the Council of Europe as the model, and his view was shared by Merkatz. In the January plenum, Dehousse also supported the 'system of qualified representation' as used in the Council of Europe, the ECSC and as planned for the EDC. Vinizio Ziino (CD) followed this line, while Brentano did not want any sudden changes in the existing treaties. Dehousse's modified proposal for the seat distribution between countries was passed with 15 votes for and 6 abstentions (9 January 1953).

Although the principles of seat distribution in the Chamber were not strongly contested, considerable parts of debating time were dedicated to two specific issues related to the borders of the Political Community, namely the overseas representation and the Saar question.

The question of overseas territories was debated already in the first meetings of the Working Party. In the original draft, France was granted 63 members in the Peoples' Chamber, as many as Italy and West Germany. On 7 October 1952, André Mutter (Lib) emphasised the problems with the inclusion of the non-European areas of the French Union (*territoire d'outre-mer*).

In the plenum on 8 January 1953, Leopold Sédar Senghor (factionless) and Jean Silvandre (Soc) demanded seats in the European Parliament for the French overseas departments. Silvandre opposed an internationalisation of overseas territories, whereas Senghor argued for giving them 'a reasonable place' in the Political Community. In an amendment, Senghor moved for 20 additional seats to France for overseas representation in the Peoples' Chamber (9 January 1953). In the Working Party of 2 February 1953, Teitgen took up the internal French dispute concerning whether the *outre-mer* should have symbolic representation in the Political Community, or whether the areas should be completely removed from the competence of the Community.

In the Constitutional Committee on 10 February 1953, Senghor responded to Dehousse's question concerning why Belgian overseas areas (Congo, Ruanda-Urundi) were not included: 'whereas French overseas areas were an integral part of the French state, the Belgian Congo was not a part of the Belgian state'. The territories were willing to open their markets to Europe, and without them France was 'split in two'. Teitgen agreed that the French Republic was entering the Community in its existing form, including its overseas departments and territories, but if it was agreed that France had 63 representatives, they could be divided between the home country and the overseas territories. Teitgen defended their having symbolic representation with 7 seats, based on the previously agreed decision of a maximum of 70 seats for the bigger countries, in contrast to Italy's and West Germany's 63 seats in the Peoples' Chamber. Such decision would also make the Statute valid within the overseas departments. Dehousse believed that the 7 extra seats for France would not disturb the overall balance, whereas other proposals for overseas areas or for the Eastern part of Germany were not presented as detailed amendments (10 February 1953).

In the plenum of 7 March 1953 Senghor regarded the 7 extra seats for the French overseas department in the Peoples' Chamber as insufficient, warning of the agitation for independence in certain African countries and therefore moving for 17 additional votes for France. Silvandre moved for 27 extra votes and was supported by Debré. On the final day of the plenum (10 March 1953), the French overseas representation was again debated, but the amendments of both Silvandre and Senghor were rejected. In the Draft Treaty, France retained 70 seats, divided between the 'overseas departments and territories' and the metropolitan France. As Senghor's warning against independence illustrates, the decolonialisation of the French empire was not yet regarded as a serious problem in the Assembly.

A politically open questions after the Second World War was the status of the Saar. It was not a state, but it was nonetheless a member of the Council of Europe. In the Common Assembly and Ad Hoc Assembly, Saar members were part of the French delegation. An agreement, the *Saarstatut* between West Germany (Konrad Adenauer) and France (Pierre Mendès France) in 1954, put the Saar under the Umbrella of the West European Union, WEU. A referendum in 1955 rejected the *Saarstatut* by a two-thirds majority, but in the *Saarvertrag* in 1956, France admitted the re-inclusion of the Saar to West Germany as an independent *Bundesland* beginning in January 1957.

In the plenum of the Ad Hoc Assembly on 9 January 1953, Heinz Braun did not accept Saar's inclusion in the French delegation as it was in the ECSC and 'urged the Assembly to appeal' to the French and German governments to resume their negotiations on the Saar. The debate on 7 February in the Political Institutions Sub-committee was opened by the letter of West German members (Hermann Kopf et.al.) on the position of the Saar in the European Parliament, requiring the suspension of their special representation in the Senate, in similar terms as in the Council of Europe. They insisted that the Saar was not a state and so its fate must be negotiated between France and West Germany. Chair Teitgen noted that Saar was not treated as a state, but represented, as an exceptional case, 'the Saar population', and he suggested that reconciliation talks be continued the next day, which Kopf accepted.

On 18 February 1953, the Sub-committee again debated the 'Saar question', which was still unresolved between France and Germany. Teitgen referred to discussions with Brentano and the Saar representative Braun, neither of them representing governments. They wanted to avoid passionate debates in the Assembly or in the Constitutional Committee, but they also wanted to keep the Saar question on the agenda. It was agreed that until its status was regulated, Saar should be represented in the Political Community – at least with a certain number of representatives in the Peoples' Chamber. Braun remarked that the exact number was not decisive for the Saar representatives.

On 25 February in the Constitutional Committee, Teitgen's and Brentano's joint proposal had as the point of departure: 'The Saar and its people shall be an inherent part of the European Community. The people of the Saar shall share rights and duties of the Community in the same way as the peoples of the Member States'. Then an interim system of representation for the Saar was sketched (3 senators; the number of members in the Peoples' Chamber was left undefined).

The Saar issue illustrates a problem that the new type of polity provoked. The area's unresolved status was in 1952/53 clearly seen as a part of the planned Political Community. A solution within the 'principles' of the Political Community was not possible, an extraordinary arrangement was needed, but an arrangement enabling the Saar to be represented in the Senate was interpreted by some of the German members as a step towards recognising the Saar as a state, whereas the Saar representative Braun declared that without such representation, the Saar would stay outside the Political Community. In other words, the issue was 'in principle' not resolvable, but the Sub-committee could, following Teitgen & Brentano's proposal, agree on a *modus vivendi* until the regularisation of the Saar's status.

From both parliamentary and supranational perspective, the debates on seat distribution in the Ad Hoc Assembly tend to lack a supranational European vision. The question was rather to get special interests represented. The common tendency in the political science of the time was to subordinate parliaments and their specific resources to elections, parties and the government vs. opposition divide. It was overdramatised in the Ad Hoc Assembly's debates on seat distribution and on electoral systems at the cost of the sovereignty of the parliament and the independence of its members from voters and parties.

8.4 The Senate

The upper house of the Parliament of the Community was a subject of controversy and differing opinions in the Ad Hoc Assembly. These concerned its parliamentary vs. governmental character, the name of the Chamber, its mode of election, composition, distribution of seats, relationship to the Peoples' Chamber, the mandate of the members as well as its powers over nominating the President of the European Executive Council. The last question will be discussed in the next chapter. Questions like the mandate and its compatibilities with respect to parliamentarism have been discussed above.

8.4.1 A parliamentary chamber

The Questionnaire of the ECSC ministers, presented in the Constitutional Committee on 24 October 1952, left the Ad Hoc Assembly to decide on the relationships between the Second Chamber, the Council of Ministers and a possible single European Executive Government.

Already on 7 October 1952, the Working Party debated the subject of the Second Chamber. The background was Adenauer's address to the Common Assembly, in which he regarded the ECSC's Council of Ministers as a Second Chamber. In the opening sitting of the Common Assembly, Giovanni Persico said of the ECSC institutions: 'Ainsi, le Gouvernement serait la Haute Autorité, nous serions la Chambre et le Conseil de ministres représenterait le Sénat' (13 September 1952).

The Working Party Chair, Brentano, did not accept the bicameral parliament if one of the Chambers would be a Council of National Ministers. Merkatz was keen to note the ambiguity in the ECSC's Council of Ministers where it would be either 'un gouvernement européen ou un Chambre des États', the latter corresponding Adenauer's view for the Common Assembly. Merkatz supported both the First and Second Chambers being accorded 'un veritable role parlementaire', while the Council of Ministers would be 'le veritable organ exécutif' (7 October 1952).

Pierre Wigny referred to building up a Council of Federal Ministers as a supranational organ, assisted by the Council of National Ministers, at least as an interim solution. Fernand Dehousse strongly opposed the view that the Council of Ministers would be a second chamber, because juridically a government could not simultaneously be a legislative organ. André Mutter completely agreed with Dehousse (ibid.).

In the Constitutional Committee meeting on 24 October 1952, Dehousse told the Committee that nobody wanted the Second Chamber to be formed of the Council of Ministers, but he left it open to debate whether it should be elected by member state governments, governments and parliaments together, or solely by parliaments. Teitgen insisted that even if the parliament-elected and directly elected chambers would not, as van der Goes had claimed, be so different in their composition, it would still be necessary in order to advance the interests of the Political Community, and a parliament-elected Second Chamber should not be reduced to a Council of Ministers.

In his Note from 16 November to the Political Institutions Sub-committee, Dehousse presented four ideal-typical alternatives for the Second Chamber according to four main 'hypotheses' of what it would be: a) a Council of National Ministers; b) which would consist of ministers and government delegates; c) be composed of representatives of both government and parliament and d) be nominated by parliament, or a by a combination of several parliaments. The committee of jurists had prioritised the fourth alternative, as was also the practice of the ECSC.

In the debate of the Sub-committee on 17 November 1952, Teitgen concluded that among the alternative ways of selecting the Second Chamber, the Council of National Ministers and the 'conference of ambassadors' were ruled out. He called for specifying the parliamentary model by asking whether only governmental majorities or also the opposition would have the right to have seats in the Second Chamber. Merkatz asked whether the Second Chamber should represent the states or political currents within them, that is, whether it would be of an executive or a parliamentary character. He supported the alternative of co-determination by governments and parliaments and moved that the parliament should present the candidates, a third of which the government would select to the Second Chamber. Teitgen stated that in France it would be difficult to let the parliament elect members to the Second Chamber without an agreement with the government. Dehousse, for his part, also regarded excluding communist membership as an important requirement for the Second Chamber (17 November 1952).

The British observer Lord Walter Layton argued that, if the UK joined the European Political Community, the government should determine the members for the Second Chamber. Dennis Healey (Labour) added that he regarded the Council of Europe model as illustrating the maximum limit of the co-operation. Neither of them was willing to accept a parliamentary bicameralism (ibid.).

Teitgen argued that in the transitory stage there would either be no Second Chamber or that it would be the Council of Ministers. Van der Goes remarked that the EDC Treaty presupposed that the Second Chamber would be only for a definitive regime. Dehousse did not like the idea of a transitory regime replacing the Second Chamber with a Council of Ministers. Merkatz supported the Second Chamber for the transition period in order to prevent the executive from being autonomous (ibid.).

The debate in the Sub-committee is a nice example of a parliamentary debate without a resolution on the agenda. Such debate allowed members to offer thought experiments and to discuss their strengths and weaknesses from different points of view, partially relying on the historical examples, but also with a willingness to listen to each other and avoid taking fixed stands.

On 20 November 1952, Brentano presented his Note (dated 18 November) to the Political Institution Sub-committee. According to it, the assemblies of the ECSC and EDC would serve as special committees of the new Parliament, which would lead to a personal union between the parliaments. When the existing institutions were retained, 'the Second Chamber would only be required to carry out primary duties...attributed to the Political Community, or which may subsequently be attributed to it'. Dehousse doubted whether it was possible to leave the existing institutions autonomous within the new Community. For Brentano, the existing parliaments should be part of the First Chamber. Even with direct election, a personal union would be possible, as the ECSC Treaty allowed election of the Common Assembly either by direct voting in member states or by national parliaments. Teitgen remarked that for creating a truly European Political Authority, certain revisions of existing treaties would be necessary. Without the possibility to expand the range of competence of the Political Community, this remained in the air. For the Second Chamber, nomination by member state parliaments in cooperation with governments, with a proportional representation including opposition members, was at that stage a position widely endorsed by the Sub-committee (20 November 1952).

In the Sub-committee on 3 December 1952, Teitgen proposed to call the Second Chamber the 'Chamber of the States' (*Chambre des Etats*). Van der Goes did not like the title because the task of the chamber was to harmonise the interests between the states and the Community, and he proposed to call it a European Senate (*Sénat européen*). Montini agree with Van der Goes, referring to his suggestion that international organisations should be represented in it. Dehousse found the term 'Senate' problematic and insisted that the states would be its key forming elements. After that, Montini wanted to stay with the 'Second Chamber'. Dehousse saw that 'Chamber' and 'Senate', would be borrowing too closely from the terms used in national level, and that 'States' Chamber' would therefore be more eye-catching. Montini disagreed, saying that was not the nature of the states in question with the Political Community.

Continuing the debate on naming, van der Goes again defended 'Senate' for the supranational chamber, since it served as a link to the Council of Europe. As Montini was also ready to this, the term 'Senate' was endorsed by decision of the Sub-committee. Despite some lingering reservations against it, the term was finally accepted (3 December 1952) due in part to its use in the parliamentary tradition, and no further disputes about it arose in later debates.

In the Constitutional Committee on 17 December 1952, P.A. Blaisse argued, like several other Dutch members, for transition arrangements. He thought that at the beginning, a single chamber and the Council of National Ministers would suffice, while the Senate could be created over time as the powers of the Community developed. Van der Goes supported the maintaining the Senate with the view that the Council of National Ministers would gradually decline in importance and fade away. Max Becker opted for a real Senate without a Council of National Ministers, as the latter would not be genuinely democratic (17 December 1952).

In the debate in the Constitutional Committee on 20 December 1952, Nicolas Margue argued for maintaining both the Committee of Ministers and the Senate. Becker opposed a government-based Bundesrat system, wishing to get all the political shades and nuances represented in a Senate whose members would not change after every change in the ministries of the member states. Gerard Jaquet's amendment was interpreted by Dehousse as containing three principles: the Senate would represent the states; it would be a second assembly of the Parliament; and it would have equal powers with the First Chamber. The amendment was passed; however, there were two abstentions against the third principle.

In the plenum of 7 January 1953, Margue argued that if the Council of National Ministers represented the national interests, the Senate 'could be constituted as a genuine Parliamentary Assembly'. Helmut Bertram (CD) had moved that the Senate should represent national governments, which would make the Council of National Ministers superfluous, but this amendment was not supported. De Menthon's motion, that national parliaments should elect the Senate and its members would also be 'qualified to sit in the Consultative Assembly of the Council of Europe', was agreed to (Plenum 8 January 1953).

In the Political Institutions Sub-committee on 6 February 1953 Dehousse insisted that the different bases for electing the members of the Chamber and the Senate also guaranteed the influence of governments through the national parliaments. He saw the senators acting more like national coalitions than the 'free men' of the Peoples' Chamber, and he regarded the Senate as also being a link to the Consultative Assembly. This was in line with his view on the priority of the Peoples' Chamber and on the Senate as a council rather than a deliberative assembly, as he put it in the Note from 16 November 1952.

The parliamentarisation of the European Political Community was not decidedly fixed in the ESCS minister's resolution, and in the early phases of the

Ad Hoc Assembly, different models for the Second Chamber were brought to the agenda. When the Constitutional Committee in December 1952 confirmed the parliamentary title of 'the Senate' and decided on its election by the member-state parliaments, these were important commitments in favour of a parliamentary system of government, as was the direct election of the Peoples' Chamber

A third pillar of parliamentarism would then be the appointment of a President of the European Executive Council by the Senate, which was agreed to after several rounds of debate in the different fora of the Ad Hoc Assembly (see Chapter 9). Letting parliaments, not governments, decide on the composition of the Senate was another step towards a parliamentary supranationalism and terminating governments' monopoly in foreign policy.

The debates on the character and the powers of the Second Chamber, were among the most intense debates ever conducted in the Ad Hoc Assembly. The need for a Second Chamber and its mode of election without a transition period as well as for a clear separation between the parliamentary chamber and the hybrid Council of National Ministers as well as the Second Chamber's powers were not self-evident matters. The Assembly agreed on them after debates without any precedent resolution. The decision of a parliamentary chamber elected by member state parliaments marks, however, the consistent striving of the Ad Hoc Assembly to combine the supranational Community with a parliamentary system of government.

8.4.2 Parity or balancing of seats

In his note from 16 November, Fernand Dehousse asked, whether the distribution of seats in the Second Chamber should be 'based on the principle of parity representation, or on that of a balanced (*pondéré*) representation of the Member States'. For him the former model neither corresponded to the reality of the states nor to the development of representation in international organisations.

In the Political Institutions Sub-committee on 17 November, Merkatz noted that the parity presupposed the sovereignty of each state, whereas in the European Political Community, as in the Norddeutscher Bund in the nineteenth century, a balanced representation should be practised. Teitgen remarked that no single country should be able to impose its will on the Community as a whole. Merkatz affirmed that balanced representation rather than parity representation had traditionally protected small states better. Teitgen, alluding to a reservation expressed by Schaus, wanted to postpone the decision, but a majority of the Sub-committee supported balanced representation in the Second Chamber.

In the Constitutional Committee on 20 December 1952, the debate was reopened. The main proponent of parity was Pierre Wigny. For him, the First Chamber represented the populations, the Second the states, and the latter could not be replaced by a Committee of Ministers with declining influence, nor could a state be represented by its governing party. One of his arguments was that the composition of a balanced parliament-elected chamber would not be sufficiently different from that of the Peoples' Chamber. Dehousse emphasised that the principle of balance in the distribution of seats would not be the same for the two chambers. Wigny's amendment was rejected by the Committee by 12 votes to 1, with 2 abstentions.

In the plenum on 8 January 1953, Wigny moved for an amendment for parity representation in the Senate in the name of providing an 'equal footing' for the small nations. Marga Klompé (CD) agreed with Wigny on parity. In debating their joint amendment, Teitgen said that after the decision on the Peoples' Chamber, he 'felt reluctant to oblige to vote in favour of parity in the case of the Senate'. He was supported by Pierre de Smet (CD) and Eugène Schaus. Wigny referred to existing federations and that the States should 'be put on equal footing'. Klompé insisted that 'the Senate be composed of members of National Parliaments', and she thought that the Senate 'would in the future be invested with the competences of the Committee of National Ministers'. Maan Sassen (CD) supported the amendment, the rejection of which 'would constitute a serious warning to the small nations'. In the vote, the amendment was rejected (9 January 1953).

In the Constitutional Committee on 7 February 1953, Wigny continued to defend the idea of electing the Peoples' Chamber based on population and the Senate based on parity, insisting that the formation of a majority against the small states should be avoided. Schaus supported *nolens volens* Wigny, as the powers of governments would decline in the Committee proposal, and he saw this as being a question about the survival of the state of Luxembourg. Johannes Semler maintained that the parity proposal lost its usefulness after it had been decided to retain the Council of National Ministers.

Still on the final plenum on 7 March, Maan Sassen and Pierre de Smet defended parity in the Senate and would see the role of the European Political Community in the economic and social field as 'merely one of supervision'. The fierce controversy over parity vs. balanced representation in the Senate did not concern just the divide between small and big countries in the Political Community. In it, the traditional federalist principle of representation in the upper chamber was opposed to the supranational idea of parliamentary representation based on different principles. The debate also involved the different electoral modes and parliamentary terms of the two chambers, as well as the opposition between a parliamentary vs. a governmental basis of representing member states.

Wigny again defended parity between member states in the Senate as being for the protection of small countries, that is, if the Council of National Ministers were to be abolished later, but he did not want to vote against the Draft. Van der Goes disputed Wigny's argument that parity in the Senate would be advantageous for small countries, as the Senate could be paralysed due to overrepresentation. In the vote Wigny's amendment was rejected (7 March 1953).

The member-state quotas in the distribution of the seats of both houses has been seen as a weak spot in the Draft Treaty. Schorkopf regards the double balancing of the seats to indicate that one of the chambers was superfluous (*überflüßig*), and that its democratic legitimisation deviated therefore from the principle of equal freedom (2023, 67). Against this view, it is possible to argue that, as unfair as such distribution might appear from the point of view of a mimetic representation of the member states, it could have strengthened the independence of parliamentarians of both chambers from their electorates, in the sense of Frank Ankersmit, according to whom representation creates both the represented and the representatives (2002, 115).

8.4.3 Membership and term length

In the Ad Hoc Assembly's debates on the membership of the Senate of European Political Community, the system for seats in the national parliaments was assumed as the starting point, but its exclusivity was disputed on different grounds. Among them were the debates on the term length of the Senate: if its composition was constantly liable to alteration due to the different rhythms of the parliamentary elections in the member states, then the composition of the Senate would be marked by a volatility that was not appropriate for its parliamentary powers. Therefore the debate on determining a term length for the Senate was put onto the Ad Hoc Assembly's agenda. Additional issues, such as the size of the Senate in relation to the Peoples' Chamber, were also debated. Behind these debates were such principles as guaranteeing the parliamentary quality and function of the Senate. This was also part of the debates on the Senate's power to choose governments. This shall be dealt with in Chapter 9.

In his Note presented to the Political Institutions Sub-committee on 14 November 1952, Pierre-Henri Teitgen argued that restricting membership to national parliamentarians 'might deprive the European Assembly from other personalities'. Therefore it would be best 'to allow a plurality of offices without making them obligatory'. For a directly elected First Chamber, restricting the membership to national parliamentarians does not make sense, but, as Teitgen insisted, nothing should prevent member state parliamentarians from being elected directly to the First Chamber.

In his Note to the Political Institutions Sub-committee from 16 November 1952, Fernand Dehousse asked: When the Chamber is elected by parliaments, should a proportional or majoritarian system be adopted? Dehousse argued that nobody supported the idea of requiring unanimous decisions, but whether a simple majority or for certain issues a qualified majority was required remained to be debated. This topic became relevant in connection with the question of votes of no confidence for the government (to be discussed in Chapter 9).

In the 17 November sitting of the Sub-committee, van der Goes asked whether members of the Second Chamber should be parliamentarians, to which Dehousse replied that this could be left to the countries, as he himself supported the possibility of including, for example, trade union-based members. Merkatz opposed this, while Teitgen concluded that a majority of the Second Chamber should consist of parliamentarians. Merkatz suggested that the Chamber could co-opt 'eminent personalities' from university or industry, and Teitgen referred to Montini's proposal to include representatives from international organisations, if a procedure of co-optation was allowed. A difference to the First Chamber would then be that the members of the Second would not be expected to be professional politicians.

In the Constitutional Committee on 20 December 1952, Becker opposed the Bundesrat-style of sole government representation in favour of representation in which the Senate would reflect the whole spectrum of political shades and nuances. Becker also felt that members should not change after every change of ministry in a member state. Brentano argued that, for co-ordination between the Community and the national parliaments, the Senators should be members of the parliament of their own countries.

In the Sub-committee Teitgen thematised the number of members in the Second Chamber. Dehousse thought that the Second Chamber should have a size of a half or a third that of the First Chamber. Teitgen took the 87-member Chamber of the European Defence Community as the model for this, and this was accepted (17 November 1952). In the plenum, Vinizio Ziino moved an amendment to double the number of senators. He defended this by saying that with this, 'the numerical inferiority of the Senate would be too marked' in the joint meetings of the chambers (9 January 1953).

In the December session of the Constitutional Committee, the relationship of the Senate with the Council of Europe was debated. The associated members would have an annual 'Conference' with the European Executive Council and the Council of National Ministers. The members of the Senate were to be allowed to serve simultaneously as members of the Consultative Assembly of the Council of Europe. Conversely, observers from the Council of Europe countries could attend Senate sittings (Draft 20 December 1952).

These arrangements led to the expectation that the Political Community would become an attractive model for European unification and that other Council countries could later apply for membership. However, Wigny refused linking the Senate to the Council of Europe (Constitutional Committee, 20 December 1952). In the plenum debate of 9 January 1953, de Menthon's motion was agreed to that, since national parliaments elect the Senate, its members would also be 'qualified to sit in the Consultative Assembly of the Council of Europe'.

Another topic debated on 6 February 1953 in the Political Institutions Sub-committee was the length of the parliamentary term. Teitgen moved that the term would be longer than that of national parliaments and asked further, what would happen if a European parliamentarian were not re-elected to the national parliament. Dehousse immediately responded that the member should continue to be a European parliamentarian. Merkatz also did not require a European parliamentarian to be a member of Parliament in their home country, but he thought that six years was too long a period, thinking that five years would be better. This debate concerned only elections to the Senate by the member state parliaments, where problems would necessarily arise when a parliamentary term was longer than in the home country. The previous debates indicated that Senators did not need to be parliamentarians from the beginning of their term, but if politicians were to be elected to the Senate, parliamentary experience could be appropriate. To resolve the ambiguities, Dehousse moved for a 5-year term for the Senate, and this was agreed.

On 11 February, however, it was agreed, as Merkatz proposed, for the parliamentary term of the Senate to follow the practice of the national parliaments which had elected them. Dehousse added that the senators would retain their seats until their successors have been elected.

On 14 February 1953, the Sub-committee returned to the term of the Senate, in view of the Senate's electing of the President of the European Executive Council. Dehousse strived for making the Senate more stable, and he proposed a fixed 5-years term for it. Antonio Azara agreed on the fixed-term, which would free the Senate from worrying about re-election, but he was afraid that including abstentions in voting when counting them, as Dehousse proposed, would paralyse the Senate. Brentano thought that, since Senators are elected by their national parliaments, their terms must end with the term of the electing parliament.

The next round took place in the Constitutional Committee on 23 February 1953. Regarding the term of the senators, that day's version of the Draft Treaty, article 16, stated that a senator not re-elected to the member state parliament shall stay in the Senate until the successor has been elected. Debré and Teitgen opposed, but Dehousse emphasised that for the Executive Council, a certain stability in parliamentary chambers would be an advantage. Merkatz opposed the principle that members who were voted out of the parliament would stay in the Senate until a replacement was elected. He was worried that this would lead to most senators being not members of their national Parliaments. This was a concern as he regarded the task of the Senate to be to harmonise the national and Community policies.

In the plenum of 7 March, the term of the Senate was again debated. For article 16, Dehousse returned to his once-agreed amendment to choose the Senate for a fixed 5-year period. The amendment had been dealt with in the Working Party on 6 March, in which Dehousse defended the amendment with the argument that the Assembly had given the Senate important prerogatives, whereas he himself had originally opted for the priority of the Peoples' Chamber. For this reason, he felt it did not work if the Senate members had a mandate of indefinite duration and consist then of a mere *Assemblée de passants*. In the Working Party, Teitgen argued against the amendment with the argument that the senators then would no longer have their 'legal bases in the Assembly'. Merkatz also noted that the amendment would change the character of the Senate, making it consist of members outside Parliament, unlike what the Committee had wanted. Chair Brentano interrupted the discussion and stated that the Working Party could not take a stand in the question.

In the Assembly plenum on 7 March 1953, Wigny supported Dehousse's amendment with the argument that membership in the Senate should be as stable as in the Chamber. Ziino also said that he would vote for Dehousse's amendment. He marked the important point that the Committee's proposal 'would be only justified if elections were held simultaneously for the Senates of all the Six States'. Georges Jean Laffargue (CD) noted, however, that the Senators would represent 'the various political trends existing in the assemblies', thus making the composition sensitive to shifts in the polities. Jean Fohrmann (Soc) proposed 'that the term of office of a Senator should expire if his national Parliament withdrew his [sic] mandate', which would have provided an interesting analogue to a vote of no confidence in senators during a fixed term.

Merkatz supported the Committee's proposal with the argument that the 'chief task of the Senate was to provide a link between the European Parliament and the national Parliaments', which was not possible if the Senate was elected for a fixed term. Hermann Kopf supported this view, citing the favourable experiences with the Council of Europe. Piet Vermeylen (Soc), whose amendment had concerned election of the President of the Executive Council by the Senate (see Chapter 9), supported Dehousse's amendment, which was agreed (26 votes for, 13 abstentions).

Fernand Dehousse had expressed his concerns in the Assembly about the Community's government would be sufficiently stable, not only due to frequent governmental changes in member states by occasional changes in the parliamentary majorities, but more generally to guarantee a certain permanency for the Executive Council as the only regularly sitting institution of the new Political Community. He had realised the strong position given to the Senate in the power to elect the President of the Council. Protecting the Senate from a dissolution of parliament would require a more permanent composition of the Senate than that resulting from the varying and partly unpredictable rhythms of the changing constellations in the member state parliaments. In the last minute, he also managed to get the support of the majority of the Ad Hoc Assembly for his amendment for a five-year Senate.

The debate on the Senate's term is another topic binding the supranational and parliamentary perspectives together. Merkatz still had reservations against a Senate that would be fully independent of the member state parliaments. Teitgen's critique of Dehousse rested on different grounds, namely the parliamentary principle of discontinuation of the mandate when membership in the electing parliament was terminated. Dehousse's argument was that, for a supranational parliament, the priority of elections is less important than the parliamentary stability and efficiency of the Senate. He combined an admission of Teitgen's argument with support for a fixed-term Senate in which membership would be, beyond the moment of election, independent of the electing parliaments and their different electoral cycles. I consider this move of Dehousse, supported by the Assembly majority, another ingenious instrument for guaranteeing parliamentary government on the supranational level. During that term, senators with a background of expertise and representation of interests could learn to act as parliamentary politicians.

Finally, it can be stated that there were no proposals in the Ad Hoc Assembly to adopt a common principle for the upper houses, namely a higher age qualification for membership. The point was not to provide a barrier against any hasty reforms of the directly elected chamber, but to accept the principle of equal powers for the two chambers. However, the debates on standing for election and dismissal of the government might have complicated this ideal (see Chapter 9).

8.5 Towards a supranational parliament

When the Ad Hoc Assembly began its work in autumn 1952, it had vague ideas on applying parliamentary principles to the European Political Community as a supranational polity. Several members had doubts about this and were unwilling to sacrifice the powers of member state parliaments to the supranational level. Against the background of the cautionary examples of powerless parliaments, the experienced parliamentarians used their political imagination and managed to render the Parliament of the Community in the Draft Treaty close to an ordinary parliament.

This did not concern so much the range of issues on the agenda, for which the guidelines remained restricted, for the members hoped to expand their powers and competence at a later stage. The point was the political form of organisation, including such elementary principles as the direct election of the

Peoples' Chamber, the exclusion of both the imperative mandate and voting by delegation, which directed the Parliament's agenda to struggles over the form of the polity and the policy direction of the European Executive Council, instead of to diplomatic negotiations between member states. Although the seat distribution remained on an inter-state basis, it transcended in both chambers the 'mimetic' ideal (see Ankersmit 1996) of the size of the population and of parity between states (which posed a danger of a *de facto* veto by member states).

Characteristic of the debates was an open mind not only for the arguments presented in the debate, but also in being willing to reconsider what had been previously agreed to. Especially regarding the second chamber, the main actors in the Constitutional Committee and Political Institutions Sub-committee, such as Fernand Dehousse, Pierre-Henri Teitgen and Heinrich v. Brentano, changed their views several times. I consider Dehousse's finally accepted amendment for a 5-year fixed-term Senate as a masterpiece of political argument, connected to the mode of electing the head of the government, the European Executive Council, by the Senate.

Of course, we can in retrospect judge that in certain respects the resulting Parliament of the Draft Treaty was not in every respect very courageous. The disputes on members state quotas illustrate the persisting limits of supranational thinking: for example, the possibility of electing citizens from other member states as representatives to either of the parliamentary chambers was not mentioned at all. The professionalisation of membership was still excluded, in terms of the sitting period and in assuming the part-time character of the Parliament's membership in both chambers (including even those who were ministers in their member state governments). The payment of members, for example, was not taken up at all in the debates or in the Draft Treaty. Nonetheless, the full parliamentary character of both chambers did contain possibilities to alter the Parliament of the Community from within.

The debates on the European Parliament and its two chambers also illustrate insights into how the somewhat conflicting demands of the supranational and the parliamentary forms of politicisation might be combined. Teitgen's and Dehousse's concerns about the stability of the European Executive Council was not only due to the potential fragility of this new type of governmental institution as such. It was partly also due to the historical experiences of a certain over-eagerness of parliamentarians in dissensus, as noted already by Bagehot, when he insisted on the position of parliamentary ministers as balancing the demands of the ministry with those of the parliamentarians (1867/72, chapter 7). Translated to the context of the Ad Hoc Assembly's debates, the combining of a stable European government and an assembly of genuinely parliamentary quality was necessary for such a balance. How this was done at the level of the details was partly solved by the bi-cameral parliament, but it depended ultimately on its type of relationship to the Government. This will be discussed in Chapter 9.

9 The European government

The High Authority of the ECSC was an example of a supranational executive. For it, there was no recommendation that the members of the High Authority should be politicians, and they were not elected by parliamentary assemblies. Although the ECSC was, like the EDC, planned to be first included in and later integrated with in the European Political Community, it provided a hardly reproducible model for a supranational European government.

As no acceptable models existed, the Ad Hoc Assembly had to invent how a democratic and parliamentary European government for the six member states could and should look. Unlike the Parliament, the executive would be a permanent institution and should be capable of the political 'leadership' of the European Political Community. It should be responsible to the parliament and consist of politicians. To fulfil these criteria, frequent changes in governments, which were still a common practice, especially in the French Fourth Republic, were to be avoided.

A politically responsible permanent executive government was a major new idea of the European Political Community. Avoiding the temptation of a 'rule by officialdom' (*Beamtenherrschaft*), which necessarily lacked the capacity to act politically, as emphasised by Bagehot (1867/72, 130–135) and Weber (1918, 225–227), was a challenge for setting up the European Executive Council. The Ad Hoc Assembly members understood well that extending the principle of parliamentary government to the supranational polity was, in principle, a precondition for a politically responsible European government. How this was to be realised was a topic of thorough debate with shifting standpoints in the Ad Hoc Assembly.

9.1 Council of National Ministers

In analysing the parliamentary chambers (above), I already discussed how the Ad Hoc Assembly dissociated itself from the Council of National Ministers as a second chamber. Before analysing the European Executive Council, I shall discuss how the Assembly finally agreed to maintain that hybrid executive and proto-parliamentary institution, inherited from the ECSC, and what kinds of powers it left to it.

As quoted above (8.4.1), Hans-Joachim v. Merkatz said that the Council of National Ministers could be interpreted either as a European government or as a chamber of the states (Working Party on 7 October 1952). Pierre Wigny took up this idea in the same sitting, seeking a balance between the will in favour of a common Europe versus the national suspicions towards it. Wigny argued that the Council of Federal Ministers with its powers of decision-making should be complemented with an advisory Council of National Ministers, 'qui donnerait son avis', to the federal Council of Ministers.

From the outset, the legitimacy of the Council was controversial in the Ad Hoc Assembly. The Political Institutions Sub-committee dealt with the executive on 18 November 1952. Fernand Dehousse spoke 'à titre personnel' against the maintenance of the Council of National Ministers. Eugène Schaus thought that the Sub-committee had already taken out too much of the governments' influence, and thus he supported maintaining the Council. Chair Pierre-Henri Teitgen proposed three alternatives: the Committee of National Ministers would form the Second Chamber; it would continue during the transition period; or it would confirm that the Executive would co-operate with the national ministers, which was the solution he preferred (18 November 1952).

On 20 November in the Sub-committee, a clear majority of members, including Georg Pelster (CD), Max Becker, Dehousse and Teitgen, turned against requiring unanimity in the Committee of National Ministers, that is, a *de facto* veto right for single member states. No opposition to this was forthcoming from Schaus either. Special cases, such as Treaty changes, should be discussed separately. Already in the 'Europe of the Six' the veto of one minister of the member states was regarded as a critical weakness to be avoided. Only by excluding the veto could the Council retain its legitimacy, and yet, several members still opted for dispensing with such a Council.

On 4 December, Dehousse expressed his preference for the title 'Council of National Ministers' over the alternative proposal, 'Conference'. Teitgen found 'Council' inappropriate because the ministers convened only in conferences. He defended the term 'conference' on behalf of the associated states on the ground that they do not have a common interest against the Community. Marinus van der Goes opposed what he saw as the Council of National Ministers' excessive level of influence. Dehousse pointed out that the Council of European Ministers would meet continuously (*en permanence*), as would perhaps the Council of National Ministers, whereas 'Conference' suggested only had periods of being in session. Schaus asked why such a conference was needed. Dehousse insisted that an executive organ cannot be a conference, and he warned that it posed the danger of paralysing (*étouffer*) the Community. In the vote, the Sub-committee agreed on European Executive Council and Committee of National Ministers. For Teitgen, federalist chances were greater if the Council of National Ministers were part of the Executive and not of the Chambers (Sub-committee 5 December 1952).

In this debate the status of the body remained unclear. The terms 'conference' and 'committee' suggest an intergovernmental meeting of ministers, or multilateral diplomatic practices based on agreements and the veto rights of governments. In contrast, 'council' indicates an institution of the Community consisting of government members, but acting as a deliberative institution, in which votes are counted and members are not bound to the instructions of their governments.

In subsequent debates, the powers of the Council of National Ministers were defended mainly by those who were suspicious of too much supranationalism, whereas several other members found it redundant or at least that it would decline in power during the establishment of the Political Community. Dehousse accepted the 'Council of National Ministers' only as a part of the compromise when no veto power for single member countries was granted (Sub-committee 5 December 1952).

In the Constitutional Committee on 20 December 1952, P.A. Blaisse thought that at the beginning that a one-chamber parliament and the Council of National Ministers would suffice, and that the Senate could be created over time along as the powers of the Community grew. To keep the Community simple, not all decisions of the Executive Council need to be submitted to the National Ministers. Sieuwert Bruins Slot argued that, due to the current economic and military problems, a Council of National Ministers instead of a Senate was needed in the bicameral system. Teitgen reported the Sub-committee's view that a Council of National Ministers would be introduced to the Political Community for facilitating its acceptance among the member states (20 December 1952).

Reporting to the Assembly plenum on 7 January 1953, Dehousse repeated the Sub-committee's view that the Council of National Ministers would form a second part of the European executive. Its task was 'approving' the decisions of the Executive Council but requiring no unanimity in the sense of a 'veto' by member states. In the later debates, the terms 'conference' or 'committee' were no longer used.

In the plenary debate on 8 January 1953, Piet Vermeylen expressed his judgement that the 'Executive of the European Community should have to be entirely independent of the national Governments', the Council of National Ministers should have 'only advisory power', and supervision by the Senate 'would ensure full protection of national interests'. For Helmut Bertram, the Senate should represent national governments, which would make the Council of National Ministers superfluous. More radically, François de Menthon said that for increasing parliamentary powers 'the Council of National Ministers should be eliminated from the European Executive; the Head of the Executive should be appointed by the European Parliament'. Marga Klompé did not want social and economic powers 'entrusted to the Government of Europe'. The Council of Ministers should not disappear, but unanimity was not to be required. Giovanni Persico wanted to remove the unanimous agreement of the Council of Ministers – it was enough sufficient if they were provided the opportunity to be heard from (8 January 1953).

In the plenum of 9 January 1953, Dehousse asked on behalf of the Subcommittee three questions: 'Should the Council of National Ministers be maintained or not? In the affirmative, should it be part of the European Executive Authority, and what powers it should have and how should it operate?' He mentioned that the Working Party (resolution 9 January) had adopted Paul Reynaud's amendment, according to which the Council 'exercises its powers to harmonise the action of the European Executive Council and that of the Governments'. The proposal also included a periodic conference between the European Executive Council, the Council of National Ministers and 'the Representatives of the Associated States'.

In the debate, Becker remarked that, as the veto right had been removed from the proposal of the Working Party, he was now willing to support the Council of National Ministers. Wigny did not regard Reynaud's text as 'adequate against the Council of National Ministers exercising a guardian's role over the European Executive'. He regretted the decision against parity in the Senate and thought that small States' representatives might be 'resolved to conserve for the Council of National Ministers a function important enough to provide the guarantee which they had been denied elsewhere'. When the parity-based Senate was rejected, Wigny regarded the Council as its surrogate in defending small states rather than defending single member states against the supranational Community. Marga Klompé asked whether 'unanimity would be required in certain cases', and Dehousse acknowledge that this might indeed sometimes occur (Plenum 9 January 1953).

In the final plenum, on 7 March 1953, Vermeylen again moved for abolishing the Council of National Ministers (Article 9). He felt that 'the Council, which would not be under the control of the Community, should not appear in the list of the Community's institutions'. This view joined supranationalism explicitly to parliamentarism and led him to assume 'that in a few years' time the Council of National Ministers would no longer be needed'. Francisco Maria Dominedò, on the contrary, insisted that 'the Council of National Ministers should be considered as an international body and not a supranational one', identifying international with intergovernmental. For Vinicio Ziino 'the Council of National Ministers was not an executive body, and was not therefore subject to Parliamentary supervision', and therefore he wanted to retain the article, although he seems not to have regarded it as an embryonic third chamber of parliament either. Dehousse defended the presence of the Council in the Statute, not as a 'federal organ' but 'nevertheless a part of the Community' when its opinion was asked for in several questions initiated by the European Executive Council. After that explication, Vermeylen withdrew his amendment (7 March 1953).

Marcel Plaisant (Lib) moved: 'The Council of National Ministers is empowered to make suitable proposal to the European Executive Council, which proposal, if not debated by it, shall be transmitted to one of the other Chambers'. With the right to initiative, the Council would act as like a parliamentary chamber (consisting only of six ministers), and the final wording indicates that Plaisant himself understood that well (ibid.).

Dehousse discussed the 'far-reaching' implications of such a view. 'It would place the European Parliament into the position of a judge in any disputes which might arise between the Council of National Ministers and the European Executive Council. Moreover, it would make the Council of National Ministers indirectly responsible to the European Parliament which would lead to impossible situations.' In other words, Dehousse understood the problems arising from dualistic governments, and he did not see any point in overloading parliaments with disputes between two executives (ibid.).

Plaisant's amendment was not seconded. He further moved the Senate to add to those bodies that could convene the Council of National Ministers, and it would be able to do so 'by a majority resolution'; however, the amendment failed to garner support (ibid.).

The questions that Dehousse had provided for the January plenum illustrate an important problem: How to serve as a mediator between the views of the European Executive Council with those of the member state governments. One alternative would have been to organise for that purpose only periodic conferences of member state ministers. Another would have been to use – as Vermeylen, Wigny or Merkatz argued – the Senate for this purpose, including, as Merkatz had proposed, both government and parliament representatives as Senators. The Council of National Ministers provided a third alternative: requiring that each government elects a minister for European affairs, as proposed by Montini in the Sub-committee on 20 November 1952, and convening the elected ministers into a Council. If it would possess a veto power, the Council would have been a diplomatic institution; if majority votes were allowed, the Council would have a proto-parliamentary character, for this would rule out an imperative mandate, as it did in the ESCS Council, and let the ministers deliberate without being bound to the instructions of governments, which instructions in any case were not always available when European issues were at stake. Understood in this manner, the Council of National Ministers would not necessarily have been opposed to a supranational European government, but instead it could serve as its advisory body.

Nonetheless, the Council of National Ministers remained a *Fremdkörper*. As the European Executive Council had, similarly to the High Authority of the ECSC, a quasi-monopoly on political initiative with respect to the Parliament and the Council of National Ministers, the Parliament's and Council's main power shares were amendments and adjournments, like those of parliamentary chambers, as well as diplomatic mechanisms of negotiation between the two parts of the executive government. Stopping a government initiative with a unanimous veto was a marginal case. No real conciliation mechanism for dissent between the two Councils were discussed, which meant that the majority view of National Ministers could have been frequently ignored by the Executive Council.

The result of deliberations in the Council were in principle independent of the member states' governments. The justification for the Council of National Ministers was for some supporters based on the assumption that the Council would express reservations against supranationalism or parliamentarism, or both, on the European level, as if the member states could form a common front against Europeanisation. In the rare cases that might require unanimity of the Council, a single minister's veto was possible. The Council of Ministers had a built-in suspicion inside the European Government, not only against the Executive Council, but also against the Executive Council's responsibility to the Parliament. From this perspective, the members who wanted to dispense with the Council of National Ministers had good grounds.

The acceptance of the Council could, as I think Dehousse's did, rely on the assumption that with a growing Europeanisation, the suspicions against a supranational government could disappear or be replaced by diplomatic negotiations between the Community and member states. In this experimental way, it could then be possible to redraw the borders between supranational and national as well as between parliamentary and governmental powers. Whether a Council of National Ministers could have served such objectives is another matter.

We could think of a 'Europeanising' moment of the current Council of EU as being visible in that, unlike in the former Council of Ministers, where only specialised 'Europe ministers' participated, nowadays practically all cabinet ministers are expected to participate in their turn in the meetings. In this way it is hardly possible to deny that the EU and a degree of supranational politics is an inherent part of member countries' domestic politics. In this sense the Council could be a place for ministers to exchange experiences and opinions on Europe with their colleagues.

If the parliamentarisation of supranational politics, as planned for the European Political Community, had been realised, also parliaments could have been included in the representation of member states. They would have not been merely a Senate-electing institution but would have institutionalised the control of their own government's European politics and policy. Renaming the 'Council of Ministers' to 'Council of the European Union' indicates the possibility of allowing each country to be represented by parliamentarians, in parity with the ministers, and contributing to parliamentarisation of the mediation between the national and supranational levels.

9.2 The European Executive Council

An innovation of the Ad Hoc Assembly was the European Executive Council, a permanent governmental institution planned to 'lead' the European Political Community. The contrast to intergovernmental institutions was most explicit in the setup of this supranational political executive under parliamentary control. It is therefore worth looking closer at both the character of this institution and the precise forms of parliamentary control, as debated in the Ad Hoc Assembly and proposed in its Draft Treaty.

9.2.1 Composition, powers, activity

The European Executive Council formed the main part of the executive government of the European Political Community. As discussed in section 6.1.3, it was understood as a European government, although this name was officially avoided, yet its members were to be called ministers. Calling the Chair Prime Minister was never discussed; however, this is not odd when considering that the French and the Italian head of government was called the President of the Council, while in Germany, the head of government was the *Bundeskanzler*.

The Political Institutions Sub-committee of the Ad Hoc Assembly had the 'Federal' Council of Ministers on its agenda on 6 November 1952. In the sitting of 18 November, Chair Teitgen spelled out the principles of how the European Executive Council should be responsible to the European Parliament, how the control of the Executive was the most important function of the Parliament, how the Executive could not consist of national ministers, and how the European ministers could not be national ministers.

Marinus van der Goes opted for calling the executive *Haute Authorité*, as in the ECSC, with the Council of Ministers as a supplement body (*co-facteur*). He was supported by Fernand Dehousse but opposed by Heinrich v. Brentano, for whom the Executive of the Community was on a different level than the High Authority of the ECSC. Hans-Joachim v. Merkatz suggested the formula of High Executive Council. Dehousse acknowledged that further debate was needed (18 November 1952).

A huge debate arose on Brentano's proposal to leave the executives of the ECSC and EDC unchanged. Teitgen saw there a danger that the High Authorities would become irresponsible technocracies and therefore the rapid creation of a political authority to assume the direction of the Political Community was needed. It was decided that the Political Community would not have a Head of State, the Executive Council should be of collegial character and its President represent it at protocolary and international occasions, and that the member states would create ministers of Europe for the Council of National Ministers (ibid.).

Michel Debré in his opposition to supranationalism was also against instituting a European government. In the Constitutional Committee on 17 December 1952, he followed a recent proposal of Adenauer by holding a meeting of the six heads of governments, which for the moment was the only possible form of co-operation. In the 1960s Charles de Gaulle as French President took up a similar proposal, which can be seen as the origin of the present-day European Council.

A first version for the statute on the European Executive Council was contained in Dehousse's Report to the Constitutional Committee, based on the debates in the Political Institutions Sub-committee, dated 15 December 1952. The point of departure was a Council of nine members. The President would choose six of the *collaborateurs* either from among the members of the European Parliament or outside it, whereas the Chairs of the ECSC High Authority and the EDC Commissariat would be *ex officio* members of the Council. A major principle was that the European Executive Council was to be organised as a permanent institution. The proposal also referred to the debates on the election of the President, which I shall deal with in the next section.

Dehousse concluded in his Report that the Sub-committee's proposal was for a parliamentary system, with the Executive Council being responsible to the Parliament of the Community, although the Swiss system of government, due to its stability, was also considered. By opting for the parliamentary responsibility of the Executive Council, the Committee 'wished to make the political institutions of the European Community conform to the constitutional principles which they [the member states, KP] themselves are applying' (Report Dehousse, 15 December 1952). A strict separation-of-powers system could not be used for a supranational polity in the same way as in national models.

The Executive Council would be in charge of the general policy of the Community, setting the political line also for the 'special communities' of the ECSC and EDC as well as negotiating the Treaties of the European Political Community. The Political Institutions Sub-committee emphasised maintaining democratic regimes and individual freedoms in the member states. Besides submitting appeals to the European Convention of Human Rights, the European Executive Council could also use other juridical instruments and support member states in maintaining democratic institutions and individual liberties. The Executive Council thus had clearly supranational competence, which Schorkopf (2023, 62) sees as the decisive supranational moment of the Draft Treaty.

In the plenum on 7 January 1953, the Constitutional Committee Chair Brentano emphasised the aim that '[t]he Political Authority to be created would be assisted by genuine Political Parliamentary Control'. The novel formula lies in the creation of a supranational governmental institution, the European Executive Council, while the Parliament is giving an 'assisting' role in the control of it. In this context, however, the point was rather seen in contrasting the 'genuine parliamentary' control of the 'Political Authority' with the 'High Authority' of the ECSC. Brentano further pointed out: 'It was the task of the Community to develop a dynamic force of its own'. Teitgen argued that the Executive should be responsible to the European Parliament as this control was most important function of the Parliament. The Executive consists of a small number of ministers, who should not he national ministers. He thereby explicitly affirmed supranationalism over intergovernmentalism (7 January 1953).

The permanent European Executive Council was the decisive link between supranationalism and parliamentarism in the Draft Treaty. It left to the Council of National Ministers no veto power; however, agreement with it was needed in certain issues. The parliamentary quality of the government was also in understanding it as a cabinet collegium of mutually equal members. The President selected the members and could also dismiss them but was only a *primus inter pares* in the collegium sittings. The ministers were at least tacitly assumed to be politicians.

9.2.2 Election and parliamentary responsibility

In the Political Institutions Sub-committee on 18 November 1952, Pierre-Henri Teitgen thought it realistic that the members of the European Executive be nominated by the Council of National Ministers. He regarded it as important that the members of European Executive Council would have the confidence of both the European Parliament and the member state governments.

On 20 November, Fernand Dehousse posed two alternatives to the Sub-committee for nominating the Executive: 1) that the member states nominate it, which raised the question of what use the Council of National Ministers would then have; 2) that, as in parliamentary government, the First Chamber elects the President, who then forms the government. Although Teitgen recognised the value of parliamentary government, he still thought that the Council of National Ministers should nominate the President as well as the members of the Council of Ministers. When Dehousse's proposal was rejected, Teitgen presented two new possibilities. The first was that the President be nominated by the national governments, but the President would then choose the ministers from among the members of the Assembly. The second was that the Council of National Ministers choose six ministers, who would elect would elect one of themselves as president. The selection of ministers would in the former case follow the Westminster practice; the second would be closer to the model of the Swiss Bundesrat (20 November 1952).

Dehousse then proposed a further alternative: the First Chamber would nominate the President, who then chooses the ministers. Brentano supported this proposal. Schaus asked whether then the Council of National Ministers would be continued. Dehousse affirmed this, but argued that that Council would be all too powerful if it elected the President of the Executive Council. Brentano also thought that the European idea would be undermined (*nuire*) if the Parliament were not given the power to nominate the President of the Executive, while the six ministers would be allowed to respect their national sovereignty, thus implying a ministerial quota for the member states. When put to the vote, the Sub-committee agreed that the First Chamber would nominate the President, who then would freely choose the members of the collegium. The European Executive Collegium would also include the Presidents of the ECSC and the EDC. Brentano added the condition that the European Executive Collegium must enjoy the confidence of the two Chambers of Parliament (ibid.).

The Political Institutions Sub-committee decided on 3 December, in accordance with the previous debates: '[With regard to] the European Executive Body...its Chairman will be appointed by methods which will be settled later, by a majority decision of the First Chamber ... the Chairman [*Président*]... will select six members of the European Executive Body from among the members of the two Chambers or from persons of high standing not belonging to either Chamber.' The executive will be reinforced by 'the chairs of the High Authority and of the EDC Commissariat'. However, 'it was agreed that the first Chairman of the Executive Body...will be appointed by the Council of Ministers. The European Parliament will have to give its assent'. (3 December 1952)

This was a compromise solution. The clear commitment to parliamentary government took a step backwards in terms of how to choose the President. However, the consent of the Parliament was required to affirm the choice. The question was not yet settled, and amendments followed later.

Indeed, the following day, Sub-committee Chair Teitgen returned to the decision and expressed his concerns that the First Chamber would elect as President the most colourless (*terne*) or most neutral, that is the most conciliant member. Therefore he suggested that perhaps it would be better to let the Council of National Ministers decide upon the President of the European Executive Council. Dehousse was afraid that that Council would seek to have a docile 'servant' (*domestique*). Teitgen argued that the Ministers would designate a personality who has a first rank record for the service to their country whereas the First Chamber would design the least important of their members. Van der Goes argued that the proposed way of nomination would give too much power to the Council of National Ministers. Dehousse and Montini did not see such danger, as it was agreed that the Council could make majority decisions. Dehousse compared this solution to the Swiss system, which would be more stable than the parliamentary system (4 December 1952).

Chair Teitgen and rapporteur Dehousse justified this move away from a parliamentary system – which took place within a single day – by their common fear that the Executive Council would not be sufficiently stable. Teitgen's fear –

that the First Chamber would elect a weak person among themselves – might be due to the experiences of the French Third and Fourth Republic. Such fears look hardly plausible, as the President for the European Executive Council would surely not been nominated suddenly and spontaneously inside the Chamber without previous negotiations between governments and party groups.

In the Constitutional Committee on 17 December, Fernand Dehousse explained the need for a stable Executive Council. In contrast to the nineteenth-century debates, he did not put this as a question of liberty against the executive. For Dehousse, the danger in this context was a government that was too weak and could not guide through its proposals and resolutions the agenda of the Parliament, leading possibly to arbitrary decisions. The European Executive Council should have collegial authority, although an authority submitted to parliamentary control.

Dehousse did not reject parliamentarism as such, but only a deformed version of it known in French as *régime d'Assemblée*. An analogous critique against parliamentary powers separated from parliamentary government can be found in the defence of British parliamentary government by Walter Bagehot. He defended ministers' retaining their parliamentary seats in order to be able to defend government against parliament and parliament against government officials. 'The parliamentary head is a protecting machine' (1867/72, 129). Replacing 'officials' with 'member state governments' gives us the main point of Dehousse's argument in the Ad Hoc Assembly.

In the Constitutional Committee on 20 December, Gérard Jaquet argued that the Parliament might tolerate a government chosen by the Council of National Ministers for a period but would dismiss it at the first opportunity. He preferred an Executive that corresponded to the wishes of both the Council of Ministers and the Parliament. Teitgen defended the proposal by arguing that it was the Council of Ministers, rather than the Parliament, that would elect strong personalities to the government. But he left the final decision to the Assembly. He seems to argue that the European Government for its legitimacy needed something of a charismatic leader and that the Council of Ministers rather than the Peoples' Chamber would presumably be able to choose such a leader (20 December 1952).

In a Report of the Constitutional Committee, dated 20 December 1952, to the January Plenum of the Ad Hoc Assembly, Dehousse repeated the Sub-committee's final views on electing the European Executive Council. He acknowledged that the Sub-committee proposed a compromise, with the European Executive Council 'entrusted with the general direction of the Community'. For electing its President, the majority had opted for the Council of National Ministers, while others considered that, 'in order to stress the political implications of the choice of the President, he [sic] should be elected by the Peoples' Chamber'. Arguing for the parliamentary responsibility of the Executive Council, the Committee 'wished to make the political institutions of the European Community conform to the constitutional principles which they [the member states, KP] themselves are applying'.

In presenting the work of the Political Institutions Sub-committee to the Assembly plenum on 7 January, Fernand Dehousse emphasised that the executive power had been more difficult to deal with than the legislative. He defended the Sub-committee's standpoint, although 'he personally was not convinced of it'. The Sub-committee had agreed 'to maintain the Council of National Ministers', without giving to it the paralysing right to veto.

In the plenary debate, the Sub-committee's proposal on the election of the President of the Executive Council by the Council of Ministers was rejected by numerous members. The democratisation of the Political Community was strongly linked with the parliamentary powers of electing, dismissal and controlling the Executive Council.

Jaquet argued for limited competence and for 'really supranational and really democratic' institutions. He disagreed with the proposed nomination of the Executive Authority and said that 'the Council of National Ministers ought not to be enabled to paralyse the Executive Authority'. Montini saw inconsistences in nominating the Executive and thought that the Council of Ministers 'would be subject to the instability of Governments in various countries', thus turning the stability argument against the Council of Ministers (7 January 1953).

In the continued debate, Francisco Maria Dominedò did not regard it as possible to set up an Executive which included 'on equal footing…the Executive of the Community, which was a supranational organ, and the Council of Ministers, which was an international organ'. The latter should be rather 'a liaison between the States and the supranational organs'. For Piet Vermeylen, the Council of National Ministers should have 'only advisory power', and the supervision by the Senate 'would ensure full protection of national interests'. He supported the election of the President of the Executive 'preferably by the Senate' and 'dismissed by either Chamber'. François de Menthon thought that if the Council of National Ministers appointed and controlled the European Executive, 'it was scarcely possible to consider making the Council responsible to the Parliament of Europe'. For increasing parliamentary powers 'the Council of National Ministers should be eliminated from the European Executive; the Head of the Executive should be appointed by the European Parliament' (8 January 1953).

In the further debate, Dehousse asked, whether the Council of Ministers would intervene only in the first appointment (as was the Sub-committee's proposal from 3 December) or as a permanent arrangement (as it supported on 4 December). Or should it rather make the proposal to the Parliament? The Assembly plenum agreed, however, that 'no intervention by the Council of

National Ministers was needed for the formation of the European Executive' (9 January 1953).

This was a decisive move of the Ad Hoc Assembly for the full parliamentarisation of the European government. The parliamentary system of government would have, as a constitutive part, the parliament empowered to appoint the Prime Minister.

In line with this principle, Vermeylen proposed: 'the President of the Executive Council would be elected by the Senate and…members would be selected by the President in the number fixed by the Community's Parliament'. The Council should 'be invested by the two Chambers before taking office' and could always be 'overthrown by a majority vote' in either of the Chambers. 'The system had the merit of simplicity and would give the Government and its President the authority they required'. Pierre Wigny was 'in favour of Vermeylen's proposal' but wanted the number of the Executive members left to the President. Vermeylen accepted this (ibid.).

Ferruccio Parri in his turn proposed: 'the Executive Council will be appointed by the two Chambers. It will remain in office a period defined in the Statute. It can be dismissed before…if a motion against it is carried by two-thirds majority in both Chambers'. Natale Santero supported this amendment. Max Becker wanted that it might be made clear 'whether the Executive Council could be compelled to resign by a no-confidence vote or whether it should be appointed for a specific period…(parliamentary or presidential system)'. In the first alternative 'it should at least be a "constructive" no-confidence vote … if the successors were simultaneously nominated'. Francesco María Dominedò could not support the aim 'to entrust the election of the President to one Chamber only'. The participation of both Chambers 'would merely help to enhance the authority and prestige' of the President. Marga Klompé asked Vermeylen, did he 'mean a simple or qualified majority' for the dismissal. Vermeylen responded that a 'simple majority should suffice' and that he held 'the system proposed by Becker and Klompé [as] too rigid'. He also supported the idea that the Parliament should be able to 'withdraw its confidence in a single Minister without withdrawing the whole Executive Council' (ibid.).

After agreeing on the parliamentary appointment of the European Executive Council, also called the Government, all proposals contained some guarantees for its stability. All agreed that frequent government changes should be avoided on the European level. Characteristically, however, there was wide disagreement over the stabilising measures. All agreed with the principle that after its formation of the Council, the government should be confirmed by a vote of confidence in both parliamentary chambers. Vermeylen put the investment of the President to the Senate because he expected the parliament-elected Chamber to be more stable than the Peoples' Chamber, but he was willing to accept its dismissal by a simple majority in either Chamber. Parri followed the ECSC practice and required a two-thirds majority for the vote of no confidence, and in addition, mentioned electing to office for certain period of time, à la Switzerland, although the government could be dismissed within this period. Becker and Klompé followed the constructive vote of confidence model of the West German *Grundgesetz* by requiring the nomination of a new candidate for the presidency. Although the previous debates had insisted on the collegial character of the Executive Council, Vermeylen was willing to allow the dismissal of single ministers without dismissing the Council itself (ibid.).

The examples illustrate not only the recognition of the need for stability but also the uncertainty over the criteria for parliamentary government on a supranational level, which was affirmed by leaving the appointment of the President to the Senate. The collegiality was linked to supranationality in so far as nobody moved for national quotas for the Ministers.

Debates and votes on the amendments ensued on 10 January 1953. Benvenuti asked about the standing of ECSC and EDC Chairs as members of the Executive Council: Did the vote of no confidence concern also them? Vermeylen admitted, as for ECSC and EDC members, 'the majority required… might…vary according to the nature of [the] questions'. Teitgen was in favour of having the ECSC and EDC Chairs serve as members of the Executive Council, 'and they should retain their personal status'. In a vote on whether the two Chambers (Parri) or the Senate (Vermeylen) should appoint the President of the Executive Council, Parri's motion was first rejected and then Vermeylen's motion adopted, as was its next part on the confirmation of the Executive Council 'by the two Chambers before assuming office' (10 January 1953).

With this decision, the Senate obtained, contrary to the principle of equal powers, the right to initiative in setting up the government, whereas the Peoples' Chamber received the joint power with the Senate to confirm the government before it took office. With the initiative of the Senate, its electors in the member states' parliaments gained indirectly powers in the Community.

For the later history of European integration, this position set an interesting precedent. Nobody proposed at this stage appointing the Council President by the Peoples' Chamber, although previously members, including Dehousse, had taken a stand for the priority of the Peoples' Chamber if the two Chambers disagreed. We could also speculate that the appointment of the President of the Executive Council was too serious to be left to the Peoples' Chamber alone, which could be interpreted as a limit to the rhetoric of popular sovereignty and an indirect recognition of the priority of parliamentary sovereignty as expressed in the parliament-elected Senate. The Ad Hoc Assembly's decision contained an element that has been later evoked when regarding member state parliaments together, besides the Council of the European Union, as the virtual third chamber of the EU.

In the further debate on Parri's motion, Wigny noted that 'there was no need to state that the Council would remain in office…It would be sufficient to that it would resign if the two Chambers passed a vote of censure'. Becker noted that a 'time-limit government', as proposed by Parri, 'could only be overthrown by a vote of no confidence of an emphatic nature (a two-thirds majority for instance) or by the Senate acting on a decision of the Peoples' Chamber'. Both alternatives were opposed to Vermeylen's motion that a dismissal could be achieved by simple majority of either Chamber. Teitgen considered that 'the two-thirds majority...would impede real control by Parliament', which control he insisted be continued also for the transitional period (10 January 1953).

Dominedò argued that 'it should not be made too easy to pass votes of no confidence'. Dehousse admitted that 'during a transitional period the Executive should be assured a certain degree of stability'. Hermann Kopf supported Becker's amendment to include a constructive vote of no confidence. In the vote on Parri's motion, Dehousse asked whether the two-third majority would be restricted to the transitional period. Parri found that this would presuppose a fixed time-limit for the Executive Council. Teitgen questioned the decision: 'To stipulate that the Executive Council could be overthrown only by a joint action of the two Chambers was to put an excessive restriction upon the powers of the Peoples' Chamber', and President Paul-Henri Spaak agreed with this. Parri's motion on the two-thirds rule was rejected in the vote (ibid.).

To sum up, a stable appointment by the Senate, a time-limit for the Executive Council, and joint action by the Chambers to dismiss the Council were accepted. Part of the decision and a guarantee of stability of the government was also the election of the members of the Senate for a five-year period, as proposed by Dehousse at a late stage (see 8.2.3).

A time-limit for the Executive Council was a redundant principle, but the requirement that the two Chambers together could dismiss it would, as Teitgen said, further weaken the standing of the elected Peoples' Chamber with respect to the Senate, in contrast to the principle of equal powers agreed elsewhere. The amendment concerning the constructive vote of no confidence was rejected (10 January 1953).

The turnaround regarding the appointment of the Executive Council by the Senate illustrated the strong support for the parliamentary government among the Assembly's members. The result of the votes on the relationships between Parliament and the Executive Council looked, in contrast, rather haphazard, because the matter of votes was not prepared by any committee work. The Assembly President Spaak reminded the members that 'the decisions...should be regarded merely as suggestions for the guidance of the Committee' (ibid.)

In Political Institutions Sub-committee, Dehousse stated that, in his judgement, the decision of the Assembly where a vote of censure would require the support of both chambers ought to be reconsidered. Teitgen found such a system to be incompatible with democratic principles, even though it would be impossible to maintain a government that had lost support in one of the chambers. Wigny did not consider the double vote of censure as undemocratic and saw in it a better guarantee of stability than what Teitgen proposed: the government should not fall by 'oppositions de passage'. Merkatz supported the view that only the Peoples' Chamber should vote on the vote of censure – a term used in the debate synonymously to vote of no confidence –, but such vote would be submitted to the Senate, whose opposition could be overturned by a two-thirds vote in the Peoples' Chamber. Teitgen found that Sub-committee was too timid and persisted in his view that a vote of censure should not require passage in both Chambers. Dehousse also argued that it would never be possible to dismiss the government if that required two Chambers, but the principle of equality between the Chambers made the vote of censure in only one of them should be sufficient (10 February 1953).

Dehousse thought that the election of the President of the Council by the Senate might be revised because rather the members of the Peoples' Chamber could be considered as candidates. Teitgen then moved for the voting to be by a common sitting of the two Chambers. Dehousse preferred a vote in the Peoples' Chamber alone. The Sub-committee finally agreed, according to the British model, that after a vote of no confidence in the Peoples' Chamber, the Executive Council would have the alternative of either resigning or dissolving the lower Chamber to try to obtain a majority in the new Chamber (ibid.).

Against Dehousse's view of a too powerful Senate, Teitgen remarked that, since the Senate could not be dissolved, it would be possible to require from it a qualified majority in the vote of censure. Merkatz supported the Peoples' Chamber dismissing government by a simple majority, with the Senate unable to that without nominating a new one. The solution arose finally from Teitgen's proposal: a three-fifths majority in the Peoples' Chamber would automatically dismiss the government without a right to dissolution, while a simple majority would give the Executive Council the possibility to consider a dissolution of the chamber. In the Senate, the appointment of an alternative Head of Government (President of the Council) was required. The Sub-committee added to that Dehousse's proposal that a majority of voters was required – that is: abstainers were counted –, which was a weaker criterion than in Germany, which required a majority of the members in the Bundestag to appoint a new government (ibid.). The wording of the Draft Treaty (Article 31) corresponds to this text passed by the Sub-committee.

9.3 A draft for a European parliamentary government

The thorough debates on the European Executive Council, on its mode of election and mode of parliamentary responsibility, complete the Ad Hoc Assembly's Draft Treaty for a European parliamentary government. In autumn 1952, committee debates resulted in support, with some reservations, for letting the Council of National Ministers appoint the chief of the European government. This was for the sake of maintaining a stable government. The majority at the Assembly plenum in January 1953 rejected this stand and rejected returning to it, so the matter was not proposed again in the later debates.

Lodovico Montini's argument, that the composition of the Council of Ministers tended to be highly volatile, depending on the electoral results and government changes in member states, was a major cause of the shift in favour of the parliament appointing the Executive Council. For this, different stability-creating measures were proposed, such as appointing the Senate for a five-year term, giving the Council a qualified right to dissolve the Peoples' Chamber, as well as different qualified majorities and the constructive vote of confidence requiring the naming of an alternative chief of government [President of the Executive Council] and counting the majorities from the Chamber membership and not from the actual number of members participating in the vote.

In other words, the Ad Hoc Assembly showed ingenuity in rescuing parliamentary government from its vulgar caricatures, well known to theorists of parliamentary government such as Walter Bagehot and Max Weber (See Weber 1919 on the January 1919 election results for the Weimar Constituent Assembly). Although no direct references to them or other theorists are documented in the debates, it may be assumed that experienced parliamentarians, being versed in political thought, constitutional law and history, were able to judge how to apply parliamentary principles and practices and avoiding their well-known weaknesses.

Why was the parliamentary government held to be superior to other models among the members of the Ad Hoc Assembly? There is no direct answer in the debates, but we can note an obvious preference for avoiding not only the weaknesses intergovernmental institutions, such as the Council of Europe, and for avoiding the dangers of technocracy, such as in the ECSC, but also a willingness to risk the experiment of applying parliamentary principles to a supranational polity.

Beyond that, a clear insight into parliamentary virtues prevailed among the members of the Ad Hoc Assembly. This was not, however, manifested in bold declarations expressing what Max Weber called mere *Redeparlament*. The Assembly was in its own procedures and practices an *Arbeitsparlament* in Weber's sense (see 1918, esp. 234), which efficiently organised its work in committees as a basis but was also able of making broad judgements in plenary sessions, such as the change in favour of the Senate electing the government. For Weber, Westminster was both a working and a debating parliament (see Palonen 2014b), and so was the Ad Hoc Assembly as well.

Following the model of a working parliament, the Ad Hoc Assembly was itself regulated by the parliamentary virtues of applying a strict procedure and timetable. The chairs and rapporteurs upheld a clear setting of agenda items but were open to dissent with them if they resulted in amendments to resolutions.

They also evinced a strong commitment to keeping deadlines, including a willingness to vote on resolutions concerning a European vision, instead of searching for compromises at any cost between the minimalists and the maximalists of the Assembly.

The parliamentary virtues also marked, in the context of the early 1950s, a distance from the *Parteienstaat* conception as propagated by Gerhard Leibholz (1951). This view operates with stable majority governments, which tend to marginalise the free mandate of members and to reduce the proceedings of Parliament to ratification or rejection of government proposals. Although parties were commonly recognised as necessary candidate-setting and parliamentary fraction-forming institutions (see Weber 1917b), in the Ad Hoc Assembly the party divides hardly played any role, and I do not think there were even any party group meetings.

In the style of Francophone parliaments, the committee chairs and rapporteurs drafted the resolutions in the Ad Hoc Assembly. As there was neither government discipline nor strict party lines, the resolutions were open to amendment and even the rapporteur of the Political Institutions Sub-committee, Fernand Dehousse, altered his stand on several occasions as well as prepared revised resolutions for subsequent meetings. It is almost certain that a similar lack of set forms could not have characterised the Parliament of the Community, but the Ad Hoc Assembly's striving to avoid a strict government vs. opposition divide could have made the Parliament of the Community more open to amendments than were member state parliaments with their *Parteienstaat* tendencies.

The limits on national governments' powers – also in issues such as the seat distribution in the Senate and the inclusion of opposition members in the Senate – aimed at limiting the member states' acting as if there were party groups inside the Political Community. This suggests that direct elections to the First Chamber would also serve in part to 'Europeanise' the ideological divides in the new Parliament. Of course, the Ad Hoc Assembly members recognised that the Europeanisation of politics does not terminate conflicts and controversies but modifies their formation and correspondingly the constellations between parties.

The Draft Treaty did not bind the new Parliament to its own procedures, practices and conventions. It may look strange that parliamentary committees were not at all mentioned in the Draft Treaty, but this should not be interpreted as if there would be none. The very practices of the Ad Hoc Assembly itself indicate that thorough committee work was inherent to the parliamentary self-understanding of the Assembly members, many of whom had already participated in the creation of committees for the Consultative Assembly and for the Common Assembly.

There were, of course, also limits to the parliamentary virtues among the members of the Ad Hoc Assembly. As I have already discussed, the most obvious of them concerned the politics of time, and the reluctance to accept the full-time professionalisation of parliamentary politics. For the members of the Ad-hoc Assembly, the 'European' interest was merely an extension to their profile, which separated them from their more provincial colleagues, but was still not a full-time profession. The permanently sitting European Executive Council was perhaps a first step towards the European professional politician.

The Assembly members were proud of being politicians themselves and understood parliamentary government as a rule by politicians over diplomats, officials, experts and specialists. Still, they seem not to have understood sufficiently the significance of sitting periods and how to work out a compatibility between spending time in the parliament or in their governmental positions, or how necessary it is to have full-time and full-paid members if the goal is to realise a parliamentary regime, especially when their adversaries regarding the priority for political judgement and action would be the full-time professionals in member state governments. The vision that Europe-level legislation and political debates would create as their by-product a full-fledged supranational and parliamentary polity – a double politicisation of 'Europe' – was still not thoroughly deliberated in terms of parliamentary time and professionalism.

Parliamentary politics since the second half of twentieth century had become increasingly the politics of time, its competent application and its fair distribution. The Ad Hoc Assembly members had well understood that they were acting within a unique *Kairos* situation for Europeanisation when they set up the European Political Community, although it ultimately turned into a missed opportunity. Did they understand that their activity marked a momentum for politicisation, combining the aspects of supranationalism and parliamentarism?

As mentioned, the Draft Treaty formulated that the powers and competence of the Political Community should be interpreted restrictively. If we look at the history of the parliamentarisation of politics, the precedents and practices have usually paved way for constitutional regulations. In this context, accepting the principle of parliamentary government meant the obvious possibility of appealing to its legitimacy in the interpretation and expansion of its competence, following the Common Assembly's practice that everything not explicitly forbidden would be allowed. P.A. Blaisse supported, in the Constitutional Committee on 17 December 1952, a modest 'auto-extension' towards a common market. In other words, it could still be possible to reinterpret the Draft Treaty's formulations to strengthen the supranational parliamentary government in specific cases, in which case the parliament could take the decision that the time has to come to overcome a restrictive interpretation of the European-level political competence.

The construction, composition and powers of supranational parliamentary government on a bicameral basis required debates on all the constitutive dimensions of the European Political Community as a polity. They concerned the political relations between a) directly and indirectly elected parliamentary chambers, b) parliamentary chambers and the government, c) the two executive institutions, d) the supranational and member state governments, e) supranational and national parliaments, f) elected representatives and voters and g) elected representatives and officials. In addition, one could also mention the relationships between parliaments-cum-governments vs. the courts as well as between the elected parliaments and the advisory Economic and Social Council.

In the debates of the Ad Hoc Assembly, each of these relationships were debated intensively. The Assembly moved thorough their debates from a vaguely sketched model of a supranational executive controlled by a bicameral representative assembly to a viable parliamentary government for the European Political Community, with a permanent European Executive Council consisting of politicians elected by a Senate and responsible to both chambers of the Parliament of the Community.

For European integration, this proposal for the parliamentary system was the Ad Hoc Assembly's major innovation, which has not been sufficiently appreciated in present-day EU politics or in the wider scholarly discourse. For parliamentary politics as well as for the studies on it, the debates and Draft Treaty of the Ad Hoc Assembly mark an extraordinary testimony of a political creativity of debating parliamentarians, which hardly has counterparts in the European politics and history.

10 Towards a supranational and parliamentary Europe

Why at the present heyday of nationalist and populist sermons against the EU has someone written on a failed plan for European Political Community in the 1950s? Is that a purely antiquarian interest of an emeritus professor, who happens to have found that the debates and documents are available at the EUI's website and can write on them comfortably from his own computer desk?

I have already referred Quentin Skinner's view of 'bringing buried treasures back to the surface' (1998, 112) as well as to Max Weber's concept of 'objective possibilities' (1906), i. e. possibilities which were not, but could have been (or could be) realised. The Draft Treaty and the preceding debates in the Ad Hoc Assembly can in this perspective be read as a thoroughly debated alternative, a supranational and parliamentary vision for Europe. Could the history of European integration have looked radically different, or even 'better', than the one that was realised? We do not know. Independently of that, the work of the Ad Hoc Assembly with the Draft Treaty deserves to be not only remembered but reassessed as a momentum for a parliamentary alternative for Europeanisation today.

10.1 Parliamentary virtues of the Ad Hoc Assembly

My primary scholarly interest lies in the elaboration of the Ad Hoc Assembly debates on the Draft Treaty for the European Political Community. That the Community was finally not realised should not diminish interest in the constitution-drafting project and practices of the Ad Hoc Assembly, which can be seen as a double politicising momentum for Europe in supranational and parliamentary terms. The scholarly contribution of this book consists above all in its detailed presentation and exposition of the thesis that the work of the Ad Hoc Assembly contains such politicising momentum, one that radically transcends conventional intergovernmental co-operation.

The Ad Hoc Assembly was practising parliamentary virtues in the unprecedented context of applying them to a supranational polity. The Assembly's thorough and nonetheless productive debates in committee and plenum provided a unique opportunity to Europeanise the politics of its West European member states with a vision towards a broader Europe. Contrary to widespread scholarly and political opinion on the incompatibility of supranationalism with parliamentary government, the Ad Hoc Assembly's work gives us a detailed illustration of how this combination could have been both possible and justified.

In opposition to the populist and nationalist prejudices against supranationalism and the EU's member states' tendency to defend their vested interests by frequently resorting to demagoguery, my *Wertbeziehung* lies in a revaluation of supranationalism and parliamentarism (see Skinner 1996). To this purpose, I have reassessed the significance of the Ad Hoc Assembly's work from the perspective of a conceptual history of Europeanisation and parliamentarisation. An open politicisation of the EU by cultivating parliamentary virtues, as well as the procedural and institutional practices around them, gives us insights into the political mood of Ad Hoc Assembly. The participating parliamentarians had the audacity to understand that they themselves possessed unprecedented possibilities for realising political actions to extending the parliamentary system of government to a supranational polity.

The parliamentary virtues of dissensus and debate contain a vision of knowledge as a mode of debating, judging issues from opposite points of view and weighing *pro et contra* the strengths and weaknesses of any motion on the agenda. The Ad Hoc Assembly's members carried out debates without governmental motions and resolutions and could therefore as politicians consider the wisdom of previous speakers' views and revise their views in ongoing debates without losing face or concerns about the media and citizenry accusing them of being turncoats.

Blaming parliaments as slow and ineffective is an old *topos* (see e. g. Mergel 2002 for the Weimar Republic). The Ad Hoc Assembly illustrates the contrary: acting as a working parliament, it managed to prepare the Draft Treaty within the planned timetable. The political identity of its members as parliamentarians was inherent to its ability to combine a willingness to debate and weigh motions and amendments from opposed points of view with efficient, quality work.

My key topic has been about understanding supranationalism and parliamentarism as politicisation moves in the process of European integration. They opened contingencies for a perspective that both reinterpreted the existing situation and offered a new European vision. The Ad Hoc Assembly's combination of these two major facets of politicisation aimed at overcoming the traditional intergovernmentalism in international politics by extending parliamentary principles to a supranational level. It relied on the insight that, in the post-war context, traditional diplomatic negotiations were not enough, but could and must be supplemented with the deliberative parliamentary style of politics. To do that required a willingness to transcend the nation-states as given polity units and their interest-based politics in favour of debating political alternatives for a supranational polity. Thinking in terms of alternatives and making use of the contingency of political orders and situations refer to parliamentary virtues, which at the same time are alien to the practices of officials and experts (see Weber 1918, 235–248; Palonen 2018).

The debates of the Ad Hoc Assembly characteristically make visible the double face of politicisation, i. e. as an intentional project and as the ability for insightful reinterpretations of changing situations and the contingencies opened thereby. The participating parliamentarians were aware of having created unprecedented possibilities by their combining of supranational institutions with a parliamentary government.

10.2 Proposals for empowering the Parliament

The Ad Hoc Assembly remains still today the most radical project for parliamentarising European integration. I have previously dealt with a failed project from 1960 to parliamentarise the membership of the European Commission by making it compatible with membership in the European Parliamentary Assembly, created after the Rome Treaty (see Palonen 2022a).

Frank Schorkopf (2023) has identified several other projects for strengthening the European Parliament from different decades. As points of comparison with the Ad Hoc Assembly, I have chosen to briefly discuss the programmatic documents of two other attempts at parliamentarising European institutions, namely, the Vedel Report from 1972 and Altiero Spinelli's legitimation speech from 1983 for a Draft for the European Union, which the Parliament accepted in 1984. Neither of them was successful, but both have contributed to later steps in parliamentarisation of the EU.

10.2.1 The Vedel Report

After partial treaty reforms on financial politics, the European Commission set up on 21 July 1971 'an *ad hoc* Working Party of independent experts to examine the whole corpus of problems connected with the enlargement of the powers of the European Parliament', as it has been similarly called since 1963 in all member state languages. The Working Party consisted of scholars and experts from the member and candidate countries, led by the French constitutional law professor Georges Vedel (1910–2002). For extending the European Community's (EC) membership and economic powers, its perspective aimed at revising the institutions, 'with a view to ensuring that Community decisions are taken within a framework of democratic legitimacy' (Vedel Report, 7). The specific tasks included:

the participation of the European Parliament in the continuous evolution of the constitution of the Community…

the participation of the European Parliament in the Community legislative process…

the definition of the European Parliament's power in budgetary matters;

the European Parliament's functions in political control over the governmental power of the Community;

the effects of increasing the powers of the Parliament on the relationship between the various Community institutions, on their structure and on their working methods;

the relationship between reinforcing the Parliament's powers and its election by direct universal suffrage' (ibid. 8).

The background for the Report was the interpretation that the European Parliament had in practice remained in a merely advisory position. The Commission's list suggested directions and steps to take to obtain elementary parliamentary power for it. Although it had the possibility to exercise a (conditional) vote of censure, this was inherited from the ECSC and the Parliament's political control remained vague, far from that of a full-fledged parliamentary government. The Commission had given proposals to the Working Party for promoting democracy and efficacy. 'The status and role of the parliament with regard to the executive are an essential part of democracy; in relation to law-making, the parliament is vested with the highest power; in one form or another, it exercises supervision over the government' (ibid. 11). Thus, only representative and legislative powers are mentioned, not the parliamentary way of doing politics.

The point about developing 'really...democratic mechanisms' on the Community level (ibid. 12) alludes to the tendency that the extension of the Community's powers had weakened the parliaments of members states without strengthening the EP. The Vedel Report quoted a resolution of the Parliament from 1970: 'any transfer of powers in economic and monetary matters from the national authorities to the Community must be accompanied, to ensure democratic control, by an increase in the powers of the European Parliament' (ibid. 18). The Report concluded that economic unification must be completed with a political unification (ibid. 20).

The situational analysis of the Report identified a deviation from the Rome Treaty: 'the Council, acting in some instances as a Community body and in others as the States in concert, has become the sole effective centre of power in the system' (ibid. 25). The Commission had also lost influence in the EC, largely due to de Gaulle's rise to power and his rejection of both parliamentarism and supranationalism in favour of intergovernmentalism, as manifested by the 'Luxembourg compromise', which brought France back to the EC's decision-making at the cost of the veto of single member states in the Council (ibid. 26–27). The Report concluded: 'there is an increasing tendency for the Community decision-making process to consist of pure, diplomatic style negotiation', and it was lacking the 'possibility of political arbitration in which the Parliament would have a real place' (ibid. 27).

The Parliament was representative but 'falls far short of fulfilling its normal tasks of expressing and shaping political opinion.' (ibid. 28) The Report wanted to make the EP act like an ordinary parliament, acting as the ECSC Common Assembly tried to do (see Wigny 1958). In the EC, the situation was according to the Report such that 'when faced with an implicit prior agreement between the Commission and the Council, the Parliament feels that its opinion can be of no substantial significance' (Vedel Report, 29). Between the Parliament and the Council there was no institutional link, nor did the Vedel Report propose any radical change in this respect:

> It would scarcely be possible, without undermining the very foundations of institutional balance, to establish a process of control giving the European Parliament a power of sanction over the Council, whose members are politically responsible before their own national Parliaments. It is, however, debatable whether all possibilities of procedures, involving questions and answers, explanations, and in brief, dialogue and communication, have been explored. (ibid. 30)

The Vedel Report recognised that there was a *Fremdkörper* in the 'foundations' of the EC (see Chapter 9.1): '[The] Council...is governmental and legislative at the same time' (ibid. 12). Unlike the Ad Hoc Assembly, the Report does not attempt to alter this. It did not render the Commission into a European parliamentary government, concentrate governmental powers in the Commission or affirm the freedom of Council members from their governments, as the ECSC's distinction of *Conseil de Ministres* versus *Conseil des Ministres* did. The proposal to use common parliamentary procedures would be a step towards making the Council responsible to the Parliament, but that would somewhat resemble the nineteenth-century constitutional states that had no parliamentary government.

The extension of the Community's powers could be realised 'only with the support of political and social forces. These forces can normally make themselves heard in the European Parliament'. The legitimisation of additional supranationalism required parliaments' support, but the 'Community directives make the national parliaments nothing more than chambers for recording decisions' (ibid. 32). To remedy the situation, the Report concluded 'The logic of a democratic system would require that this loss of parliamentary power at national level should be compensated at the European level.' Furthermore, 'the European Parliament is the institution *par excellence*' for reconciliation of interests disputes in general' (ibid. 33). For new long-term projects, such as the principles regional policy '[t]he Parliament must have its say when it comes to fixing these normative frameworks' (ibid. 35).

The Vedel Report well understood that both democracy and efficiency demand increasing the powers of the Parliament. Without radically extending legislative powers or parliamentary responsibility, the Report did identify a range of items for increasing parliamentary powers and the deliberative style of politics as a counterweight to the Council's intergovernmental diplomacy or the Commission's expert-based supranationalism.

The Report stressed that when the EC moves towards an economic and monetary union, 'the losses of power by national parliaments must be compensated'. The Working Party argued that 'strengthening the role of the Parliament will fill up not only a sort of democratic vacuum but also certain gaps in the efficient working of the Community', also because 'the Parliament is the only Community institution where the parliamentary oppositions of the Member States are represented' (ibid. 36–37). This is in line with Ad Hoc Assembly's proposals, but still no vision for a European parliamentary government.

The Report did not question that, for the Community, 'the Council is its legislature'. This idea was adopted in the Treaty of Rome, while in the ECSC the High Authority was the main legislature, the Council of National Ministers had the sole veto right to its policy decisions, and the Common Assembly had a qualified right to a vote of censure. The Vedel Report proposed a second legislative power, 'a real power of codecision based on the Parliament's ability to accept or reject Council decisions' (ibid. 37–38).

With EC's expected powers of an economic and monetary union in view, the Report considered 'whether the Parliament's intervention should not be recommended in these cases, either by way of consultation or by way of codecision'. In the Community's long-term plans and programmes, 'the European Parliament ought to be heard, at least in a consultative capacity'. No extension was proposed in 'a common short-term economic policy or a monetary policy', but 'ex post control' should play a role in it (ibid. 38–39).

The Report proposed increasing the powers of the Parliament in two stages. The first (List A) 'covers questions which materially involve either the Community's constitutive power or its relations with other persons in international law' (ibid. 40). These included 'revision of the Treaties; implementation of Article 235 of the EEC Treaty and analogous provisions in the ECSC and Euratom Treaties; admission of new members; ratification of international agreements concluded by the Community' (ibid. 39).

List B proposed 'a greater power of consultation consisting in the right to ask the Council to reconsider a subject and hence a suspensive veto in enumerated policy fields' (ibid.). In the EEC Treaty, there were suspicions about Parliament's competence to handle pure policy questions, which were frequently considered quite technical. As the

amendment of the Treaties…presupposes democratic endorsement since ratification in accordance with the constitutional rules of each Member State implies approval by the national parliaments…it is highly desirable that the Community's own constituent process should make provision for like approval by the European Parliament, which is the democratic institution of the Community as such. (ibid. 41)

Here the Report proposed empowering the supranational European Parliament enabling it to act like a genuine parliament. The new parliamentary powers proposed were procedurally specified as including not only veto power, but also the power to make amendments and to make decisions before waiting for approval by the member state parliaments.

[The] approval of the amendment by the Assembly would set the seal of the Community's Parliament on the texts adopted by the Council in pursuance of the proposal... before the national parliaments are called upon to speak and this would undoubtedly make it easier for them to give their assent. (ibid. 41)

The power to amend treaties seems to have been the Vedel Report's most important move. It could give to the EP a temporal priority over the national parliaments, which would remain closer to merely ratifying institutions regarding the treaties. 'Finally, the entry of new members into the Community affects both the constituent power and international agreements. This justifies the Parliament's intervention' (ibid.). A legitimising power was given to the Parliament. The list B's issues are divided into 'harmonization of legislation' and 'questions of principle affecting *common policies*' (ibid. 42), and these should include the possibility to make amendments.

The procedural powers of the Parliament were identified as 'co-decision, consultation and suspensive veto' (ibid. 44), and their application was divided into an 'initial' and a 'second stage' (ibid. 44). The Report discussed the case in detail and concluded that dealing with items on the agenda does not necessarily have to follow the order 'Commission –> Council –> Parliament'. Especially the power of co-decision promoted an improvement of both democracy and efficiency in the EC's politics:

Preliminary consultation of the Parliament on Commission proposals would make it easier for the power of co-decision to be exercised in a harmonious manner. Knowing that approval by the Parliament determines the decision-making process, the Commission and the Council would find it in their interests to be informed in good time of the Parliament's point of view. Furthermore, the Parliament may propose, in advance, amendments to the draft text. (ibid. 47)

The Report further stated: 'The Parliament is already able to propose initiatives affecting legislation by means of resolutions requesting the other institutions of the Community, especially the Commission, to take action.' (ibid. 48). This would roughly correspond to the practice of the Common Assembly of the ECSC. The Report was not willing to alter the Commission's quasi-monopoly on parliamentary initiative: 'It is in the Commission that the Treaties vest the role of initiator and promoter of Community norms' (ibid. 48). This was not far from the practices in most post-war parliaments, but it was alien to the Westminster-style, including with respect to the power of initiative of individual MPs.

The Working Party saw a danger in extending the EP's powers to what in Westminster are called bread and butter questions: 'Its work would be overloaded by tasks of secondary importance, which would adversely affect the degree of attention which it should give to fundamental or important decisions' (ibid. 49). This failed to address the question, who and how would it be determined which are the 'tasks of secondary importance'? Without allowing the Parliament to decide about its own agenda, there would be a danger of it being in merely patronised in relation to the Council or the Commission.

One debate in the context of the Vedel report considered the Parliament's budgetary powers. The Report prioritised investing it with co-decision powers: 'Since the Parliament will exercise a power of co-decision in the acts which are at the basis of Community expenditure and will be associated with the establishment of pluriannual estimates, it will share with the Council the financial responsibility resulting therefrom'. This would make separate disputes on the budget 'disappear' and the Report found it necessary 'to give the Parliament a power of co-decision on the budget as a whole equal to that which it will then be exercising in legislative matters' (ibid. 55).

As for parliamentarians' questions, Council's reports and Parliament's committees, the Working Party emphasised the use of procedural techniques for parliament to increase its powers.

All these procedures, which are a part of parliamentary techniques, will develop and become consolidated as the Parliament acquires new powers, particularly powers of co-decision. The history of parliaments shows that as soon as a parliament begins to play a real part in the legislative process, it assumes *ipso facto* an authority and an influence which guarantee it the power to watch over the government's actions and to demand the supply of all necessary information. (ibid. 57)

For the ECSC Common Assembly, all that was not forbidden was seen as allowed. The European Parliament after the Treaty of Rome was less willing to take this approach, partly due to the Council's extended powers. Since the Community's powers had increased well beyond the limits given to the Ad Hoc Assembly, this extension was submitted to a strict intergovernmental control by the Council, which envied the Parliament's powers, so the Report proposed an increase of parliamentary powers within the Treaties.

Regarding the 'Investiture of the President of the Commission', the Working Party directed attention to an asymmetry: 'Curiously enough, the Treaties which give the Assembly the power to overthrow the Commission do not provide for its intervention in the nomination of its members which is decided only by agreement of the Member States' (ibid. 58) This was again inherited from the ECSC. The next paragraph denied, however, that radical change would be possible:

The nomination of members of the Commission by the Parliament cannot be envisaged. The institutional relationships between the Commission and the Council and the

Commission's position with regard to the national governments necessitate, for the very maintenance of its authority, that its members be chosen by the governments. (ibid.)

While the Ad Hoc Assembly proposed as a parliamentary and supranational principle the empowering of the Senate to nominate the President of the European Executive Council, the Treaty of Rome left such powers of nomination to the national governments. The Vedel Report upheld this to affirm the Commission's authority. In the language used in the Report, this marked a priority of intergovernmental diplomacy over parliamentary sovereignty, which the Ad Hoc Assembly had proposed. The next paragraph took, nonetheless, a half step in the parliamentary direction:

It could, however, be conceived that the Parliament should receive a power of co-decision in this matter too. This would be normal and logical, would have the advantage of stressing the political importance of the Commission, and would perhaps orientate the choices of governments towards outstanding political personalities. (ibid.)

The power of co-decision was justified in terms of strengthening the Commission politically at the cost of the Council. That parliament, rather than the governments alone, could orient 'towards outstanding personalities', was contrary to the fear of Pierre-Henri Teitgen in the Ad Hoc Assembly. The Working Party tacitly admitted that Council diplomacy had led to a choice of only technocrats instead of politicians to the Commission's presidency. The Report further stressed the value of involving Parliament in the election of the president, and this would: '[give] the choice of President a political character… providing a solid basis for his authority and…giving him a say in the formation of the Commission. This is clearly an instance where the criteria of democracy and effectiveness coincide completely.' (ibid.) Even if the Parliament would receive merely a veto power over the governments' candidate, this half step towards parliamentarisation was seen by the Report as marking a politicisation of the Presidency, strengthening the Commission over the Council, and perhaps forming an alliance with the Parliament to challenge the overwhelming powers of the Council's intergovernmental diplomacy.

The Report referred to article 138 of the EEC Treaty, moving to elect the Parliament by universal suffrage, which the Council had prevented. It mentioned the 'widespread view' that the '[e]lection of the Parliament by direct universal suffrage would therefore constitute a precondition for any increase of its powers' (ibid. 59). This was also the Ad Hoc Assembly's view. However, 'The Working Party has plainly and emphatically opposed this assumed precondition' (ibid.). The Report states: 'even without its recruitment procedure having been changed, the European Parliament has managed to acquire new and legally important budgetary powers'. (ibid.) The Working Party's proposals for the strengthening of the Parliament's powers 'would in themselves endow the Assembly with sufficient prestige to attract a good many influential parliamentarians from the Community's Member States' (ibid. 59). It argued that it would be better not to wait until the Council agreed to accept direct elections, but rather, changing the powers should start as soon as possible, not waiting for the creation of 'a "real" European Government' (ibid. 60).

The Working Party regarded direct European elections as nonetheless justified: 'Direct elections would considerably contribute to the Community's democratization and consequently, to its authentication, its legitimation. It should promote a closer union between the European peoples.' (ibid. 61). Direct elections could strengthen the supranational Community, independently of Parliament's powers. The Working Party seemed to give direct elections more of a plebiscitarian than a parliamentary colour, in line with the French Fifth Republic.

The Report adhered further to a traditional view of the European Parliament in relation to national parliaments: 'For a long time to come, the careers of politicians will be built up in a national context'. (ibid. 65). The Report wanted to avoid a competition between parliaments:

It will thus be possible for a two-way movement to emerge which would be of the utmost benefit to the parties in either process: the national parliaments will support the European Parliament and the European Parliament will be able to make its policies felt and perhaps exert a coordinating influence on national parliamentary life. (ibid. 66)

The simplest way to combine the interests would have been the dual mandate. However, 'the increase in the European Parliament's activities, in itself a happy circumstance' made this very difficult. It 'deters the national political groupings from sending to the European Parliament too large a number of top rank national parliamentarians' (ibid.). Unlike the Ad Hoc Assembly, the Working Party recognised that the longer sitting time indirectly demanded professional parliamentarians. The increased powers of the EP would attract more 'outstanding politicians', while another benefit would be '[a]n increase in the number of members of the European Parliament', which would be 'reducing the drawbacks of absences' (ibid. 67).

Another device to strengthen the inter-parliamentary links could be that 'the chairmen or certain members of the national parliamentary committees dealing with problems relating to the Community should automatically be members of the European Parliament' (ibid. 68). This would be valid only so long as the national parliaments elected the EP members. A long-term solution would be 'joint meetings of the specialized committees of the national parliaments and the European Parliament to study important problems' (ibid.). The Report opted for 'committees for European affairs, which would have the task of coordinating the national parliamentary work relating to Europe' (ibid. 69). The Ad Hoc Assembly did not yet deal with such options.

The Working Party's Report was the first major attempt to expand the powers of the European Parliament from the inside. It aimed at obtaining the best possible outcome from the existing Treaty and EC's institutional balance, and in this it was following the ECSC Common Assembly's strategy rather than that of the Ad Hoc Assembly's Draft Treaty for parliamentary government. The Working Party consisted of academics and officials, and therefore lacked parliamentarians' willingness to bold moves.

Until the early 1970s, the European Community had expanded its supranational competence and was expected to go further in economic and monetary policy by means of the Council's intergovernmental diplomacy. The Vedel Report aimed at redressing the institutional balance. Its proposals for empowering both the EP and the national parliaments relied on the procedural and legitimising resources in the parliamentary tradition. It aimed at realisable results, without waiting for direct EP elections or turning the Commission into a proper European government.

10.2.2 The Spinelli Project

Whereas the Vedel Report aimed at strengthening the EP in policy questions, the Spinelli Project attempted a reform of the polity. Its strategy was to increase its political legitimacy through the European Parliament, which in 1979 was directly elected, and to gain additional legitimacy among the member state parliaments by circumventing the intergovernmental Council.

Altiero Spinelli was an Italian *Resistant,* the author of the Ventotene Manifest and one of the main ideologists of the federalist European movement (see Chapter 5.1). In 1972 he was elected European Commissioner for industry, and in 1976 and 1979 direct elections as an independent on the list of the reformed, pro-European Italian Communist Party. He was also member of the Italian Parliament. After the 1979 European elections he collected a cross-party 'Crocodile Group' – named after a Strasbourg restaurant – and in 1981 led the Institutional Affairs Committee, which the EP had set up, for preparing a new Treaty. The draft for founding the 'European Union' received majority support in the EP on 18 February 1984, and it was intended to be legitimated in the second direct election of the EP but was ultimately ignored by the Council (see Schorkopf 2023, 167–173). Schorkopf judges that 'die Mehrzahl der Regelungsinhalte heute Primärrecht sind' und 'die Abgeordneten setzten ein starkes Signal, die Primärrechtsänderungen…parlamentarischer Logik zu unterwerfen' (ibid. 168).

I analyse Spinelli's Jean Monnet lecture at the EUI a on 13 June 1983 (English translation), supplemented with references to the Draft Treaty passed by the Parliament on 14 February 1984. Spinelli opened his speech by alluding to the EP's undertaking 'to propose a reform designed to turn the Community into a true political and economic union, equipped with the competence and the institutions it needs in order to be able to tackle effectively and through democratic procedures the serious and growing problems shared by our peoples'.

He prepared answers to three questions: '1) Why did the European Parliament take on this task? 2) What was the substance of the proposal that the Parliament was about to advance? 3) What would the Parliament have to do in order to ensure that its proposal was adopted by the member states and brought into effect?' (Spinelli 1983).

In Spinelli's view of the EP at the time was of 'an observatory before which all the problems relating to the establishment of European responsibilities are brought and discussed'. He saw the initiatives to it as coming from elsewhere, and the first directly elected Parliament showed its powers by rejecting the budget in December 1979. This was, however, a 'blunt sword', of which the Commission and the Council had little to worry about. The powers between institutions were as weird as they have been viewed in the Vedel Report 11 years earlier:

> While the Commission, in its unquestionable freedom, would sometimes take into consideration suggestions made by the Parliament and include them in the proposals that went before the Council, the Council, in turn, would always ignore, entirely and disdainfully, the Parliament's proposals, and base its decisions solely on agreements reached or not reached in intergovernmental negotiations between member states. (ibid.)

With its various initiatives the Parliament had shown 'that it is possible to gather considerable political consensus around these proposals, both on the left and on the right'. The Council 'disregards entirely the proposals advanced by the Parliament'. Parliament's opinions in international problems had led to nothing. It had proposed to the Commission and the Council to reform the institutions, but the Council has not paid 'any attention' to the Parliament's reform ideas. Finally, '[e]very six months, the Council's incoming president sets out, before the Parliament, all that the Council proposes to do', but 'the power to decide which rulings and directives are introduced and how they are applied, which policies are adopted and which are not, and which decisions and reforms are proposed and which are not, is practically all in the hands of the Council of Ministers' (ibid.).

Next, Spinelli depicted a caricature of the future EC that some persons were striving for:

> If the political and economic questions, internal and international, that face the Community and demand to be resolved through common actions were few in number, of secondary importance, and even on the decline, then today's inefficient system could be tolerated, or indeed simplified. The Parliament, with its cumbersome periodic elections and its demands to be involved in decision making, could be suppressed. The Commission, with its independent administration, could be reduced to a streamlined secretariat serving the Council. The few common actions needed would be undertaken only by those wishing to undertake them, and could be entrusted to specialist agencies controlled by intergovernmental committees. (ibid.)

For Spinelli, the fault lay in the intergovernmental method: 'Intergovernmental decisions are thus very often impossible, and on the rare occasions when they are reached, they are reached late, and are inadequate, disconnected from one another, and lacking in any guarantee of continuity.' It was '[t]he glaring contradiction between...the need for more Europe, and...the incapacity of the Europe of the Council of Ministers to respond to this need'. To respond to this contradiction, 'the European Parliament, on behalf of the citizens that had elected it, took on the task of drawing up and proposing a global reform of the Community and of its other collateral structures'. (ibid.)

Spinelli reported that the Committee on Institutional Affairs had prepared a resolution for the future Treaty to be debated in the Parliament, after which 'the Committee will transform it into a clear draft Treaty establishing the European Union'. The Committee had done something not expected by either the Council or Commission, but not forbidden by the treaties: it used its indirect ways of using parliamentary initiative to propose the founding of a new European Union.

The Committee had rejected the ordinary route of amending treaties and drafted 'a Treaty formally establishing the Union from scratch, an approach that allowed it to decide coherently the Union's structure and competence, as well as the stages in and manner of its creation' (ibid.). He justified the naming: 'The new political body will be given the name Union, because this is the expression that has been used, ever since 1952, to indicate the ultimate objective of the European constitution' (ibid). Spinelli saw the advantage of the Draft in that 'it brings the entire European edifice under the banner of the Union' (ibid.)

The new Treaty contained both the 'sphere of intergovernmental cooperation' and that of the 'common actions' for the Union institutions. The relationships were described with the Catholic doctrine of subsidiarity, no longer with delegating national sovereignty, but neither with a supranational language. 'The transfer of competences from each of these areas to the next is governed by the principle of subsidiarity. In other words, it occurs only when tasks are more effectively carried out by the member states acting in concert, as opposed to separately, or when they can only be carried out in concert'. (ibid., see also the Preamble of the Entwurf 1984)

In the new Union, the Gaullist invention of the European Council was planned to become 'an institution of the European Union' (Spinelli 1983, see Entwurf 1984, Articles 31–32). Spinelli believed that 'The European Council can decide to transform some forms of cooperation into common actions'. He argued that 'force of circumstance will very often lead the heads of government to see the need for common actions, but...they will be required not to entrust their own ministers and national functionaries with realising their vision'.

The Draft had, in accordance, proposed that 'The European Council, in choosing the president of the Commission and inviting him to form the Commission, also fulfils a role similar to that of the heads of state' (Spinelli

1983; Entwurf 1984, Article 32). Against the Ad Hoc Assembly's proposal of a full parliamentarisation of the Commission presidency, the Spinelli project retained it on the intergovernmental level, but by entrusting the political leaders of the member countries and not the Council of their ministers. In line with the Vedel Report it was further proposed:

The Council of the European Union...is made up of government representatives, who... will make decisions by more or less qualified majority voting, but never by unanimity. The Council of the Union and the Parliament will share legislative powers and, together, will be responsible for approving the budget and giving the Commission its mandate. The Parliament will cease to be a purely consultative body and will become a branch of the legislative and budgetary authorities. (Spinelli 1983; see Entwurf 1984, Articles 16 and 21)

The Commission will become a true centre of government with a political physiognomy and political responsibilities. It is formed by a president, nominated by the European Council. (Spinelli 1983; see Entwurf 1984, Article 28)

As a voting institution, the Council would gain a proto-parliamentary quality when abandoning the veto of member state representatives. The Commission was presented as a political government, and 'the Parliament has the faculty to dismiss the Commission on the basis of a motion of censure passed by a large majority', but according to the Swiss model of 'a directorial government', meaning that a vote of no confidence is possible only in 'major conflicts between the Parliament and the Commission'. (Spinelli 1983; Entwurf 1984, Article 29). The guarantee of a stable government would be different from that of the bicameral Parliament proposed by the Ad Hoc Assembly.

Another novelty was taking away all executive powers from the Council: 'The Commission becomes the Union's sole executive body'. (Spinelli 1983) Referring to the fate of the preceding projects, including the Ad Hoc Assembly, Spinelli insisted: 'The Parliament must realise that its battle for the European Union, far from ending, will, in reality, begin with its definitive approval of the draft Treaty' (ibid.). His strategy to avoid wilful ignorance or dismissal of the Draft consisted in referring to a common principle applied for passing constitutions:

As a rule, it is parliamentary assemblies that vote on constitutions, because it is in parliamentary assemblies that the different political families to which the citizens belong freely exchange their views, and freely find the convergences around which the greatest possible degrees of consensus can be gathered. There is no reason why the Constitution of the European Union should not come into being in the same way. (ibid.)

Spinelli thus appealed to an 'unwritten political right of parliaments' and referred to histories of West European constitutions: 'there is no legal obstacle preventing the draft Treaty from being drawn up by a parliamentary assembly (rather than the usual intergovernmental diplomatic conference) that adequately represents the citizens of the state it will be called upon to ratify' (ibid.). Spinelli put his trust in the EP elections of 1984 and the campaigning on behalf of the new Treaty. He came to be disappointed with these elections.

Altiero Spinelli's speech marked a new strategy for the parliamentarisation of Europe. Instead of delegating sovereignty, Spinelli spoke of a transfer of competence. The figure of subsidiarity referred to a kind of natural division of labour between the units, but marked for Spinelli rather a principle of expediency, which can be tested in practice and could allow for both upward and downward transfers. Of course, the criteria for what should be regarded as efficient or expedient are thoroughly political. In that sense, his appeal to the principle of subsidiarity hides the disputes and does not see the value of procedures for dealing with such disputes.

In the Spinelli project, the counter-concept for Europeanisation had shifted from national sovereignty to the vested interests of the member states, protected by the powers of the Council of Ministers with a veto. There was no resistance against further transfers of power to the Community, but the Luxembourg compromise has taught all member states to protect their interests. The removal of the veto from the Council was, like in the Vedel Report, a part of Spinelli's programme. The powers of the Council were submitted to a control from above by officialising a European Council of the 'heads of state or government'. The belief that they would be more Europe-minded than their ministers in the Council does not sound especially convincing.

A major proposal in Spinelli's speech concerned the concentration of the governmental powers to the Commission by terminating the hybrid legislative-executive character of the Council, which the Vedel Report still accepted. This was a step towards the parliamentarisation of government and it strengthened the Council's and European Council's proto-parliamentary character as voting chambers without a veto. Despite this, letting the European Council choose the President of the Commission instead of Parliament deciding, as the Ad Hoc Assembly had proposed, left the parliamentarisation of the government halfway.

The most original and almost revolutionary move in Spinelli's reform programme was realising the programme through parliaments, accepting it on the European level and creating legitimisation by letting the member state governments debate and ratify it before applying the official procedure through the Commission and the Council. Using the 1984 direct European elections as a quasi-referendum, Schorkopf calls the Spinelli project 'plebiscitarian' (2023, 167–168). While the Vedel Report still appealed to the existing institutions' view towards removing the Council's veto and to effect other reforms, the Spinelli project found justification in the historical forms of parliamentarisation as an unwritten, but legal procedure.

10.3 The legacy of the Ad Hoc Assembly

Whether the Ad Hoc Assembly's work on the Draft Treaty has been used later, for example, in the long debates on directly electing the European Parliament, would deserve another study. As several members of the Assembly were later involved in European institutions, it seems plausible that they would have used some proposals of the Ad Hoc Assembly. Independently of that, I shall speculate in which respects its legacy could be reactivated today.

One legacy of the Ad Hoc Assembly could consist of successful prevention of a one-party European government. In the plans for the European Political Community, opposition parties were included in the Senate and provisions against a single-party European Executive Council were included when its programme was to be approved by both chambers. For the full parliamentarisation of the Commission, the government vs. opposition divide should not be allowed to dominate in European politics. The political competence and imagination of individual MEPs should be fully applied committee work by welcoming members' initiatives and amendments as well as cross-party parliamentary initiatives and amendments (on Westminster see e.g. Wright 2012), not simply pushing through the stands of the Commission.

The bicameral Parliament of the Draft Treaty has seldom been discussed. The Council of National Ministers model of proto-bicameralism persists in the Council of the European Union, although this alternative was almost unanimously rejected by the Ad Hoc Assembly in favour of a parliament-elected Senate. Joschka Fischer proposed in 2000 that 'eine Kammer durch gewählte Abgeordnete besetzt wird, die zugleich Mitglieder der Nationalparlamente sind...Bei der zweiten Kammer wird man sich zwischen einem Senatsmodell mit direktgewählten Senatoren der Mitgliedsstaaten oder einer Staatenkammer analog unseres Bundesrates zu entscheiden haben' (Fischer 2000, see the quote from Griffiths 2000, 17 in 4.2). Even in this respect, the Ad Hoc Assembly's model was more radically supranational.

By adopting the Ad Hoc Assembly's model, the Senate could strengthen itself as the second parliamentary chamber. Even the Ad Hoc Assembly's model for electing the President of the European Commission by the Senate would then be worth considering, giving voice to parliamentarians elected to the Senate. It could make the President of the Commission resemble more a prime minister in a parliamentary regime than a proto-plebiscitarian President.

As mentioned in Chapter 9.1, the renamed Council of the European Union, could be interpreted to allow each country to be represented by a representative of the parliament and a minister (for example, a post like 'chair of the committee for European affairs'). If the government's parliamentary majority is narrow, it would be convenient to nominate the second representative of the opposition to the Council. Even if the parliament's representative were from the government coalition, this would prevent the Council from becoming a rubber stamp of the governments.

An idea debated in passing in the Ad Hoc Assembly but postponed for later consideration concerned border-crossing electoral districts. As an additional step towards supranationalism, it would no longer allocate the seats in the directly elected chamber based on the member states, but on mixed constituencies of at least two countries, at least for a portion of the chamber. This kind of de-naturalisation of electoral districts would strengthen the independence of MEPs against their electorate's immediate interests, as the electorates would be nationally heterogenous. Correspondingly, strict national quotas for the MEPs could also be abolished: already today, several MEPs in the European Parliament represent countries other than that of their citizenship. How such a reform could be realised – for example, whether the European regions would serve as the bases for the cross-border electoral districts, or whether the electoral districts would be formed by a radical deconstruction of state borders by means such as rotation or lottery – could be left to be debated between the parliamentarians.

A further idea discussed in the Ad Hoc Assembly was European citizenship. It was also included in the Draft of the Spinelli project (Entwurf 1984, Article 3), and has today been realised in the burgundy colour of European passports, in the right to vote and stand as a candidate in European and local elections, and in the Schengen Area for the free movement of persons. Besides the EU institutions of the Court, the Central Bank (with the eurozone as a currency union) and the Ombudsman, there already exist numerous institutions independently of nationality within the EU and beyond, including European cultural capitals, the Interrail and the European club competitions in football. Although the borders of these practices are not always identical with the EU and they may be organised independently, they contribute to the strengthening of the European thinking and weakening of the national identity of the citizens. It would be possible to continue these kinds of policies without, however, moving in the direction of ignoring or dismissing the nationality.

One way worthy of consideration for strengthening the parliamentary aspect could be to hold joint meetings of the EU committees with those of the member state parliaments, as suggested in the Vedel Report. This could allow for another level for the strengthening of parliamentary powers, one in which opinions on Europe could be exchanged among member state parliamentarians, as a supplement to the present system where single parliaments have only the possibility to take a stand vertically on proposals 'in the possession of' (to use a Westminster expression) the European Commission or Parliament. The point would be to allow parliamentary initiatives to come from the joint meetings of the member state parliaments. This would complement to the long-standing desire and efforts of many individual MEPs to reduce the Commission's practical monopoly on the parliamentary initiative.

When compared with the Vedel Report and the Spinelli Project, the Ad Hoc Assembly's Draft Treaty applied a more consistent way of combining parliamentary government with supranationalism. The concepts were not used in these later attempts at parliamentarisation, partly due to their points of departure in the situations prevailing at the time, whereas the Ad Hoc Assembly was aiming to set up a new polity. Today both the work of the Ad Hoc Assembly and the different later attempts should be included in the political imagination of politicians for EU parliamentarisation.

I have identified the Ad Hoc Assembly's debates and the Draft Treaty as having marked a momentum that combines supranational and parliamentary politicisation for European integration. The lost opportunity of this endeavour was the failure to realise a European Political Community, the failure to follow the parliamentary path proposed by the Ad Hoc Assembly when writing the Draft Treaty for the Political Community. If we understand this momentum in the Weberian sense of a *Chance,* it is in a historical analysis possible to speak of a partially taken and partially lost chance. Already the identifying of a momentum is a sign that something of it has been taken up; conversely, never in history has there been a momentum that has been followed in every respect. In this sense, the momentum of the Ad Hoc Assembly lives on in its potential to inspire future possibilities for supranational parliamentarism.

All politicising moves have their limits. The joint moment of supranationalism and parliamentarism in the Ad Hoc Assembly relied on delimiting the project for the European Political Community to the specific themes of the economy and foreign policy, which could be amendable, but were 'interpreted restrictively' in the Draft Treaty. In other words, the narrow range of policy topics might have facilitated acceptance of radical supranational parliamentary government among the polity.

The actual history of European integration, however, led to an expansion of policy fields to be Europeanised. The Vedel Report and the Spinelli Project arose out of the experience that intergovernmental diplomacy had gained the upper hand in the polity at the cost of both the parliamentary and the supranational dimension. While the focus on a greater number of policy issues was supranational, this was depoliticised by the veto power of the member states, which reduced supranational powers and restricted politicking to struggles between the member states. The two attempts aimed at re-politicising European institutions for coping with the expanded policy range, but even these, as such, remained far behind the supranational parliamentarism proposed by the Ad Hoc Assembly.

From today's perspective perhaps the main strength of the Ad Hoc Assembly lies in its practice of the parliamentary virtues of dissent and debate. A precondition for that was, however, a willingness and competence to transcend national parochialism and other vested interests and adopt a broader vision, *erweiterte Denkungsart* in Kantian and Arendtian (1982) terms. I present two quotes from Arendt's posthumously published Kant lectures, in which she interpreted Kant's concept of *Urteilskraft* (judgement) as a political concept. In order to reproduce Kant's quotes in the original, I also use the German edition of the lectures.

The 'enlargement of the mind'…is accomplished by 'comparing our judgements with the possible rather than actual judgement of others and putting ourselves in the place of any other man'. The faculty that makes this possible is called imagination…Critical thinking is possible only when the standpoints of all others are open to inspection'. (Arendt 1982, 42–43)
Die 'Erweiterung des Geistes'…wird dadurch erreicht, 'daß man sein Urteil an anderer, nicht sowohl wirkliche, als vielmehr bloß mögliche Urteile hält, und sich in die Stelle jedes andere stellt'. Das Vermögen, das dies möglich macht, wird Einbildungskraft genannt. (Arendt 1985, 60)

'Enlarged thought' is the result of…'abstracting from the limitations which contingently attach to our own judgment', of discarding its 'subjective, private conditions… to which so many are limited', that is, discarding what we usually call self-interest'. (Arendt 1982, 43)
Die 'erweiterte Denkungsart' ist…das Ergebnis einer Abstraktion 'von den Beschränkungen, die unserer eigenen Beurteilung zufälligerweise anhängen', einer Mißachtung der 'subjektiven Privatbedingungen…wozwischen so viele…wie eingeklammert sind', d. h. der Mißachtung dessen, was wir gewöhnlich Selbstinteresse nennen. (Arendt 1985, 61)

My point is that the extended judgement referred to has its best historical approximation in parliamentary procedure and debate. Thorough debating in several rounds, each from different perspectives, is the best-known way of getting rid of prejudices, weighing the stands and arguments of others, and extending one's own as well as other members' horizon of political judgement beyond the narrow interests. What such a widening of horizons leads to must not be named but understood as itself a part of the topic to be debated. 'Enlarged thought', according to Arendt, 'does not tell one *how to* act' (Arendt 1982, 44). Replacing the national point of view with the supranational European perspective is an excellent example of using 'enlarged thought', and the debates of the Ad Hoc Assembly provide us a fine example of how such enlargement of the horizons of political judgement have been practised.

Studying the Ad Hoc Assembly's debates has given me an even greater respect for politicians who act in a parliamentary manner. When faced with the ambitious and unprecedented undertaking of writing a constitutional draft for a new type of polity, the members of the Ad Hoc Assembly showed an astonishing degree of political innovation and judgement.

In his *Liberty before Liberalism,* Quentin Skinner describes the intellectual historian as 'acting as a kind of archaeologist, bringing buried intellectual treasure back to the surface, dusting it down and enabling us to reconsider what we think of it' (1988, 112). Skinner did not want to apply the seventeenth-century neo-Roman concept of liberty to the contemporary world, but he did hold the concept to be worth remembering and reconsidering as a possible contribution to current debates. As he borrowed from Nietzsche, 'you need to be able to ruminate' (1998, 118). This study might be understood in similar terms.

References

1 Documents

Historical Archives of the European Union, (https://www.eui.eu/en/academic-units/historical-archives-of-the-european-union)
—. L'Assemblée Commune de la CECA, https://archives.eui.eu/en/fonds/152?item=AC
—. The Assemblée ad hoc, https://archives.eui.eu/en/fonds/1853?item=AH
Assemblee Ad hoc, AH.AA Activité de l'Assemblée, https://archives.eui.eu/en/fonds/1854?item=AH.AA
— Dossiers spéciaux de la Commission constitutionnelle, https://archives.eui.eu/en/fonds/1855?item=AH.AA-DV%2FCCON_1952
—. Procès-verbaux des réunions de la Commission constitutionnelle, https://archives.eui.eu/en/fonds/1858?item=AH.AA-PV%2FCCON_1952
— Dossiers spéciaux du groupe de travail de la Commission constitutionnelle, https://archives.eui.eu/en/fonds/1856?item=AH.AA-DV%2FCOGT_1952
—. Procès-verbaux des réunions du Comité de rédaction, https://archives.eui.eu/en/fonds/1859?item=AH.AA-PV%2FCOCR_1952
—. Procès-verbaux des réunions de la sous-commission des attributions, https://archives.eui.eu/en/fonds/1863?item=AH.AA-PV%2FSCAT_1952
—. Procès-verbaux des réunions de la sous-commission des Institutions juridictionnelles, https://archives.eui.eu/en/fonds/1864?item=AH.AA-PV%2FSCJU_1952
—. Procès-verbaux des réunions de la sous-commission des Liaisons, https://archives.eui.eu/en/fonds/1865?item=AH.AA-PV%2FSCLI_1952
—. Procès-verbaux des réunions de la sous-commission des Institutions politiques, https://archives.eui.eu/en/fonds/1866?item=AH.AA-PV%2FSCPO_1952
—. Procès-verbaux des réunions de la séance plénière, https://archives.eui.eu/en/fonds/1867?item=AH.AA-PV%2FSEANCE
—. Rapports de la Commission constitutionnelle, https://archives.eui.eu/en/fonds/1868?item=AH.AA-RH%2FCCON_1952
—. Rapports du groupe de travail de la Commission constitutionnelle, https://archives.eui.eu/en/fonds/1869?item=AH.AA-RH%2FCOGT_1952
—. Rapports de la sous-commission des attributions, https://archives.eui.eu/en/fonds/1870?item=AH.AA-RH%2FSCAT_1952
—. Rapports de la sous-commission des Institutions juridictionnelles, https://archives.eui.eu/en/fonds/1871?item=AH.AA-RH%2FSCJU_1952
—. Rapports de la sous-commission des Liaisons, ps://archives.eui.eu/en/fonds/1872?item=AH.AA-RH%2FSCLI_1952
—. Rapports de la sous-commission des institutions politiques, https://archives.eui.eu/en/fonds/1873?item=AH.AA-RH%2FSCPO_1952
Draft Treaty Embodying the Statute of the European Community. http://aei.pitt.edu/991/1/political_union_draft_treaty_1.pdf
La Haye (1948): Congrès inaugural européen https://archives.eui.eu/en/fonds/158711?item=ME.45.01=
— Document divers, ME–1264.pdf
— Session pleniere, ME–0388.pdf

— Session pleniere, ME–0421.pdf
— Session pleniere, ME–0570.pdf
Briand Plan 1930. League of Nations. Documents Relating to the Organisation of a System of European Federal Union, https://www.europarl.europa.eu/100books/file/EN-N-B-0014-Memorandum.pdf
The Coming Century of Supranational Communities. Robert Schuman's speech 16 May 1949, https://www.schuman.info/Strasbourg549.htm
Commission of the European Communities 1972. Report of the Working Party examining the problemof the enlargement of the powers of the European Parliament <<Report Vedel>>, http://aei.pitt.edu/5587/
Le congrès de l'Union européenne des fédéralistes à Montreux (27 au 31 août 1947) https://www.cvce.eu/education/unit-content/-/unit/7b137b71-6010-4621-83b4-b0ca06a6b2cb/3f668d4f-d854-4518-8aa1-eb0ec412905a
Documents on the History of European Integration, eds Walter Lipgens and Wilfried Loth. Berlin: de Gruyter.
–Vol. 3. 1988. The Struggle for the European Union by Political Parties and Pressure Groups in West European Countries 1945–1950.
–Vol. 4. 1991. Transnational Organizations of Political Parties and Pressure Groups in the Struggle for the European Union.
European Defence Community Treaty, unofficial translation, https://aei.pitt.edu/5201/1/5201.pdf
Europäisches Parlament, Entwurf eines Vertrages zur Gründung der Europäischen Union, angenommen am 14. Dexember 1984 (Spinelli-Entwurf), https://www.politische-union.de/eu-vertragsentwurf1984.pdf
Fischer, Joschka 2000. *Die Rede des Bundesministers des Auswärtigen Joschka Fischer am 12. Mai 2000 in der Humboldt-Universität Berlin*, https://www.bundesregierung.de/breg-de/service/bulletin/rede-des-bundesministers-des-auswaertigen-joschka-fischer-808150
Inter-Parliamentary Union. Main Areas of Activity of the Inter-Parliamentary Union.
Journal official de la Communauté européenne du carbon et de l'acier. Débats de l'Assemblée Commune, Compte rendu in extenso de séances, 1952–1953, http://aei.pitt.edu/64508/1/A6595.pdf
Schuman Declaration, du Mai 1950, https://www.robert-schuman.eu/fr/declaration-du-9-mai-1950
Spinelli, Altiero 1983. Towards the European Union, https://www.thefederalist.eu/site/index.php/en/essays/1996-towards-the-european-union#_edn1
Statement by Anthony Eden (19 March 1952): https://www.cvce.eu/en/obj/statement_by_anthony_eden_19_march_1952-en-5b2bfb47-d200-49e5-bdf7-25a4e16ad831.html.
The Statute of the Council of Europe, 5 May 1949, https://scienzepolitiche.unical.it/bacheca/archivio/materiale/143/Storia%20integrazione%20europea/Statute%20of%20the%20Council%20of%20Europe%201949.pdf
The Statute of the Council of Europe, Signed at London, on 5 May 1949, https://treaties.un.org/doc/Publication/UNTS/Volume%2087/volume-87-I-1168-English.pdf
Traité instituant la Communauté européenne du charbon et de l'acier, traité CECA, https://eur-lex.europa.eu/legal-content/FR/TXT/HTML/?uri=LEGISSUM:xy0022
Union des Fédéralistes Européens' (https://www.cvce.eu/education/unit-content/-/unit/7b137b71-6010-4621-83b4-b0ca06a6b2cb/3f668d4f-d854-4518-8aa1-eb0ec412905a

United Nations Parliamentary Assembly, https://en.wikipedia.org/wiki/United_Nations_Parliamentary_Assembly.

The Ventonome Manifesto. Towards a free and united Europe – a draft manifesto [1941], https://web.archive.org/web/20050408162709/http://www.federalunion.org.uk/archives/ventotene.shtml

Vertrag zur Gründung der Europäischen Gemeinschaft für Kohle und Stahl, EGKS-Vertrag,

Werdegang der Artikel des Entwurfs eines Vertrages über die Satzung der Europäischen Politischen Gemeinschaft 1953. Luxemburg: Sekretariat des Ministerrates 15. April 1954.

Zusammensetzung der Gemeinsamen Versammlung der EGKS (Erste Sitzungsperiode 10–13 September 1952 https://www.cvce.eu/de/obj/zusammensetzung_der_gemeinsamen_versammlung_der_egks_erste_sitzungsperiode_10_13_september_1952-de-69d13dd6-cbdf-469c-bf23-a9f3e90daf42.html

2 Literature

Agnoli, Johannes 1967. 'Die Transformation der Demokratie', in Johannes Agnoli and Peter Brückner, *Die Transformation der Demokratie,* Frankfurt/M: Europäische Verlagsanstalt, 5–87.

Andrén, Nils 1947. *Den klassiska parlamentarismens genombrott i England.* Stockholm: Almqvist & Wicksell.

Ankersmit, F.R. 1996. *Aesthetic Politics.* Stanford: Stanford University Press.

— 2002. *Political Representation.* Stanford: Stanford University Press.

Arendt, Hannah 1961. *Between Past and Future.* New York: Viking Press.

— 1982. *Lectures on Kant's Political Philosophy.* University of Chicago Press.

— 1985. *Das Urteilen. Texte zu Kants politischer Philosophie.* München: Piper,

Bagehot, Walter 1867/1972 [2001]. *The English Constitution.* Cambridge: Cambridge University Press.

Beck, Ulrich and Edgar Grange 2004. *Das kosmopolitische Europa.* Frankfurt/M.: Suhrkamp.

Beyen, Marnix and Henk te Velde 2016. 'Passion and Reason. Modern Parliaments in the Low Countries', in Pasi Ihalainen, Cornelia Ilie and Kari Palonen (eds), *Parliament and Parliamentarism.* Oxford: Berghahn, 81–96.

Borchert, Jens. 2003. *Die Professionalisierung der Politik.* Frankfurt/M: Campus.

Buchstein, Hubertus 2009. *Demokratie und Lotterie.* Frankfurt/M: Campus.

Burke, Edmund 1774. 'Speech to the electors in Bristol', in *Selected Works of Edmund Burke,* vol. 4., 4–14, https://oll.libertyfund.org/title/canavan-select-works-of-edmund-burke-vol-4.

Butler, Judith 2015. *Notes toward a Performative Theory of Assembly.* Cambridge, Mass.: Harvard University Press.

Campion, G.F.M. 1929 *An Introduction to the Procedure of House of Commons.* London: Allen & co.

Canihac, Hugo 2020. 'From Nostalgia to Utopia: a genealogy of the French conceptions of supranationality (1848–1948)'. *Modern Intellectual History* 17, 707–736.

Cohen, Antonin 1998. 'Le Plan Schuman de Paul Reuter entre communauté nationale et fédération européenne', *Revue française de science politique*, 46, 645–663.
Colclough, David 2005. *Freedom of Speech in Early Stuart England*. Cambridge: Cambridge University Press.
Conti, Gregory 2019. *Parliament the Mirror of the Nation. Representation, Deliberation and Democracy in Victorian Britain*. Cambridge: Cambridge University Press.
Dicey, A.W. 1885 [1961]. *Introduction to the Study of the Law of the Constitution*. London: Macmillan.
Duroselle, Jean-Baptiste 1966. 'General de Gaulle's Europe and Jean Monnet's Europe', *The World Today* 22, 1–13.
Evans, Paul ed. 2017. *Essays on the History of Parliamentary Procedure*. London: Bloomsbury.
Forsyth, Murray 1964. *Das Parlament der Europäischen Gemeinschaft*, Bonn: Europa Union Verlag.
Gehler, Michael 2002/2014. *Europa. Von der Utopie zur Realität*. Innsbruck: Haymon.
Gottschalch, Wilfried 1968. *Parlamentarismus und Rätedemokratie*. Berlin: Wagenbach.
Grey, Henry George 1858, *Parliamentary Government Considered with Respect to A Reform of Parliament*, (https://www.google.com/search?client=safari&rls=en&q=1858+Parliamentary+Government+Considered+with+Respect+to+A+Reform+of+Parliament.+An+Essay.&ie=UTF-8&oe=UTF-8)
Griffith, J.A.C. and Michael Ryle 2003. *Parliament. Functions, Practices, Procedures*. 2. edition by Robert Blackburn and Andrew Kinnon. London: Sweet and Maxwell.
Griffiths, Richard T. 2000. *Europe's First Constitution. The European Political Community, 1952–1954*. London: Federal Trust.
Guerriri, Sandro 2008. 'The start of European integration and the parliamentary dimension: the Common Assembly of the ECSC (1952–1958)'. *Parliaments, Estates & Representation* 28, 183–193.
— 2014. From the Hague Congress to the Council of Europe: hopes, achievements and disappointments in the parliamentary way to European integration (1948–51). *Parliaments, Estates & Representation* 34, 216–227.
Gunn, J.A.G. 2009. *When the French Thought They Were British*. Montréal: McGill University Press.
Gusy, Christoph ed. 2008. *Demokratie in der Krise: Europa in der Zwischenkriegszeit*. Baden-Baden: Nomos
Haapala, Taru 2022. 'Saving European Democracy. British debates on European unification 1948–49', in Niilo Kauppi and Kari Palonen eds *Rhetoric and Bricolage in European Politics and Beyond. The Political Mind in Action*. London: Palgrave Macmillan, 59–88.
Haapala, Taru & Álvaro Oleart (eds) 2022. Tracing the Politicisation of the EU: The Future of Europe Debates Before and After the 2019 Elections. London: Palgrave Macmillan.
Haapala, Taru & Hanna-Mari Kivistö 2023. 'A Missed Opportunity. The Drafting of European Political Authority in the Consultative Assembly of the Council of Europe, 1949–1951'. *Parliaments, Estates & Representation* 43, 306–321.
Habermas, Jürgen 1962. *Strukturwandel der Öffentlichkeit*. Neuwied: Luchterhand.
Hexter. J.H. 1992. *Parliament and Liberty*. Princeton: Princeton University Press.
Ilie, Cornelia and Cesar Ornatowski 2016. 'Central and Eastern European Parliamentary Rhetoric since the Nineteenth Century: The Case of Romania and Poland', in Pasi

Ihalainen, Cornelia Ilie and Kari Palonen (eds). *Parliament and Parliamentarism.* Oxford: Berghahn, 192–217.

'Initiation á l'idée du "supranational"' 1955. *Chronique de politique étrangère* 8, 637–645.

Kapteyn, P.J.G. 1962. *L'assemblée commune de la communaute européenne du charbon et acier.* Leiden: Sijthoff.

Kauppi, Niilo, Kari Palonen and Claudia Wiesner 2016. The Politification and Politicisation of the EU. *Redescriptions: Political Thought, Conceptual History and Feminist Theory* 19, 72–90.

Kiljunen, Kimmo 2004. *The European Constitution in the Making.* Brussels: Centre for European Policy Studies.

Kissling, Claudia 2006. *Die Interparlamentarische Union im Wandel.* Frankfurt/M: Peter Lang.

Kluxen, Kurt 1956. *Das Problem der politischen Opposition.* Freiburg: Alber.

Kluxen, Kurt 1983. *Geschichte und Problematik des Parlamentarismus.* Frankfurt/M: Suhrkamp.

Koselleck, Reinhart 1959 [1973]. *Kritik und Krise.* Frankfurt/M.: Suhrkamp

— 1972. 'Einleitung', in *Geschichtliche Grundbegriffe*, Bd. I. Stuttgart: Klett, xii–xxvii.

— 1979. *Vergangene Zukunft. Zur Semantik geschichtlicher Zeiten.* Frankfurt/M: Suhrkamp.

Koskenniemi, Martti 2001. *The Gentle Civilizer of Nations. The rise and fall of International Law 1870–1960.* Cambridge: Cambridge University Press.

Krumrey, Jakob 2018. *Symbolic Politics of European Integration. Staging Europe.* London: Palgrave Macmillan.

Leibholz, Gerhard (1951 [1967]). 'Repräsentativer Parlamentarismus und parteienstatliche Demokratie', in Kurt Kluxen ed. *Parlamentarismus.* Köln: Kiepenhauer & Witsch, 349–360.

Leinen, Jo and Andreas Bummel. *Das demokratische Weltparlament.* Bonn: Dietz.

Maier, Charles S. ed. 1987. *Changing Boundaries of the Political.* Cambridge: Cambridge University Press.

Mergel, Thomas 2002. *Parlamentarische Kultur in der Weimarer Republik.* Düsseldorf: Droste.

Müller, Christoph, *Das imperative und das freie Mandat.* Leiden: Sifthoff.

Otto, Volker 1971. *Das Staatsverständnis des Parlamentarischen Rates.* Düsseldorf: Droste.

Palonen, Kari 1998. *Das 'Webersche Moment'.* Wiesbaden: Westdeutscher Verlag.

— 2003. 'Four times of politics: Policy, polity, politicking and politicization'. *Alternatives: Global, local, political* 28, 171–186.

— 2006. *A Struggle with Time. A conceptual history of 'politics' as an activity.* Münster: LIT.

— 2010. *"Objektivität" als faires Spiel. Wissenschaft als Politik bei Max Weber.* Baden-Baden: Nomos.

— 2012. *Rhetorik des Unbeliebten. Lobreden auf Politiker im Zeitalter der Demokratie.* Baden-Baden: Nomos.

— 2014a. *The Politics of Parliamentary Procedure. The formation of the From Oratory to Debate. Parliamentarisation of Deliberative Rhetoric in Westminster. Westminster procedure as a parliamentary ideal type.* Leverkusen: Barbara Budrich.

— 2014b. 'Was Max Weber Wrong about Westminster?' *History of Political Thought* 34, 519–535.

— From Oratory to Debate. Parliamentarisation of Deliberative Rhetoric in Westminster. Baden-Baden: Nomos.
— 2018. Parliamentary Thinking. Procedure, Rhetoric and Time. London. Palgrave Macmillan
— 2019a. 'Four aspects of politics in Max Weber's Politik als Beruf'. Journal of Classical Sociology 19, 331–345.
— 2019b. 'Parliamentary and Electoral Decisions as Political Acts', in Daniel Bessner and Nicolas Guilhot (eds). The Decisionist Imagination. Oxford: Berghahn, 85–108.
— 2020. 'Aspects of conceptual history of parliamentary politics', in Cyril Benoît and Olivier Rozenberg eds Handbook of Parliamantary Studies. Interdisciplinary approaches to legislature. Celtenham: Edward Elgar, 67–85.
— 2021a. 'Parliamentarisation as Politicisation', in Rethinking Politicisation in Political Science, Sociology and International Relations, ed. Claudia Wiesner. London: Palgrave Macmillan, 75–80.
— 2021b. Politik als parlamentarischer Begriff. Perspektiven aus dem Deutschen Bundestag. Leverkusen: Barbara Budrich.
— 2022a. 'A Lost Opportunity to Parliamentarisation of the European Commission. Bagehot, Weber and a debate in 1960', History of Political Thought 43, 382–403.
— 2022b. 'Paradigms for Political Action. A draft for a repertoire'. Redescriptions 25, 97–112.
— 2023. 'We Politicians: Translation, Rhetoric, and Conceptual Change', in Luigi Alonzi ed. History as a Translation of the Past. London: Bloomsbury, 121–140.
Palonen, Kari and José María Rosales (eds) 2015. Parliamentarism and Democratic Theory. Leverkusen: Barbara Budrich.
Palonen, Kari, José María Rosales and Tapani Turkka (eds) 2014. The Politics of Dissensus. Parliament in Debate. Santander: University of Cantabury Press.
Pierre, Eugène 1887. De la procédure parlementaire. Étude sur le mécanisme intérieur du pouvoir législatif. Paris: Maison Quantin.
Piodi, Franco 2017. Towards a Single Parliament. The influence of the ECSC Common Assembly on the Treaties of Rome. Historical Archives of the European Parliament. https://historicalarchives.europarl.europa.eu/files/live/sites/historicalarchive/files/03_PUBLICATIONS/03_European-Parliament/01_Documents/towards-a-single-parliament-en.pdf
Redlich, Josef 1905. Recht und Technik des Englischen Parlamentarismus. Leipzig: Duncker & Humblot.
Ridard, Basile 2018. L'encadrement du temps parlementaire dans la procédure de législative. Étude compare: Allemagne, Espagne, France, Royaume-Uni. Paris: Assemblée nationale.
Rittberger, Bernhard 2005. Building Europe's Parliament. Democratic Representation Beyond the Nation-State. Oxford: Oxford University Press.
Robert, Cecile 2021. 'Depoliticisation at the European Level: Delegitimisation and circumvention of representative democracy in Europe's governance', in Claudia Wiesner (ed.) Rethinking Politicisation in Politics, Sociology and International Relations. London: Palgrave Macmillan, 201–222.
Roussellier, Nicolas 1997. Un parlement d'éloquence, Paris: Presses de Sciences-po.
Roussellier, Nicolas 2015. La force de gouverner. Le pouvoir exécutif in France. Paris: Gallimard.
Schlochauer, Hans-Jürgen 1953/55, 'Von der Association zur Integration Europas'. Die Friedens-Warte, 1–18.

Schmitt, Carl 1941[2022]. *Völkerrechtliche Großraumordnung mit Interventionsverbot der raumfreien Mächte.* Berlin: Duncker & Humblot 2022.
Selinger, William 2019. *Parliamentarism from Burke to Weber.* Cambridge: Cambridge University Press.
Skinner, Quentin 1969. 'Meaning and Understanding in the History of Ideas', *History and Theory* 8, 3–53.
— 1974. 'Principles and Practices of Political Opposition: The case Bolingbroke versus Walpole', in *Historical Perspectives,* ed. Neil McKendrick. London: Europa, 93–128.
— 1998. *Liberty before Liberalism.* Cambridge: Cambridge University Press.
— 2002. 'A Third Concept of Liberty', *Proceedings of the British Academy* 117, 237–268.
— 2007. 'Paradiastole', in Sylvia Adamson et al. (eds), *Renaissance Figures of Speech.* . Cambridge: Cambridge University Press, 149–163.
Soininen, Suvi and Tapani Turkka (eds) 2012. *The Parliamentary Style of Politics.* Helsinki: The Finnish Political Science Association.
Soutou, Georges-Henri 2021. *Europa! Les projets européens de l'Allemagne nazié et de l'Italie fasciste.* Paris: Tallendier.
Tanchoux, Philippe. 2004. *Les procédures électorales en France.* Paris: Comité des travaux historiques et scientifiques.
Tiilikainen, Teija 2011. 'The Role of European Parliament in EU's Political Order', in Claudia Wiesner, Tapani Turkka & Kari Palonen (eds). *Parliament and Europe.* Baden-Baden: Nomos, 2540.
Tiilikainen, Teija and Claudia Wiesner 2016. 'Towards a Political Theory of EU Parliamentarism', in Pasi Ihalainen, Cornelia Ilie and Kari Palonen (eds). *Parliament and Parliamentarism. A comparative history of a European Concept.* Oxford: Berghahn, 292310.
Turkka, Tapani 2007. *The Origins of Parliamentarism. A study on the Sandys' motion.* Baden-Baden: Nomos.
Ullrich, Sebastian 2009. *Der Weimar-Komplex.* Göttingen: Wallstein.
Vieira, Ryan 2015. *Time and Politics. Parliament and the culture of modernity in Britain and the British world.* Oxford: Oxford University Press.
Wassenburg, Birte 2013. *History of the Council of Europe.* Strasbourg: Council of Europe.
Weber, Max 1904 [1973]. 'Die "Objektivität" sozialwissenschaftlicher und sozialpolitischer Erkenntnis', in *Gesammelte Aufsätze zur Wissenschaftslehre,* ed. Johannes Winckelmann. Tübingen: Mohr, 146–214.
— 1906 [1973]. 'Kritische Studien auf dem Gebiet der kulturwissenschaftlichen Logik', in *Gesammelte Aufsätze zur Wissenschaftslehre,* ed. Johannes Winckelmann. Tübingen: Mohr, 215–290.
— 1917a [1973]. 'Der Sinn der 'Wertfreiheit' in soziologischen und ökonomischen Wissenschaften'. in *Gesammelte Aufsätze zur Wissenschaftslehre,* ed. Johannes Winckelmann. Tübingen: Mohr, 489–540.
— 1917b |1984]. 'Wahlrecht und Demokratie in Deutschland', in *Max-Weber-Studienausgabe* I/15, eds Wolfgang J. Mommsen and Gangolf Hübinger. Tübingen: Mohr, 155–189.
— 1918 [1984]. 'Parlament und Regierung im neugeordneten Deutschland', in *Max-Weber-Studienausgabe* I/15, eds Wolfgang J. Mommsen and Gangolf Hübinger. Tübingen: Mohr, 202–302.

— 1919 [1991]. 'Der Reichspräsident', in *Max-Weber-Studienausgabe* I/16, eds Wolfgang J. Mommsen and Wolfgang Schwendtker. Tübingen: Mohr, 75–77.
— 1922 [1980]. *Wirtschaft und Gesellschaft*, ed. Johannes Winckelmann. Tübingen: Mohr.
Wiesner, Claudia ed. 2019. 'Rethinking Politicisation: Critical Exchanges', Special issue *Contemporary Political Theory* 18, 248–281.
Wiesner, Claudia ed. 2021. *Rethinking Politicisation in Politics, Sociology and International Relations*. London: Palgrave Macmillan.
Wiesner, Claudia, Taru Haapala and Kari Palonen 2017. *Debates, Rhetoric and Political Action. Practices of Textual Interpretation and Analysis*. London: Palgrave Macmillan.
Wigny, Pierre 1958. *L'Assemblée Parlementaire dans l'Europe des Six*, http://aei.pitt.edu/39007/
Wilde, Pieter de and Michael Zürn 2012. Can the Politicization of European Integration be Reversed? *Journal of Common Market Studies* 50, 137–153.
Wittgenstein, Ludwig 1953 [1971]. *Philosophische Untersuchungen*. Frankfurt/M: Suhrkamp.
Wright, Tony 2012. *Doing Politics*. London: Biteback.
Zürn, Michael 2016. 'Opening up Europe: Next Steps in Politicisation Research'. *West European Politics* 39, 164–182.

Erratum

The references in this book do not contain all the titles mentioned. Please note the additions listed below. We apologize for this mistake!

Additions to References:

Ad Hoc Assembly 1953. *Ad Hoc Assembly instructed to work out a draft treaty setting up a European Political Community, Session of January 1953. Report of the Constitutional Committee*. Paris, 20 December 1952. http://aei.pitt.edu/33690/

Schorkopf, Frank 2023. *Die unentschiedene Macht. Verfassungsgeschichte der Europäischen Union 1948–2017*. Göttingen: Vandenhoek & Ruprecht.

Ullrich, Sebastian 2009. *Der Weimar Komplex. Das Scheitern der ersten deutschen Demokratie und die politische Kultur der frühen Bundesrepublik 1945–1949*. Göttingen: Wallstein.

Palonen, Kari 2024. *At the Origins of Parliamentary Europe: Supranational parliamentary government in debates of the Ad Hoc Assembly for the European Political Community in 1952–1953*. Opladen, Berlin, Toronto: Verlag Barbara Budrich. ISBN 978-3-8474-3066-7

Index of actors

Adenauer, Konrad 59f., 62f., 74, 76, 91f., 98, 135, 156, 158, 177
Azara, Antonio 65, 75, 80, 98f., 117, 133, 142, 145f., 166

Becker, Max 78, 80, 101, 113, 119f., 148, 161, 165, 171, 173, 182–184
Benvenuti, Lodovico 78, 80, 85f., 94, 97, 101, 109f., 115–120, 122f., 125f., 142, 183
Bergmann, Giulio 79f., 86, 97, 122
Bertram, Helmut 80, 161, 172
Bertrand, Alfred 80, 109, 123
Bidault, Georges 38, 73, 92
Blaisse, Pieter Alphons (P.A.) 64, 76, 80, 85, 96, 109, 115, 117, 119, 122f., 133, 140, 148, 161, 172, 188
Braun, Heinz 81, 153, 157
Brentano, Heinrich von 71, 76, 81, 85, 93, 96, 98f., 113, 118f., 123, 125, 140f., 146, 155, 157f., 160, 165–167, 169, 176–179
Bruins Slot, Sieuwert 81, 85, 110f., 136, 146f., 172

Churchill, Winston 25, 30f.
Coudenhove-Kalergi, Richard 25, 31, 34

Debré, Michel 23, 60, 75, 77f., 81, 86, 88, 93, 96, 98, 102f., 108–110, 112f., 128f., 134, 140, 156, 166, 177
Dehousse, Fernand 69, 76, 78, 81, 85f., 93f., 96f., 99–101, 103, 112–114, 118f., 123, 125, 127, 129, 133, 135–143, 145–150, 152f., 155f., 159–169, 171–181, 183–185, 187

Delbos, Yves 81, 96, 119, 152–154
Dominedò, Francesco Maria 81, 115, 125, 173, 181f., 184

Eden, Anthony 68f.

Giovannini, Alberto 81, 76, 88, 110
Goes van Naters, Marinus van der 82, 85, 98–100, 112, 115, 117, 119, 122, 126, 129, 136–138, 146–149, 152f, 159–161, 164f., 171, 178f.

Jaquet, Gerard 82, 122, 126, 161, 180f.

Klompé, Marga 82, 59, 127, 163, 172f., 182f.
Kopf, Hermann 82, 96, 98f., 127, 140, 146, 157, 167, 184
Korthals, Henk 82, 117, 154

Layton, Walter 136, 140, 159
Lefevre, Theo 76, 82, 98, 147, 149

Margue, Nicolas 75, 77, 82, 101, 109, 112, 115, 122, 137, 149, 161
Maroger, Jean 76, 82, 109
Menthon, François de 35, 77, 82, 94f., 97, 123, 125–127, 161, 165, 172, 181
Merkatz, Hans-Joachim von 76, 82, 85, 110–112, 125, 133, 136f., 146f., 149, 151, 155, 158–160, 162, 165–168, 170, 174, 176, 185
Mollet, Guy 47, 77, 82, 96f., 101, 114f., 126
Monnet, Jean 45, 48, 50–52, 59–61, 63, 66, 79, 97f., 106–108, 135, 200

Montini, Lodovico   82, 100, 113, 115, 136, 140, 145, 152, 154f., 160f., 165, 174, 179, 181, 186
Mutter, André   83, 96, 123, 155, 159

Nederhorst, Gerard   83, 116, 122

Parri, Ferruccio   83, 116, 125, 182–184
Persico, Giovanni   76, 83, 85, 96, 112f., 140, 152, 158, 172
Plaisant, Marcel   79, 83, 173f.
Preusker, Victor Emmanuel   83, 122, 137f.
Pünder, Hermann   78, 83, 85

Reynaud, Paul   83, 150, 173

Santero, Natale   79, 83, 150, 152, 182
Sassen, E.M.J.A. (Maan)   76, 83, 163
Schaus, Eugène   83, 99, 112, 136, 140f., 151, 153, 162f., 171, 178
Schuman, Robert   23, 26, 38, 45, 48–51, 69, 72f., 93, 107f.
Semler, Johannes   84, 85, 112f., 140, 163

Senghor, Léopold Sédar   84, 79, 129, 155f.
Silvandre, Jean   84, 79, 129, 155f.
Spaak, Paul-Henri   13, 65, 69, 75, 78f., 85, 91f., 95, 111, 115, 120, 153, 184
Spinelli, Altiero   24f., 69, 106f., 192, 200–204, 206f.
Struye, Paul   84, 63–66, 75, 89

Teitgen, Pierre-Henri   84, 75, 85, 93f., 99–101, 103, 112, 116, 118f., 123, 125, 133, 135–138, 140, 142, 145–147, 150–154, 156f., 159f., 162–169, 171f., 176, 178–180, 183–185, 198

Vedel, Georges   24, 192–198, 200f., 203f., 206f.
Vermeylen, Piet   84, 115, 143, 167, 172–174, 181–184

Wigny, Pierre   57f., 67, 84f., 94, 96, 100f., 113, 115, 119, 122f., 133, 135, 138, 145–149, 159, 163–165, 167, 170f., 173f., 182–184, 194

Ziino, Vinizio   84, 123, 155, 165, 167, 173

Index of concepts

Ad Hoc Assembly 9–12, 15–16, 19–24, 27, 46–48, 54, 66–192, 194, 195, 197–200, 203–208
- Constitutional Committee 23, 71, 79f, 85–89, 93–94, 98, 108–115, 119, 122, 124, 126, 134–138, 140, 142f, 148, 150 153–159, 161–163, 165f, 169, 173, 177, 180, 188
- Constitutional draft 9, 19, 21–23, 29, 68, 71, 108, 127, 208
- Draft Treaty 9, 11, 21–23, 71–74, 88, 94, 97, 102, 108f., 111f., 115, 120f., 125, 127–129, 132–136, 139, 141f., 144, 150, 156, 164, 166, 168f., 176–178, 185, 187–191, 200, 202f., 205, 207
- Members 9–11, 64, 66–68, 77–86, 91, 95–99, 101, 103, 106, 109–117, 120f, 123, 125–130, 132–139, 143–147, 149, 152, 156f., 160f., 171f., 175, 181, 183f., 186–188, 205, 208
- Observers 20, 23, 79f., 94, 103, 113f., 136, 140, 163,165
- Plenum, plenary 9, 21, 23, 72f., 78f., 85f., 89f., 91f., 94–97, 101, 109–112, 115–118, 120, 122f., 125, 127, 129, 134–138, 141f., 145f., 149, 152–157, 161, 163, 165, 167, 172–174, 177, 180f., 186, 190
- President 79, 85, 115, 184
- Sub-committee for Attributions 85, 87 101, 109, 115, 133, 142
- Sub-committee for Political Institutions 23, 85–89, 93, 99–101, 112f., 118, 129, 135–138, 140f., 145–150, 153, 155, 157, 159–161, 164–166, 168, 171f 174–179, 181, 184, 185, 187
- Working Party 23, 85–89, 94, 96, 111, 116–118, 123, 125–127, 134f., 139, 142f., 155f., 158, 167, 170, 173

Constitutions, Political systems
- Britain s. Parliaments/Westminster
- France 47, 50, 52, 96, 140, 151, 153–156, 174, 180, 184, 199
- Switzerland 36, 37, 53, 131, 181–183, 203
- United States 36.f, 92, 98, 127, 147
- West Germany 26, 31, 49, 56, 62, 77, 103, 119, 132, 143, 183, 187

Council of Europe 10f., 16, 20, 22–24, 28, 35, 38–48, 51, 55, 57, 62f., 65–70, 72, 79f., 92f., 97–99, 113f., 120f., 126–129, 132, 138, 141, 146–148, 150f., 155, 157, 159, 161, 165–167, 186
- Committee of Ministers 40–47, 51, 68, 113f., 118, 125
- Consultative Assembly 11, 23, 38–47, 62, 65, 68f., 74f, 92, 97f., 103, 114, 126, 128, 138, 141, 161, 165f., 187

European Coal and Steel Community (ECSC) 10f., 14, 17, 20, 22–24, 45f, 48–72, 74–80, 91–95, 97f., 100f, 106–108, 111–114, 116f., 121, 123, 125, 128f, 131–135, 137f., 140–142, 144–146, 151, 155, 157–160, 170, 174, 176–179, 183, 186, 193–197, 200
- Common Assembly 10, 14., 16, 20, 23, 45–48, 51f., 54–57, 59–69, 71, 74–77, 79f., 91, 93, 97–99, 108f., 113, 132, 134f., 138, 144,

156, 158, 160, 187f., 194–197, 200
- Council of Ministers 23, 48, 51f., 54–57, 59f., 62f, 67, 69, 76f, 108, 158
- High Authority 10f., 16, 23, 48, 50–67, 69, 93, 99, 106f., 112–114, 126, 128, 136, 170, 174, 176–179, 195
- Paris Treaty 10, 48, 51f, 67

European Defence Community (EDC) 10, 23, 69f., 72–75, 92–95,100f., 116f., 119, 121, 124f., 129, 133, 140, 142, 147, 155, 160, 165, 170, 176f., 179, 183

European Political Community (EPC) 9–11, 14, 16, 20–23, 46, 48, 68, 70–74, 77, 79, 88, 91–103, 109–117, 119, 121f., 124–130, 132, 134, 136–140, 147, 150, 159, 161, 168, 170, 175f., 188–190, 207
- Council of National Ministers 136, 141, 148, 158f., 161–165, 170–175, 178–181, 186, 195, 205
- Direct elections 99–102, 117, 137, 141f., 145–151, 159, 164, 168, 187, 189, 199f.
- Distribution of seats 145, 149, 155–158, 162–164
- Draft Treaty (see Ad Hoc Assembly)
- Economic and Social Council 23, 54, 93, 133, 189
- European Executive Council/ European government 11, 71–73, 99–103, 118, 124–126, 137, 139f., 143f., 149, 165, 169–189., 198–200, 205
- Legal status 16, 23, 116, 124
- Membership, Association 23f., 69f., 79, 109, 126f., 129, 143, 165

- Parliament [of the Community] 71, 91, 97–103, 117–120, 130–177, 179–185, 187, 189–192
- Peoples' Chamber 100f., 120, 129, 138, 141–143, 145–158, 163f, 167, 169, 180, 182–186
- President of European Executive Council 100, 143, 176, 178–183
- Senate 42, 72f., 76, 100–102, 114, 126, 135f., 139, 141–143, 148, 154, 157–169, 172–175, 181–187, 189, 198, 205

European Union (EU) 9f., 20f., 24f., 48, 72, 74, 92f., 105, 107, 130, 139, 175,183, 190–192, 200, 202f., 206f.
- Council of the European Union (formerly Council of Ministers) 175, 183, 193–206
- European Commission 16, 137, 140, 192–198, 200–206.
- European Council 141, 177, 202, 204
- European Parliament 9, 16, 139f., 142f., 154, 192–202, 205f.

Federal/–ism, federation 25–31, 33–37, 44–47, 49f., 60, 62f., 68–70, 72, 76–78, 88, 91, 97, 106–112, 114, 117, 128, 130, 163, 171, 173, 176, 200
- Confederal-/ism, confederation 30, 47, 70f., 91, 93, 107, 109–111

Parliamentarism 9, 14f., 17, 19f., 22–25, 31, 39, 46, 67, 74, 103, 107, 118, 129–132, 150, 158, 162, 173, 175, 178, 180, 188, 191, 207
- Parliamentarian 9f., 22f., 25, 27, 31, 33f., 37, 42f., 46f., 51, 55–57, 59, 63, 66, 68, 71, 77–80, 89, 102, 105–108, 132f., 135, 137–139,

143, 164–166, 168f., 175, 186, 189, 191f., 197–200, 205f.
- Parlamentarisation 9, 12–14, 16f., 19–21, 23f., 38, 45, 47, 66f., 82, 85, 118, 126, 131f., 142, 150, 161, 175, 188, 192
- Parliamentary government/system 9, 11, 18, 25, 34, 72f., 99f., 102f.,106, 116f., 128, 131–133, 168, 178f, 183f., 188f.
- Parliamentary debate/rhetoric 14f., 18–20, 24, 38–40, 49, 65, 90f., 133f., 143f., 148, 183
- Parliamentary elections 14, 17, 19, 99, 132, 141f., 145–155, 158, 164,
- Parliamentary freedom, free mandate 14f., 17, 20, 30, 39f., 41, 52f, 55, 58, 61f., 102, 119–121, 129, 133, 135–139, 169, 174, 187, 194
- Parliamentary initiative 67, 75, 78, 97, 116, 125, 142–146, 174, 183, 196, 201f., 205f.
- Parliamentary procedure 11, 13–17, 22, 26, 41–43, 55, 57, 63–67, 78, 85, 110, 125, 133f. 129, 186f., 194, 197, 208
- Parliamentary representation 16f., 19, 26, 40, 54, 58, 140–142, 145, 148, 152, 155–158, 160, 162–168, 175
- Parliamentary responsibility/ 33, 35, 40, 45, 61, 99, 101, 149, 177f., 180, 185, 194
- Parliamentary time 14, 18, 20, 55, 61, 102, 138f., 164–169, 188
- Parliamentary, vote of censure/of no confidence 37, 47, 54, 56f., 60–62, 66, 128, 132f., 167, 182–185, 193, 20

Parliaments
- Assemblée Nationale/Sénat (France) 15, 17, 21, 34, 65, 72
- Bundesrat (West Germany) 135f., 161, 165, 178, 205
- Bundestag (West Germany) 134f., 139, 151, 185
- Parliament/House of Commons/ Westminster (UK) 13, 16–19, 32, 35, 37, 43, 55, 58, 64f, 95, 134, 136, 143, 178, 186, 197, 205f.

Parties 14, 18f., 40, 42, 46, 50, 60f., 72, 77, 79f., 143, 147–155, 158, 187, 199, 205
- Christian Democrats 60, 78, 80
- Communists 42, 78, 134, 145, 150–153, 159
- Liberals 20, 60, 80, 85, 153, 155
- Socialists, Social Democrats 19f., 46, 56, 80, 88, 119, 126, 153, 155

Politics 9–22, 24–26, 28, 32, 38, 42f., 47, 55f., 58, 62, 65f., 78, 89–91, 95, 97, 102f., 106f., 111, 119, 121–124, 128–130, 132–134, 139, 146, 149, 154, 175, 187–193, 195f., 205
- Policy 12f., 20, 26, 28f., 32, 46, 49, 52, 56f., 60, 62, 64, 68f., 70, 72, 77, 92, 95, 102, 106, 108, 114, 116, 118f., 121–126, 128–130, 148–150, 162, 166, 169, 175, 177, 194–196, 199–201, 206f.
- Politician 10f., 38, 44, 46, 52, 63, 77, 79–84, 94, 106, 108, 119, 136, 165f., 168, 170, 178, 188f., 191, 198f., 207f.
- Politicisation 9, 12–24, 27, 66, 95, 117, 119f., 127–130, 149, 169, 188, 190–192, 198, 207
- Politicking, doing politics 10, 12f., 17, 19–22, 58, 128, 193, 207
- Polity 9, 11–16, 18, 20, 22, 24, 28f., 34–36, 38f., 52, 66f., 73, 78, 88, 95, 100, 102–131, 133, 144, 149, 157, 167–170, 177, 186, 188, 190f., 200, 207f.

223

Sovereignty 16, 28, 30f., 35f., 54f., 60, 62, 68, 75, 100, 105f., 109–111, 115–120, 122, 127, 129, 145, 148, 158, 162, 179, 183, 198, 202, 204
- Delegation, transfer, sacrifice 16, 29–31, 35f., 44, 60, 109, 111, 114–116, 118, 122, 125, 127, 168, 189, 202, 204
- European 64, 96, 116f., 127, 129
- State, national 16, 31, 35, 56, 105f., 109–111, 115f, 162, 179, 202, 204
- Parliamentary 34, 55, 62,75, 76, 158, 183, 198
- Popular 54, 96, 120, 145, 148, 183

Supranational/-ism 9–24, 26f., 29–31, 33–35, 37f., 40, 42, 44–46, 48, 50–53, 57–59, 61–64, 66f., 69f, 72–78, 85, 88, 90–96, 98–100, 102f., 105–133, 135f., 139, 143f., 146, 150, 155, 157, 159, 161–163, 168–170, 172–178, 181, 183, 186, 188–193, 195f, 198f., 202, 205–208.
- Europeanisation 10, 12, 15f., 19f, 32, 48, 60, 66f., 73, 75f.,103, 107f., 110–114, 118–121 124f, 128f, 130, 132, 139, 148f., 153–155, 175, 187f, 190f., 204, 207
- vs. intergovernmental/-ism 12, 16, 23, 25, 28f., 38–41, 44f., 47, 57f., 60, 68, 90, 95, 107, 110–114, 119. 124,128, 135 139, 171, 173, 176, 178, 186, 190f., 193, 195, 197f., 200–203, 207
- vs. international 16, 25, 39, 44, 62, 76f., 90, 107, 114, 124f., 128f. 134, 138, 149, 160, 162, 165, 173, 176, 181, 191, 195f., 205
- vs. nationalism 17, 20, 22f., 28, 32, 35, 39, 46, 48, 70, 78, 104f., 107–110, 124, 128, 191, 207
- parliament[arism] 11, 15, 17, 19, 24, 38, 62, 107, 130, 150, 168f., 188, 207